A Narrative Community

A Narrative Community

Voices of Israeli Backpackers

Chaim Noy

Wayne State University Press   Detroit

© 2007 by Wayne State University Press, Detroit, Michigan 48201.

Manufactured in the United States of America.

11 10 09 08 07   5 4 3 2 1

Library of Congress Cataloging-in-Publication Data

Noy, Chaim, 1968-

A narrative community : voices of Israeli backpackers / Chaim Noy.

p. cm. — (Raphael Patai series in Jewish folklore and anthropology)

Includes bibliographical references and index.

ISBN-13: 978-0-8143-3176-7

ISBN-10: 0-8143-3176-9 (pbk. : alk. paper)

1. Backpacking—Social aspects. 2. Youth—Israel—Social life and customs. I. Title.

GV199.6.N68 2006

796.5108992'4—dc22

2006025936

Published with the assistance of a fund established by Thelma Gray James
of Wayne State University for the publication of folklore and English studies.

Designed and typeset by Maya Rhodes
Composed in Warnock Pro

CONTENTS

ITINERARY

So we decided on playing this game.
The truth is we invented it on the spot, but I'm sure it was also invented before us.

  Meirav

In this combination of elements—the mountain, the mind, and society—exists a circumstance, an option, a fantasy which is ancient.

  Michael Tobias

I still consider myself a narrativist in the romantic sense: one who is truly fascinated with how people conjure up and create realms of being through storytelling; how people convey the deepest recesses of their lives through stories, by and by re-creating selves for themselves. The stories that mesmerized me at the onset of this research lay at the very core of romanticism—stories of travel and adventure. Indeed, it was my initial fascination with travel that had moved me to backpack extensively in Asia some fifteen years ago, similar to the backpackers whose excited stories I heard later. The profound stories I first heard and later recounted were the phenomenological dynamo that stirred me to undertake another kind of travel, an academic one, of which this book is a travelogue.

Along the route of academic socialization I had transformed from a traveler to a researcher, from a romanticist to a modernist—and perhaps even to a postmodernist (Noy 2003b). For one thing, I had come to realize that the structure of the travel narratives was profoundly related to their content—to the literally wonderful sights and scenes of the trip. The skyscraping peaks of the Annapurna Mountains in Nepal, the brilliantly colorful lagoons of the Torres Del Paine reserve in Peru, the Indian Ganges at dawn—all required, but also afforded, the use of unique vernacular and forms of expression.

Spellbound by the diversity of genres of human narrative imagination, I became absorbed with the social production of the stories, in which form and content fuse to become a moving performance. Years of sobering academic socialization have framed and tamed my romanticist fascination and have directed my attention away from the story to its performance. Thus, I began to inquire into how such performances were socially produced, what their intended effects were, how they implicated their audience, what ideologies they promoted in a specific discursive sociocultural context, and what role the particular texts (the travel narratives) played in these performances. Although I did not completely forsake my fascination with incredible scenes of soaring peaks, titanic glaciers, and roaring avalanches, I gradually began to concentrate on the communicative and constitutive aspects of these breath-capturing stories—on the storytelling occasions themselves in their capacity as communal rituals that dialogically facilitated negotiation and construction of meaning, authority, and identity. In other words, becoming a "social scientist" meant foregrounding the social and cultural aspects of the backpacking narrative community, thus construing the dramatic mountainous scenery as the backdrop against which a social drama developed. I came to view the haunting texts that captured heightened touristic scenes as resources that made the performances so subtly compelling.

Another vital aspect of the transition from romanticism to (late) modernity concerns the highly institutional context of contemporary travel. Addressing backpackers' stories comprehensively entails acknowledging the institutional setting in which and through which their trips take place. Since the global tourism industry has successfully monopolized both the material aspects and the semiotics of travel, a "thick" inquiry into the experiences and stories of backpackers offers insights into tourism in general (as a forerunner of the late modern condition) and into the language and performance of tourists in particular.

In addition, since it has been charged that tourism research lacks a systematic theoretical framework, by attending to tourists' words, stories, and performances in light of current sociolinguistic theories of interaction, this book aims to rectify this situation and to provide a much-needed contribution to the particularities of the language(s) of tourists, focusing on what is unique in their descriptions of their (touristic) experiences.

At the core of this book's inquiry lie the performance of quotations, the dialogues constructed by these quotations, and the social voices they convey—all of which play a crucial role, linking the backpackers' stories intertextually. Serving as interpersonal anchors, the voices of others persuasively web the individual into a tightly knit tourist community, endowing those participating in the "great journey," as it is called, with communal authority and with a sought-after sense of shared communal experience and belonging.

The opening section of this volume (site I) provides a sociocultural account of the emergence of widespread backpacking tourism in Israel (chapter 1) and explores the persuasive genre underlying ideological aspects of backpackers' narrative performances (chapter 2). The central chapters (site II) are then dedicated to the performance of quotations and social voices. These chapters are arranged according to a simple characteristic of the quotations the narrators cite: their attribution. Hence, following chapter 3, which is a sociolinguistic introduction to the performance of quotations in narrative, chapter 4 explores social space created by quotations of choral or group voice versus individual voices; chapter 5 explores the voices of Others—instances in which quotations designate those who are positioned outside the tourist community, namely "natives" and "tourists"; chapters 6 and 7, which constitute the centerpiece of this section, explore the unique collective voice: the impersonal and highly authoritative voice of the community itself; finally, chapter 8 deals with a consequence of this state of heightened polyphony: the communal sonority that is composed of the overall sounds of communal voices and the relation of this sonority to space and collective identity.

The concluding section (site III) suggests that the narrators frame and perform their travel experiences in terms of identity and self-change (chapter 9) and provides concluding assessments (the epilogue). Thus the structure of the book reflects its subject: the central chapters in this volume (site III), which deal with quotations and social voices, are framed—like quotation itself—by two inquiries that do not focus on quotations but shed light upon the socionarrative context within which voices emerge so vibrantly and plentifully.

Two short intermezzo pieces, acting as theoretical transitions between the sections, account for the performative connection between quotations and social voices and for the dialogical genres of persuasion and self-change. Additionally, five short diary entries reflect, sometimes humorously, upon the different perspectives I have on the matters discussed.

The book, then, is the product of an academic journey and might be construed as a travelogue of fascination with the language of immersion into profound sceneries (Tobias 1979). This travelogue is truly interdisciplinary—a consequence of my academic trajectory and of the crystal-like quality of the backpackers' performances, which reflect differently when viewed from different disciplinary perspectives. The book brings together knowledge and methods from the fields of linguistic anthropology, discourse analysis, and communication. Chapter 2 (persuasive performances), chapters 6–7 (authoritative communal voice) and chapter 9 (identity and self-change) rely mainly on ethnographies of speech and performance, as these have been studied in folklore and linguistic anthropology (Bauman; Hymes; Tedlock) as well as on the notion of performance in communication studies (Langellier). Chapters 3–5 (quotations and voices) and, to some extent, chapter 6 identify and explore narrative quotations and dialogues with the help of discourse analysis (following Becker and Tannen).

These subdisciplines raise different questions and search for answers through different means and in different places. For instance, while a performance framework views the narrations as constitutive rituals in and of themselves, discourse analysis generally stresses the linguistic composition of the narratives: the way voices and dialogues are constructed in and reflected by the narratives. Essentially, however, these disciplinary perspectives converge in this book on live speech and narrative performance as these unfold dialogically. This convergence or fusion amounts to a multidisciplinary cross-fertilization that presents a social and cultural account of the backpackers' narrative performances.

I should point out that very little of the itinerary just described was in fact planned at the outset of this research. The terms *persuasion, community, quotations,* and even *performance,* which are important sites in this journey, were signally absent from the doctoral proposal that I signed on July 22, 1997. As I have discussed elsewhere (Noy 2003b), I had to allow my work (and myself) to drift away from my initial expectations and from my contractual obligation, which was a frightening process of breaching the doctoral proposal. I "lied" (to use Metcalf's [2002] term), and the findings reported in this book, whether depicting the social reality I encountered, my own sensitivities and hidden agenda, or, most probably, an interaction of the two, are mostly emergent: unexpected and novel.

The sites visited during this journey, however, are not only academic disciplines but people. First and foremost among these are the backpackers themselves, who opened the doors of their narratives and enthusiastically shared their profound experiences with me. The other people who served as significant "sites" along this journey, and to whom I am deeply grateful, are mentors and colleagues whose works and thoughts, conversations and stories have touched, inspired, and provoked me. These include Amia Lieblich, Yoram Bilu, Zali Gurevitch, Erik Cohen, Galit Hazan-Rokem, Ken Gergen, Dan Ben-Amos, Shoshana Blum-Kulka, Tamar Katriel, and Yael Maschler. I am also indebted to Gonen Hacohen and to the two anonymous reviewers who made insightful comments on later versions of this manuscript.

Finally, some who have inspired my academic and intellectual itinerary in formative ways, and to whom I feel personally indebted, I have never met face-to-face. These include Victor Turner, Mikhail Bakhtin, and William Labov. The three have left enduring impressions upon me, which underlie the ensuing chapter and resonate, explicitly and implicitly, throughout this book.

Victor Turner's (1967, 1969) anthropological contribution builds upon Arnold van Gennep's (1960) early (originally published in 1909) model of rites of passage, entailing three stages: departure from familiar surroundings, or commencement; a state of liminality; and a return home, or closure. This influential model, which I first studied when I was a (clinical) psychology graduate student, brought the full thrust of anthropological thought into my worldview of people's experiences and transformations and brought into focus the interrelations between the cultural and the personal spheres. It had a powerful impact on me primarily because it lent itself so easily, even invitingly, to narrative framing (as Turner himself elaborated [1980]). But it also accorded well with my initial interest in travel-induced phenomenology and in sites simultaneously physical (geographical) and symbolic where social and cultural change was taking place.

Reading Mikhail Bakhtin's works (especially 1981 and 1986) for the first time was exhilarating—and, surprisingly, aroused a calm feeling of being at home (rather than intellectually traveling in terra incognita). Bakhtin's texts provided me the rare and precious experience of reading someone else's words and feeling as though I myself had written them. In addition, although I had not seriously studied semiotics, pragmatics, or sociolinguistics before reading Bakhtin, his works were a delicious introduction to all these fields and to their points of convergence in real occasions of talk and social interaction (Bakhtin's theory of utterance). Indeed, it was the attention he paid to lively occurrences of language in actual social interactions that I found so familiar and at the same time so refreshing and provocative. Within this perspective other things I liked about Bakhtin were covered, mainly his humanist pragmatism.

William Labov's famous work (1972) on narratives of personal experience was my first encounter with narrative scholarship. I read it as an undergraduate psychology student writing a seminar paper on life stories of people of different personological "attachment types," and it had an immediate appeal. The work's structuralist dimensions, which were influenced by and were part of a respected tradition of folkloristic research into diverse narrative structures (Propp 1968), suggested the existence of an easily discernible structure that made interpreting every narrative of personal experience manageable thereafter. This structure was comprised of six parts: abstract, orientation, complicating act, evaluation, resolution, and coda. Yet the impact (and popularity) of Labov's work is attributed—correctly, in my opinion—not only to the clear structural analysis he promoted but to its location between purely structural theory, on the one hand, and later post-structural and processual conceptualizations, on the other (Bamberg 1997; Bauman and Briggs 1990; Langellier 1999).

Particularly, Labov's notion of "evaluation" (especially "external evaluation")—those utterances in which, stopping the unfolding of the plot for a narrative instant, the narrator addresses the audience directly and expresses her or his own view of the significance of the story and what is important in it—suggested an initial conceptualization of narration as a site of interaction and contestation of meanings of various types and magnitudes; or, from a different perspective, these utterances suggested the door through which Labov's structural model could evolve and transform into a poststructural contribution.

Indeed, the following period of my life, shortly before I began my doctoral studies, was a time of personal scholarly transition from structural perspectives to more intricate notions of performance and intersubjectivity. This transition explains why I treasured Labov's works but also why I drifted away from their influence as well as from the influence of Turner's structural model.

Before proceeding, I would like to return from the realms of high theory to the world of material concerns to express my indebtedness to three generous consecutive postdoctoral fellowships—Rothschild (Yad-Hanadiv), M. Ginsberg (Social Sciences Faculty, Hebrew University), and the Post-Doctorate Fellowship of Budgeting and Planning Committee (Vatat) of the National Council for Higher Education (Social Sciences Faculty, University of Haifa)—that provided me with the time this journey required.

Meirav's words in the epigraph above reveal part of what is fascinating in the stories recounted by the backpackers: their view of the trip suggests that it is a creative and playful activity occurring within a symbolic and reflexive context. They play backpacking. The form of playfulness that emerges in Meirav's words is particularly relevant because she speaks of creativity and innovation while referring to repetition; she thus acknowledges the fact that cultural innovation rests on the mastery of tradition. Meirav supplies an illuminating maxim for the phenomenon of backpacking: the youthful tourists are simultaneously inventing and repeating, traveling off and on the beaten track, arriving at genuinely new sites ("virgin," "exotic," "authentic") that they learned from battered-from-use stories shared with them by friends and acquaintances. Quotations, coupled with the social voices that emerge through performing them competently, constitute both a part of and an appropriate metaphor for this process: the narrators are authors and creators of new (language) games, while at the same time they are engrossed in repetition and replication.

Since backpackers are "sure" the game they are playing was "also invented before," as Meirav puts it, this is a case of traditionalization (Bauman and Briggs 1990). This paradoxical term suggests that a community is constantly being created and recreated. The backpackers performatively extend their cultural roots and identities "backward" in time, as it were. In performing backpacking they create a tradition that endows their identities with authority and with considerable narrative (sociocultural) capital. In this context, quotations serve a diachronic and a synchronic purpose simultaneously: diachronically, they create a past—a taleworld from which words are borrowed into the present—and synchronically, they establish a performative state during the interviews and position the interviewee-audience powerfully, as they wish.

SITE I

Introduction
Persuasion

1

Performing Backpacking Narratives

Travel has its canonized great traditions, its formalists (insisting that destination is unimportant), and its modernists (proclaiming the imminent end
of the art).

Judith Adler

Backpacking the Israeli Way: A Brief Cultural History

Backpacking, or *Tarmila'ut,* presently constitutes a time-honored rite of passage in
Israeli society. For three decades now, scores of youths, after completing their man-
datory service in the army, make the "great journey" (*hatiyul hagadol*), backpacking
extensively to explore "exotic" and "authentic" destinations. These are typically located in "third world" regions; in Asia itineraries include India, Nepal, and Thailand,
and in Central and South America popular destinations are Colombia, Ecuador,
Peru, and, proceeding southward, Brazil, Chile, and Argentina.

From modest beginnings in the early 1970s, in the form of a trickle of alienated
drifters who traveled solo for extended periods of time, backpacking has turned
into a widely practiced popular custom (Noy 2006a; Noy and Cohen 2005b). In
fact, among secular Jewish youths it nowadays carries both *normative* and *collective*
characteristics. Normatively, youths are expected to travel; they see a need to justify themselves if they choose not to. Collectively, participation in the trip amounts
to a ticket—an entrance rite—into a subculture, allowing for the assumption of a
desired identity. In the heated competition over cultural and identitary resources
that is part of the politics of identity in contemporary fragmented Israeli society,
the liberal-modern images acquired by the backpackers via travel are of vital importance. By and large, the rite embodied in the great journey positions the youths
advantageously as a collective within a turbulent sociocultural climate. Beyond the
sheer numbers of youths who participate in backpacking, the narratives, images,
and institutional arrangements that surround the trip all point to the uniqueness of
this phenomenon in contemporary Israeli society.[1]

Historically, the massive participation in the great journey is rooted in societal
changes that followed the Yom Kippur War (1973) and were partly consequential

3

to it. In those early days of backpacking, which lasted from the 1960s to the mid-1970s, the few who traveled were perceived as "drifters" or "wanderers" (Cohen 1973). They came from the socioeconomic "centers" or elites of Israeli Jewish society, against which they were reacting. From those years, and especially later (during the war in Lebanon in 1982), a severe social schism erupted and widened, taking the form of growing alienation between various sectors of society and the hegemonic Zionist ideology (embodied by the nation-state).

These changes were both part and product of a larger historical course that led to the decline of the sociopolitical and cultural hegemony of the Sabra culture. It also brought about the sectorialization, as well as the polyphonization, of the Israeli public sphere. The decline of communal-socialist ideologies, and with them the degeneration of the image of the "melting pot"—according to which the many Jews who immigrated to Israel from various diasporas were supposedly "equalized" under a hegemonic identity of the native Sabra—had a fundamental impact on a range of spheres of individual and communal lives in Israel.

These transformations were pertinent to the ensuing phenomenon of backpacking because they suggested a motivation, a "push" factor, in the form of alienation and protest. This, coupled with considerable economic growth, a proliferation of leisure time, and the initial emergence of consumer society during the late 1970s and early 1980s, contributed to youths' motivation to take "time off" in the form of backpacking. At the same time, the aforementioned weakening of hegemonic ideology resulted in a decrease of control over individuals who chose to leave Israel, either temporarily and permanently. In earlier times, for example, people who emigrated from Israel were described as *yordim,* or "descenders" (connoting disloyalty). Similarly, embarking on tourist activities was viewed disapprovingly, as a frivolous "bourgeois" practice.

While these processes suggested "push" factors, rebellious youth movements worldwide suggested a "pull" factor—a direction, a site, namely Asia (and specifically India, where the Beatles, for instance, visited in 1968). The pilgrimage of Western youths to India, among other sites, suggested a direction for disillusioned Israeli youths who wished to partake in contemporaneous global youth culture.

While research on backpackers of the 1970s suggests that they engaged in counterculture practices, studies on their later counterparts show that from the 1980s to the present, backpackers, far from exhibiting countercultural worldviews, share features with mass institutional tourists. Moreover, solo travelers have become infrequent, occupying the fringes of the backpacking population, which usually travels in groups.

During the 1980s, backpacking was embraced by the global tourism industry and its respective local organizations. In this decade, many more youths took on the rite of passage embodied in the great journey, and the phenomenon began to receive serious media coverage in Israel. Backpacking attained the form of a *collective and normative cultural rite of passage.* Toward the end of the 1980s backpackers had clearly turned into "backpacking tourists," and backpacking had become "the backpacking phenomenon." Although the colonial myth of the "pioneer," "explorer" backpacker remained active, as did echoes of counterculture ideologies, institutionalization and commercialization nonetheless governed the backpacking industry. Nowadays, there are many travel agencies in Israel that specialize in various areas of expertise *within* backpacking tourism and that organize an assortment of excursions to "traditional" as well as more recent backpacking sites, all of which are aimed at the heterogeneous patterns of backpacking-related consumption.

From the 1990s to the present, backpacking underwent additional changes, which both facilitated and were facilitated by an impressive quantitative expansion and by further institutionalization. Presently, the full impact of *mediatization* is apparent, and the role assumed by the *culture of backpacking* in public life in Israel is enhanced. It is not only that there are daily reports in the news about the dangerous, adventurous, and mischievous—and sometimes tragic—undertakings of backpackers. Books are published about backpackers (some by celebrated authors), to backpackers, and by backpackers. Television networks broadcast programs and series resting on backpackers' adventures and experiences, and the local film industry has produced movies concerning backpacker culture. These instances point to the impact that culture has had on the home society by way of an "import" of culture into mainstream society. Concurrently, celebrated Israeli performers regularly perform in backpackers' enclaves abroad, a fact that illustrates the "export" of Israeli culture (albeit not to other, non-Israeli cultures, but to enclaves of Israelis).

These recent developments thrive due to the enclavic nature of the travel of Israeli backpackers, and at the same time, they strengthen this nature and contribute to its insular character. Previously, Israelis would congregate in designated guesthouses and participate in certain activities on the basis of their own word of mouth; now Israeli backpacking operators and facilitators have it all organized. With the taking over by Israeli entrepreneurs of local tourist businesses and the management of transportation and accommodation, the institutional circle surrounding Israeli backpackers and mediating their itineraries, activities, and experiences is nearly complete and hermetic—a point that evokes the notion of the "end-of-tourism" (Rojek and Urry 1997) with regard to the phenomenon of Israeli backpacking.

Institutionalization, however, does not necessarily bring with it the homogenization of tourists or of the activities in which they partake. On the contrary, the processes of institutionalization and commercialization lead to backpacking becoming "more composite and multifaceted than ever" (Sørensen 2003, 848; see also Uriely, Yonay, and Simchai 2002). Indeed, over the years, the sociodemographic and religious backgrounds of the backpackers have become increasingly varied and their travel motivations and experiences more and more diverse. Needless to mention, this has made backpacking all the more interesting a tourist phenomenon.[2]

As backpacking is pursued immediately after a lengthy period of service in the Israeli army, the manner of travel displays considerable militaristic overtones carried over from the time the youths spent in uniform (approximately two years for women and three years for men). Scholars researching militarism in Israeli society observe that backpackers travel in a "military" mode, which includes precise planning of their routes, walking in small cohesive groups, and repeated tests of their abilities to withstand hardship and take risks (Ben-Ari 1998, 116; see also Lieblich 1989, 189; Lomsky-Feder 1996, 57). Similarly, in a single reference to Israeli backpackers in the general literature, Anders Sørensen (2003, 848) characterizes them as "fresh out of the military service." More generally, when considering Israeli backpacking as a local phenomenon, the semimilitaristic conduct of the backpackers can also be attributed to wide-ranging pro-militaristic trends in contemporary Israeli society, which converge variants of chauvinism and colonialism (Noy 2003a).

Whether it is because of their actual service in the military or more abstract sociocultural proclivities, some backpackers view the trip as a ludic reaction to a demanding and "serious" military service, while others view it as expressing continuity. Obviously, both perspectives hold some validity: they are both possible under the heterogeneous activities and experiences encompassed by backpacking. Among various individuals and groups, and amid the various activities the great trip entails, youths have plenty of opportunities to perform both a reaction to military service—which is usually exhibited on an expressive, conscious level—and militaristic extensions into civic-tourist (yet colonial) practice—which are usually implicit in the backpackers' conduct, patterns of socialization, preoccupation with achievement, the vernacular they employ, and so on.

While the brief sociological history above sketches the background and central characteristics of Israeli Tarmila'ut, I now turn to a brief examination of the *cultural roots*—the spatial fantasies and embodied narratives—of backpacking culture. The origin of these narratives in fact precedes the 1960s and 1970s and suggests that the ensuing backpacking culture is a manifestation—a reincarnation, perhaps—of much earlier cultural tenets and fantasies. From this perspective, the first drifters were in effect revitalizing earlier images of nature and adventure that preoccupied early Sabra culture (see Noy 2006b). More important, at stake are the sociocultural patterns of storytelling, which complemented and augmented the adventurous physical achievements and amounted to an elaborate tradition of storytelling. In other words, when the first Israeli youths embarked on lengthy trips in remote, "exotic" regions in the early 1970s, they had cultural narratives to draw upon and to revive: the early Sabra tradition had reserved a unique place for romanticist, mountainous nature hiking and the pursuit of adventurous activities and, no less crucially, to the "tall tales" that granted their narrators the status of cultural heroes.

As early as the second decade of the twentieth century, groups of wanderers (called *agudot meshotetim*) had undertaken extensive hiking tours across the Land of Israel in a ritual through which groups of travelers experientially got to "know" the land to which they or their pioneer parents had recently immigrated. In the ensuing heyday of the Sabra culture, Katriel (1995, 6–7) observes, traveling at length by foot was an "important element in the complex of ritualized cultural practices which have been appropriated and cultivated during the Israeli pre-state . . . and which form the core of Israeli 'civil religion.' . . . [It carries] a special aura in Israel public culture . . . as a native-Israeli form of secular pilgrimage."[3]

Indeed, a significant aspect of the emerging Sabra tradition was the performance of adventurous, sometimes highly risky, trips throughout Israel. This quality further intensified with the shift from the ethos of the "farmer" to that of the "warrior"—a point in time at which hiking had absorbed the meaning of a quasi-military reconnaissance activity (Shapira 1999). These adventures, which in extreme cases included transgressing the borders of neighboring (hostile) countries at considerable risk, were pursued vehemently by various youth institutions, including youth movements of German and English origins.

The rise of semi-institutional, state-organized hiking reflects the "institutionalization of an ethos"—that of the wanderer—and also reflects the ideological conviction that traveling by foot is a highly "educational" and "patriotic" activity (Zerubavel 1995, 119–25). In fact, to this day, all grades in all Jewish public (secular and religious) schools embark on an annual trip (*tiyul shnati*), hiking and touring the country for several days.

One of the well-known sites that served as a major destination for pilgrimage is Masada, located in the southern part of the Judean Desert. Masada's location on the summit of a steep mountain played an important role in turning its strenuous physical ascent into a meaningful symbolic rite. As noted by Yael Zerubavel (1995, 125), "The dramatic ending of the field trip served as a last test of the pilgrims' courage, commitment, and persistence. Masada's topographical shape was clearly instrumental in enhancing the sacred character of the new pilgrimage tradition."[4] Much the same can be said about other mountainous sites in Israel, to the summit of which youths have climbed time and again, thus simultaneously performing embodied patriotism, determination and willpower, and repeated "conquering" of the land (Gurevitch and Aran 1991). These ascents play out key cultural metaphors, wherein the "'ultimate' Zionist pilgrimage—immigration to Zion" (Zerubavel 1995, 126)—is performed.

Notably, the Sabra variation of the myth of the romanticist explorer was uniquely pursued by and embodied in *highly cohesive groups* (and not by individuals). In fact, the culture of ritualistic traveling was as much about strengthening the bond between the Sabras themselves as it was about strengthening the bond between the people and the land. This is clearly evinced among present-day backpackers, who travel in large groups and gravitate toward Israeli enclaves. Put differently, while the socialist collective ideology has completely declined, ethnocentric collectivism has emerged in its stead. The patterns of socialization characteristic of the latter ideology are particularly salient against the international setting of global backpacking tourism.

The cultural significance of these strenuous and embodied performances is only half understood if we do not take into consideration the communicative, discursive environment in which they were practiced and which they sustained. The point is that performing these adventurous rites made for *narrative realms* in the form of tall tales. Such performances suggest not only the actual deeds that were prescribed for Zionist youths but also the unique interpersonal dimensions of the Sabra culture in which the stories of these accomplishments were shared and com-

pared. In fact, part of the livelihood of the manly Sabra culture was tied to the performance of recounting adventures—from minute mischievous acts through travel
to exotic locations to exciting and risky military raids—all of which were narrated
in social settings, such as around the legendary bonfires of the Palmah (the major
pre-state military organization).[5]

The role assigned to both adventure and adventure narration meant that performing these activities competently had the potential to position narrators in a
uniquely esteemed social standing. Occurrences pertaining to travel, adventure,
and risk indicated their narrator's virtuous "character," the extent to which he (it
was typically a male) embodied the role of the hero. On a different level, it suggested
an epistemic relationship between stories and events: the adventure-travel narrative
is a genre replete with "actual" events. This is indicated by one of the key terms of
the Sabra culture—*tahles*, literally meaning "factual" or "matter-of-fact." Tahles indicates that Sabra culture highly values factuality and that the accounts supplied by
individuals should be "true" and "real" occurrences in which they themselves took
part. Narrative is viewed as a "transparent" medium, one that should convey the
mere tahles of the story in line with a nonstylized, nonchalant type of performance
(Katriel 1986) conveying "straight-talk realism" in an optimal way (Hazan 2001b,
57).

Though seemingly egalitarian (drawing on socialist morals), Sabra culture promoted and prescribed ways by which individuals could claim esteemed social status
by competently embodying the ideal and hegemonic images of the epoch and just as
competently telling about them. The fusion of adventures and the stories recounting
them with ideologies and identities was set for later generations of youths to follow (Katriel 2004). The adventurous ethos and the ethos of performing adventurous
narratives would later be collectively invigorated and reincarnated by backpackers. This reappearance calls to mind a significant and critical observation Edward
Bruner (2005, 22) recently made: "Tourism is not that innovative in inventing narratives but rather seeks new locations in which to tell old stories."

Global Backpacking Culture: Experience and Expertise

Once international tourism began booming after World War II, the concept of "tourist" became more complex, no longer signifying a simple generic category. Tourism
scholars drew distinctions among types of tourists on the basis of manner of travel
(for example, individual versus group, consumption of expensive versus inexpensive
products and services), travel motivations ("pull" versus "push" factors), travel experiences, and so on (Cohen 1972, 1973, 1979).

These efforts at classifying tourists on more or less formal grounds have contributed to the ensuing scholarly appreciation of tourism and its complexities, yet
they have not been productive in and of themselves and by and large have not yielded
further explorations (but see Uriely, Yonay, and Simchai 2002; Wickens 2002). In
this vein, I will begin with a formal definition of backpacking tourism, only to suggest a more updated, conceptually nuanced and processual alternative.

The traditional view is that backpackers are self-organized, noninstitutionalized mass tourists who pursue a multiple-destination trip of a relatively long duration (significantly exceeding the duration of annual cyclical holidays). They are commonly designated as youths who travel to "third world" destinations and hold countercultural views. The travelers have a loosely planned itinerary (or no planned itinerary) and travel on a "tight" budget, a fact that carries consequences regarding the choice of transportation (a preference for local transportation versus more luxurious air-conditioned vehicles used by "mass tourists") and accommodation (a preference for low-cost facilities, such as youth hostels and YMCAs versus deluxe international hotel chains).

Recent findings show that backpackers vary greatly in age, that backpacking is a long-standing tradition of travel in the West (particularly in mainland Europe), and that backpackers actually rarely adhere to antiestablishment worldviews anymore. For instance, Laurie Loker-Murphy and Philip Pearce (1995) show that, contrary to the commonly accepted view of backpackers, of the various groups of tourists who enter Australia, backpackers came with the greatest amount of money (out of ten categories)!

The difficulties that arise from using formal definitions are not exhausted, however, by such occasional inaccuracies. Rather, in line with recent innovative contributions, a meaningful definition of backpackers should not rely only on "hard" sociological parameters (Elsrud 2001; Richards and Wilson 2004a; Sørensen 2003). Instead, the category "backpacker" can fruitfully be construed as an emergent sociocultural category, one that is performed and established from "within," as it were; it encompasses experiences and narratives as much as it does behaviors in an intricate institutional context. In the words of Sørensen:

> If viewed as a *social category*, the term backpacker offers analytical qualities to supplement the predominantly descriptive use of the term in the literature. For although many do not meet the descriptive characteristics, these nevertheless describe how backpackers tend to view themselves: they form the outline of a travel ideology. The category makes sense from the insider's point of view. Being both an individual perception and a socially constructed identity, "backpacker" is more a social construct than a definition. (2003, 852; emphasis in the original)

The narratives by which tourists interpret their practices and endow them with meaning—including sharing these narratives with travel companions—amount to a "bottom-up" creation of both the "social organization" and the "culture" of backpacking (Bruner 2005; Clifford 1997; Giddens 1984). In other words, the experiences of consumers cannot be left outside the ethnographic inquiry of "backpackers' culture." Rather, a constructive tension arises between formal-structural characteristics, on the one hand, and experiential-subjective ones, on the other hand (Uriely, Yonay, and Simchai 2002). While neither can adequately conceptualize various tourist categories by itself, recognizing the complex scheme of interrelations between these features is highly productive.

By *travel culture* or *travel ideology,* a conceptualization is promoted in order to address what has traditionally been explored under more behavioristic and operational terms (*motivations, attitudes,* and so on). The terms *culture* and *ideology* integrally encompass the entire tourist-related repertoire, including motivations, experiences, practices, narratives, patterns of socialization, perceptions of what constitutes a "tourist" and a "native," and more. This holds true in relation to the trip itself as well as to its consequences: how the trip is reconstructed and incorporated in hindsight into one's biography and one's sense of identity. Exploring travel culture and travel ideology "allows for the culture continuously to create and re-create the backpacker as category" (Sørensen 2003, 855). I would add that it also allows the category of "backpacker" to continually re-create both the culture of travel and aspects of the traveler's broader (home) culture.

This continual re-creation of a social category is achieved by way of recurrent social interactions—everyday interaction rituals that comprise storytelling and storyhearing. Indeed, from the early works on backpackers until the present, research has repeatedly suggested that a central characteristic of backpacking is frequent and recurring social interactions among the travelers (Cohen 1973; Loker-Murphy and Pearce 1995; Riley 1988). While some ascribe these frequent interactions to the exchange of knowledge and the gathering of information through word of mouth (Murphy 2001, 50), I would suggest that knowledge and information can be viewed productively as central components in—or even justifications for—the performance of the category "backpacker," as a part of the process of production and reproduction of the social system of backpacking.

Indeed, Elsrud's (2001) work points to the narrative quality of the interactions that regularly take place among backpackers. In these frequent and recurrent meetings, backpackers' word-of-mouth communications are expressed as a part of sharing stories with one another, stories that commonly depict risk and adventure. Perhaps even more significantly, in these stories travelers construct episodes of risk and adventure—a late modern touristic variation of the romanticist travel narrative—wherein they themselves are the heroes, in a setting that affords an "excellent arena for such creative construction" (Elsrud 2001, 603). Comparatively, it could be said that the notorious loquaciousness of tourists is evinced in the case of backpackers in the oft-told travel narratives of risk and adventure: these make for the backpackers' own variation of "what is worth telling about," of "adventures [pursued] in order for satisfactory life stories to be constructed and maintained" (Schiebe 1986, 131; see also Bruner 2005, 19–27).

These recent trends clearly illustrate why a constructionist view of backpacking lends itself naturally to a narrative, performance-sensitive appreciation. Although the authors cited above do not explicitly refer to backpackers in performative terms, their writings lend themselves readily to the idea that travelers cleverly utilize the setting (formal characteristics) of backpacking tourism in order to publicly produce social meaning.

Performing Narratives of Personal Experience

One can legitimately argue that tourism is grounded in discourse.
Graham Dann

At the beginning of my meetings with backpackers—and even later, when I approached the voluminous transcribed texts (facing the dreadful "1,000-page question" [Kvale 1996])—I admittedly was not attempting to research "backpacking performance." Rather, as my notes, drafts, and research proposal from the time indicate, I was out to explore the profound experiences that backpackers were narrating, which I conceptualized along the lines of Victor Turner's popular notion concerning traditional and modern pilgrimages. I was also seeking to inquire into various "narrative aspects" pertaining to *how* these stories were structured in order to convey their narrators' significant travel experiences.

Soon, however, my attention turned from what the backpackers were talking *about*, from the referential content of the narrative, to what was going on *in the interview meetings*. The emotive, experiential, and ultimately ontic state of these meetings carried an impact that compelled me to explore beyond the "information" I had sought to flesh out of the accounts. I came to see that in these sites of elicitation, face-to-face interactions were taking place that were, in fact, a substantial part of what I was out to research. It was this consideration of the interview event itself as a meaningful social occasion, coupled with my long-standing interest in matters linguistic and my preoccupation with the semiotics of representation, that led me eventually to gravitate toward viewing the stories narrated by backpackers as "tourist performances."

It was a sobering moment when I realized that the backpackers were, in fact, "tourists"(!) Backpackers themselves (myself included) construct the identitary category of "backpacker" by ardently opposing it to "tourist" or to "mass tourist," and in their manners of travel—and travel narratives—they repeatedly promote this distinction, assuring themselves and their audiences that they are backpackers, not tourists. Nonetheless, the conceptualization of backpackers as tourists was a fruitful one, even if it meant I had to view what the informants said from a quite different standpoint than they themselves had viewed it.

Together, these two pivotal research insights—the consideration of narrative communication (not merely narrative content and structure) and the viewing of backpackers as a type of tourist—suggested that the phenomenon I was researching was "tourist performances." It was an occasion in which backpackers' culture and identity, and the narrative capital engulfed therein, were embodied and cached in a performance that occupied the ritualistic sites of face-to-face interaction (à la Goffman).

Historically, the folkloric theorizing of oral storytelling performance placed central emphasis on the narrator's assumption of responsibility for the stories that she or he narrates. Following Roman Jakobson's influential work on style and parallelism (1960; Jakobson and Halle 1971), on the one hand, and considering Walter

Benjamin (1968) on representation, on the other hand, Richard Bauman (1986) has influentially proposed that performance "resides in the assumption of responsibility to the audience for a display of communicative skill, highlighting the way in which communication is carried out, above and beyond its referential content. . . . [It] calls forth a special attention to the heightened awareness of both the act of expression and the performer" (3). Similarly, Dell Hymes (1975, 18) describes performance, or moments of "breakthrough" into performance, as a "cultural behavior for which a person assumes responsibility to an audience." Though both Bauman and Hymes stress the responsibility of the narrator, they are nonetheless occupied with the consequences of these (experiential) states of accountability, which they closely associate with the referential order and with the performative moment that transcends it.

Within this framework, Hymes (1975, 70) importantly anchors the discussion of performance in the perpetuation and survival of communal knowledge. The emphasis on the vital role of performance in culture draws the folkloric discussion well into the research of backpackers, members of a speech community who confirm their membership through the repetition of travel narrative performances. Further, the vital communal performance is attainable due to the "realization of known traditional material," where "the emphasis is upon the constitution of a social event, quite likely with emergent properties" (Hymes 1975, 13; see also Briggs 1988, 275). Again, the contention is that tradition is not only represented in performance, it is also acted and enacted in it; it is *experientially realized* by those attending the performance. In relation to storytelling, Hymes observes that "performance is a mode of existence and realization that is partly *constitutive* of what the tradition is. The tradition itself exists partly for the sake of performance; performance is itself partly an end" (19; emphasis in the original).

Since performance breaks with the referential order and is, in effect, creative and constitutive, the responsibility borne by the narrators is that of members of a community who both know the tradition and know how to *do it*. At stake here is not (only) personal responsibility—say, for "saving face" in a Goffmanesque fashion—but a responsibility that is imbued with social, communal, and historical dimensions: in a word—agency.[6]

Thus viewed, performance inhabits a ritualistic site in which tradition and culture are convincingly manifest, realized, and improvised upon, innovated and negotiated. Performance supplies metacultural commentary that reproduces hegemonic norms while probing and contesting them. Indeed, in the burning politics of identity in Israeli society (described above), perpetuation of sociocultural assets is very much at the root of the travelers' zealous practices and in the meaning their performances encapsulate.

Bauman, Hymes, and others touch shyly upon matters of subjectivity (presently viewed in terms of experience and emotion). Yet accounting for what emerges in performance cannot leave the realm of the subjective—or that of the intersubjective—aside. Rather, it is the interchange between "acts" and "experiences," between (social) reality and (social) subjectivity as it emerges interactionally between narrator(s) and interlocutor(s) that lies at the core of performance.

A revealing expansive treatment of the relationship between intersubjectivity and the performance of storytelling is pursued in the work of folklorist Katharine Young (1987). Young's early work, which is inspired by Erving Goffman's (1974) work on interaction and William Labov's (1972) work on narrative, on the one hand, and by a phenomenological tradition, on the other hand, forcefully brings intersubjectivity into the notion of everyday performance. Young argues that "the lodgment of stories in speaking situations returns attention to the mutuality of their construction, shifting interest from monologue to dialogue" (14). Storytelling occasions do not have merely an inherent dialogic interpersonal quality, they also revolve upon participants' awareness and involvement.

By "intersubjectivity" Young means a mutual reflexive awareness, experienced by both narrator(s) and interlocutor(s). Both parties to the interaction are experientially and emotionally "engaged" in acts of storytelling and storyhearing (the storyrealm) and in the events conjured up therein (the taleworld). "We are implicated in a world together," as worded by Young (1987, 5). In a successful performance participants are drawn into the text, as it were, and are implicated or enlisted in different ways and to different degrees of tensions of consciousness. These stretch "from full awareness in the reality of everyday life to sleep in the world of dreams" (Schutz, cited in Young 1987, 10). Whichever term we employ, the point remains that dialogical states of awareness are both the prerequisite for and the processual outcome of being implicated in the narrative or in the taleworld conjured up performatively and persuasively by the narrative.

A phenomenological narrative implication has *metapragmatic* consequences. Here I evoke ideas presented by Erving Goffman, combined with the notion of "linguistic ideology" (Silverstein 1976, 1979). In this capacity, a narrative implicates the audience and draws it into what is "told," suggesting that the audience is also a character in a tale—a tale that is, in effect, still occurring in the here-and-now (the convergence of the storyrealm and the taleworld). In other words, a narrative performance is characterized by *simultaneously indexing two realms,* two separate and disparate spatiotemporal contexts. This interactional linguistic capacity is what establishes the "double reference" quality of narrative communication (Silverstein 1996), the "two conceptual structures" (Wortham 2001, 36); it simultaneously denotes, refers to, tells and evokes, enacts, shows. In the semiotics of tourism, these twofold structures are evinced in two separate yet intricately interrelated performances: those transpiring during the excursion and those transpiring upon the return from the excursion (that is, either the daily return from excursions to the location of the accommodation during the trip or the return from the trip as a whole. (See my discussion of "excursion narratives" in Noy 2005, 127–31; see also Bruner 2005, 19.)

Experientially, "enclaves" are established during performance, which possess a "double orientation: stories are events themselves and they refer to events that are not themselves, to fictive realms or past worlds, taleworlds conjured by the telling" (Young 1987, 12, following Berger and Luckmann 1967). In every passing moment of narrative performance, two "destinations" are simultaneously indexed. In a society whose linguistic ideology strongly adheres to the abyss between referential and performative, signifier and signified, this experience of performance is dizzying.

The metapragmatic negotiation that occurs during performance concerns the language ideology held by performer and audience. The participants' linguistic ideology touches on the pragmatics of the very language they employ, or, in other words, touches on the relationship between language and (extralinguistic) "reality." As observed by John Lucy (1993b, 21) with respect to metapragmatics, a "verbal art is a form of creative metalinguistic play with the power to affect social reality."

Such cultural metapragmatic commentary evokes Goffman's work (1974) on "frames" that supply our everyday experiential epistemology. It is through these frames of experience that people make sense of what unfolds around them on interactional occasions, and it is through these frames that things are felt to be real, including a sense of one's own selfhood. In this vein, a "Goffmanesque embarrassment," which is commonly (and rightfully) taken to refer to one's losing face, is also an *epistemological embarrassment.* "When individuals attend to any current situation," Goffman writes, "they face the question: 'What is going on here,'" the exploration of which directs us to the "basic frameworks of understanding available in our society for making sense out of events" (8, 10). It is not so much about losing face, then, as it is about losing sense of reality.

More recent theorizing points to the centrality of language and dialogue in establishing the experience of subjectivity and selfhood in narrative performances. Whether inspired by the influential works of Judith Butler (1993, 1997a, 1997b) or by the folkloric-anthropological tradition, these works show how in various social settings, such as the family, the classroom, or the workplace, performance indicates the constitution of social events and social reality. If two decades ago, Bauman (1986, 4) tentatively suggested that performance "carries the potential to rearrange the structure of social relations within the performance event and perhaps beyond it," then current research corroborates that both social relations and social reality are primarily constituted in and through performances. From a communication perspective, Kristin Langellier (1999, 129) contends that "the *personal* in personal narrative implies a performative struggle for agency rather than the expressive act of a pre-existing, autonomous, fixed, united, or stable self" (emphasis in the original). Thus, the notion of narrative performance engulfs a radically constructionist approach whereby descriptions of happenings and experiences that occurred in different spatiotemporal context(s) are linked to the present *constitutively.* "In performativity," Langellier further notes, "narrator and listener(s) are themselves constituted" (129).

In sum, everyday storytelling makes an excellent case for demonstrating referential qualities of language. When people elaborate a personal narrative—when they talk about something that happened to them sometime/somewhere—they effortlessly cross an abyss and bridge the following paradox: how do people tell in one place and at one time what transpired in another place and at another time in a meaningful way? How do people *enliven* that which they tell about and instill their telling with something—popularly called "drama"—that endows the telling with uniqueness, realness, and authenticity? In accomplishing this, in resolving this paradox, we become performers, albeit ad hoc ones; in the capacity of performers we create out of the telling of both ordinary and nonordinary everyday stories occasions in their own right. At stake here is the sense of realness and of reality, which are linguistically mediated and constructed; hence, performances attempt to achieve pragmatic or, more precisely, metapragmatic negotiation and eventually mutual "calibration" shared by the participants (Benjamin Whorf, cited in Young 1987, 206).

The picture remains incomplete, however, as long as the power relationship between those attending and giving performances is not singled out for attention. Indeed, the ability to performatively impel others and to constitute what "reality" is (and what it is not), as well as what "identity" is (and what it is not), is by no means devoid of sociocultural power and authority. In fact, performance is precisely the site where such power is embodied and occurs. Inspired by both Michel Foucault and Jacques Derrida, Judith Butler has reiterated how authority and power, enmeshed in discourse, are the conditions by which subjectivity may be constructed as well as stifled (1993, 1997a, 1997b). More than any other scholar, she cogently directs attention to inequalities in the authority of the performative agent, which refer to her or his very possibility of being an "agent." Butler (1993, 225) succinctly contends that "performance is one domain in which power acts *as* discourse" (emphasis in the original). Although she discusses performance within the broader context of gender construction and inequalities, what she points to is deeply characteristic of constitutive performances in general. In particular, her attention to oppressive and subversive discursive forces within the arena of performance as well as to the "histories" of these authorities, histories in which a given performance is a link, sheds necessary light on the capacity of performances to be "successful": namely, to be constitutive and to implicate others in their ideology.

Having established this broad notion of performance, our inquiry now turns to *tourist* performance. The following section considers whether touristic performances are distinguishable from other performances, and if they are—what are the particular institutional characteristics that endow them with a specific hue.

Tourist Performance: Where Is "Tourism"?

From the older sociodramaturgical model of tourism to recent theorizing, tourism has continually been appreciated as transpiring within an inherently theatrical arena (Bruner 2005; Kirshenblatt-Gimblett 1998; MacCannell 1976; Urry 1990). Theatricality, such authors contend, supplies the semiotic and methodological premise on which we may begin to address and to understand modern tourism and the role language plays in it.

Nevertheless, applying a performance-sensitive approach to tourism is an admittedly tricky matter. It runs counter to the common (and commonsensical) notion that tourists are the observers-consumers of performances and not their objects; they are the spectators and not the spectacles. It is only recently that the active roles played by "guests" and not only "hosts" on the international stages of tourism are being studied. Hence, it is ironic that tourists, too, have become the objects of the touristic gaze; or, to borrow from tourist discourse, that tourists themselves performatively transform into "attractions."

It is the *public nature* of touristic sites, destinations, and activities that grants them their performative qualities. In the epoch of mass (re)production and mass transportation, the various sites visited by tourists are public in the sense that they are readily accessible for the consumption of many. Hence, the diverse activities in which tourists partake acquire the status of public performances. Amplified by an unprecedented state of commercialization and mediatization, the public aspects of tourism, as well as the central role spectatorship plays therein, all lend the semiotics of tourism aptly to a performative-based appreciation.

Judith Adler has suggested that contemporary travel, akin to other forms of art, is both performed and consumed publicly, which is the sphere where its meaning is generated. As in artful performance, the significance of travel is dependent on context and audience: "The audiences for whom travelers perform are crucial to any travel world, and anticipations of their responses, as well as of their direct interventions, play a constitutive role in the production of journeys. Travel audiences are also one source of explicitly articulated standards of performance, as they voice expectations regarding the honor of various itineraries—and the manner in which performances should be 'marked'" (1989, 1378). Artful practices—travel included—beseech responses from designated audiences. In this regard, Adler creatively coins the term *travel audiences* to designate both audiences who are traveling and the particular characteristics of audiences (or audienceship) that attend travel performances (which may or may not have traveled).

This discussion carries at least two relevant implications. First, practiced in a public space, tourism is an ideal activity by means of which collective identity can be established, negotiated, and innovated. Tourism institutionally constructs public spaces that are most suitable for dynamic social interaction and exchange—social public spaces of the type depicted by Bakhtin (1968)—as well as for the performance of identities and their refractions.

Second, the end of the quote above from Adler (1989, 1378) implies that performances also establish the very norms by which they are defined and appraised. In this vein, too, touristic public spaces are ideal for competitively comparing performances. As we will see, while the performances of backpackers make use of various touristic resources that are available in the public spaces of tourism, competing and comparing performances are an *intratourist affair*, conducted within the backpacking community.

This notion is echoed in subsequent works that explore the in situ practices of tourists. Sørensen's (2003) ethnography of backpacker culture suggests that the travelers ceaselessly engage in a process of "hierarchization." By this term Sørensen is suggesting that they repeatedly compare and compete with one another in order to establish their valued "road status" and to position themselves more advantageously within the community. Interestingly, the process of hierarchization, albeit competitive, is by no means exclusive—quite the contrary: through establishing shared norms that pertain to the appreciation and evaluation of performance, the process of hierarchization does not have "anyone on the bottom rung" (858). Rather, the establishment of these hierarchic and competitive norms is the social glue that binds the performed category "backpacker" to produce a shared experience of identity.

While research on tourist performances in general naturally focuses on the conduct of the travelers in situ—that is, in destination sites—this book attends to narrative performances that take place *after* tourists *return* from the trip, once they are back in their everyday lives, activities, and spaces (Harrison 2003). In this regard, the present perspective is less inclined to an ethnographic exploration of what is traditionally designated as the "field."

This type of inquiry is intricate because it adds representations to a semiotic scene already saturated with representations. Within a heated nexus of narratives and images, the present exploration deals with how tourists represent that which they saw, experienced, and did elsewhere. In line with the constitutive effect of performance, the performances of tourists actually render problematic the notion of in situ altogether, a notion commonly equated with "destination" (or, in ethnography, with "field"). It is here that the contribution of a performance-based inquiry is most illuminating, for it brings to the fore the highly contextualized event of tourist narration, in which meaning and semiotic values of places, peoples, and times are conjured and constituted. Touristic excursions and the unique experiences they endow supply the means by which performances establish a sense of place, for example, "home" and "hereness," the qualities of which are associated with those of the destination (Kirshenblatt-Gimblett 1998, 7). To paraphrase Adler (1989), at stake is an inquiry concerning the interlinking of two performances: "the art of travel" and "the art of travel narrative" (cf. Bruner 2005, 19).

Yet in the performative capacity, these travel narratives amount to "off-site" markers, which make for "the first contact that a sightseer has with a sight" (Dann 1996, 9; see also MacCannell 1976, 109–33). These stories then amount to a "narrative sequence in which the tourist first hears or reads about a sight through an off-site marker . . . and then follows the directions given him by subsequent markers until arriving at the on-site markers (such as a memorial plaque) which trigger his recognition of the sight" (van den Abbeele 1980, 4). In this vein, the performances of tourists can also be construed as a type of "trigger" or "marker," which in itself constructs an attractive site to which tourist "artifacts" are brought, including memories, pictures, and narratives. Such a perspective is inspired by the poetics of extraction (in the Kirshenblatt-Gimblett sense), whereby tourists' bodies are conceptualized as embodied souvenirs—they are witnesses of their own (and of others') unique travel experiences and adventures. As pointed out by Susan Stewart (1993,

135), narrative performance typically bridges abysses: "We need or desire souvenirs of events that are reportable, events whose materiality has escaped us . . . events that thereby exist only through the invention of narrative."

The literature on backpacking experience points to how touristic adventures become narrative resources, employed performatively in the capacity of (re)constituting experience, identity (the "experiencer"), and a sense of social belonging in the tourists' home societies. Researching tourists visiting the Grand Canyon, Mark Neumann observes that "the meaning and significance of travel assume value in the *moment of recollecting* for others the experiences that occur away from home . . . [which] *materialize in the moments of storytelling*" (1992, 179–80; my emphasis. Cf. Coleman and Crang 2002); and Edensor succinctly concludes that "as performers, tourists are informed by representations yet *produce representations of their own*" (1998, 61; my emphasis). Tourist performances, then, amount to creative events within which cultural tenets are constituted and maintained. Hence we shall see how the profound experiences that backpackers narrate and the very sense of profundity develop in the course of the performance intersubjectively, and how it is accomplished with regard to the unique qualities of the destinations of which they narrate.[7]

Indeed, performances often constitute spaces or sites that meaningfully effect identity. In tourist performances narrative capital is galvanized while authoritative claims of and for identities are made. Elsrud (2001, 606) observes of backpackers' stories of adventure and risk that "through establishing a (mythologized) image of Otherness, a story about self-identity can be told." Desforges (2000, 927) adds that upon the tourists' return home, "touristic stories are used to present new self-identities." Elsrud and Desforges indicate that the semiotics that endow touristic performance with meaning and influence rest on the role played by metonymy, particularly when *off-site* performances are at stake. Metonymy is the thread connecting the two types of tourist performances: those that occur in the destinations—the there-and-then of narrative—and those that occur after the trip—the here-and-now (posttravel) of narrative. As artists practicing the "art of the metonym" (Kirshenblatt-Gimblett 1998, 19; see also Bruner 2005, 19), tourists try to conjure or construct in the "here-and-now" of their performances something of the "there-and-then" of events narrated, events in which they themselves played the role of heroes.

It is with this notion of the here-and-now of posttravel narrative performance that we proceed to the next section, dedicated to the context of the (touristic) interview encounter and to snowball sampling methods.

Sampling and Interviewing Tourists

> Poring over our fieldnotes, there is plenty of time to discover crucial questions that we failed to ask, and remember kindnesses that can never be repaid. These are the preliminaries to writing ethnography.
> P. Metcalf

During 1998–99 I conducted forty-one interviews with forty-four Israeli backpackers who had recently (within five months) returned from "the great journey" as a basis for my Ph.D. dissertation. The interviews took place in Israel, usually at the backpackers' homes (or, to be accurate, at their parents' homes), which were located in large cities, anywhere between Beersheba in the south and Haifa in the north. The interview conversations were in depth and open ended (see Fontana and Frey 2000; Kvale 1996) and typically lasted between one and three hours. I met with twenty-three female backpackers and twenty-one male backpackers—all middle-class, secular Jewish Israelis, aged twenty-two to twenty-five. Seventeen women and twelve men were of European origin (Ashkenazi), while six women and nine men were of Oriental origin (Mizrahi). All but two had been born in Israel. They all had traveled for at least three months in the countries typically frequented by Israelis in Asia (mostly India, Nepal, and Thailand) and in South America (mostly the Andes, Argentina, Chile, and Brazil), in trips that took place shortly after completion of their obligatory military service in Israel.

I reached these veteran backpackers through employing a sampling method that is known as "snowball" sampling, by which interviewees referred me to friends and acquaintances of theirs, who in turn gave me further names, and so on (Noy 2002, 2006b, 96–102; O'Leary 2004, 114; Rosenthal 1993). The first few backpackers I met through mutual acquaintances and through several visits I made to a photography store located in the center of Jerusalem, which backpackers frequented in order to develop the many reels of film they had taken during the trip.

The snowball sampling procedure has substantial advantages, yet it is not without its weaknesses. Central among its advantages is the fact that the researcher moves within a naturally existing social network. As is the case with other "bottom-up" or "respondent-driven" sampling procedures (Heckathorn 1997; Heckathorn and Jeffri 2001), the researcher is led along active social chains of friends, acquaintances, and even siblings, who, in this case, regularly exchanged travel information and travel experiences. Traveling along social routes from one interviewee to the other affords the researcher some sense of entering a community and interacting within it.[8]

Snowball sampling is a method commonly employed in order to estimate the sizes of "hidden populations" (such as HIV carriers). While the backpackers are surely not a hidden population, the second advantage of this sampling procedure is that it makes it possible to sample tourists who cannot be reached via demographic data (see note 1). Hence, the "site" I explored is social, not geographical, and is embodied precisely in these lively social networks (see appendix 1).[9]

The snowball sampling method is also called "ascending methodology" (Faugier and Sargeant 1997). In the present study, this "ascending" movement touches upon the interrelations between what is commonly called micro and macro spheres of sociality. By following the backpackers' organic social networks, I "ascended" from the sphere of the individual (with whom I met in the interview) to the sphere of the community (about which I heard in the interview). As noted by Dell Hymes (1974, 51), any attempt to define a speech (or narrative) community runs the risk of being tautological. Communal tenets, symbols, and narratives inspire a shared worldview by which social interactions and networks are possible. These interactions and networks, in turn, maintain the community's social vitality.

This tautology can be avoided by employing constructionist sensibilities. While interpersonal networks are a given (observable) social fact, which functioned in this research as a convenient infrastructure for traveling between travelers, a community is a socially constructed entity. It is generated in and through the backpackers' performances, endowing the narrators with a sense of identity and belonging. They accomplish generating a communal experience by intertextualizing their performances, thus populating the duo encounters with a polyphony of social voices: with various wes, yous, and theys (backpackers, locals, tourists, and so on; see chapters 3–7). In this vein, Alessandro Duranti (1997) suggests abandoning the notion of a speech community as "an already constituted object of inquiry" (82) and conceptualizing it instead as a "product" of communicative activities. When it is thus conceptualized, Duranti stresses that researchers should "recognize the constitutive nature of speaking as a human activity that does not only assume but builds 'community.'"

In retrospect, I am surprised at the nerve I demonstrated then, contacting people who were complete strangers, asking them to allocate a few hours of their free time, during which—for a cup of coffee or tea and some sweets—they openly shared personal experiences. Undoubtedly, my own "backpacking genes" were at work, pressing me to meet younger backpackers who had participated in the same rite of passage as I. Yet there were also power dynamics involved, resulting from the fact that I arrived at the interviews as a "doctoral candidate." These dynamics resulted from and took shape through the similarities and differences of the two elitist institutions and discourses of tourism and academia. Academically, the motivation that propelled me in these efforts was mainly phenomenological: I was interested in the depths of the experiences the great journey supplied these youths with. This is why the interviews were conducted *shortly after* the return from the trip, at a point in time when—as a few of the backpackers put it—"we've returned but we're still there": when the experiences of travel were still of the quality of "magma" (and not "granite"), to use a metaphor occasionally evoked by Bakhtin.

Indeed, the conversations provided ideal posttour settings (Bruner 2005, 26), in which the backpackers could recount and relive the experiences of the great journey. The conversations were planned so as to provide a convenient occasion for recollections of both a holistic nature—referring to the entire trip—and an anecdotal and thematic nature—referring to particular incidents and recollections, such as gender-related experiences. (See appendix 2.)

Occurring shortly after they had concluded the trip, this inquiry into backpackers' tales and experiences may be conceptually situated between large-scope biographical research, which inquires into the interviewee's life in its entirety, and particularly into his or her travel biography, on the one hand, and tourist ethnographies, which are conducted in situ and investigate the actual conduct during the excursion, on the other hand.

Very little has been published about posttour (Bruner 2005) or posttrip (Dann

1996) interpersonal communication and storytelling. Indeed, one of the most enduring biases of tourism scholarship is the inclination to locate "tourism" in the destination sites or to equate tourism with its destinations, in much the same way as the tourists themselves do (I will return to this point later). This exclusion produces a rather partial picture of the intricate play of tourism and the semiotics of "things touristic" in various societal and cultural spheres. As a result, precious little attention has been paid to pre- and posttravel experiences or to the experience of travel (transportation) itself (Bruner 2005, 15).

In one exception, Julia Harrison observes the pros and cons of the method of posttour interview conversations. She notes that while "I would not see first hand how they acted as tourists while away . . . I would have access only to what they remembered," the information that would be gained "was valid in its own right: it could shed light on the meaning of the travel experience to these people, for it was these memories that spurred them on to plan their next trip" (2003, 5).

As Harrison indicates, she explores in her research the travel biographies of "travel enthusiasts," who are older than the backpackers and are always in between trips—concluding the last one while anticipating the next. Yet the present consideration of backpackers examines narrations by travelers who had recently returned from what they typically called "a once-in-a-lifetime experience" (rather than a lifetime of experiences). The youths to whose stories I listened were very much under the impression—or the spell—of the overwhelming experience(s) of the trip—still within the experiential "halo effect" of the great journey. This fact might account for the ritualistic character of their performances. At this juncture in their lives, they were hardly beginning to anticipate how they would join society as adults and assume civic responsibilities therein, where their trips would take them in the future, and what or who they would become. (See chapter 10.)

The Art of the Metonym: A Note on Transcription

The irony is that a more exact science and method make accidental details essential.

Dell Hymes

The role of metonymy in tourism presently touches upon yet another representation, that of transcribed travel narratives. Although transcription—the process of "translating" oral material into printed matter and simultaneously translocating it—seems to be a neutral procedure, it is in fact semiotically tricky: soon after I began to transcribe narratives, it became clear to me how theory-ridden this process really is. This is why this methodological practice has troubled anybody researching oral material in Western research traditions (the core, if not sole, representation avenue of which is in the form of written publications).

From nineteenth-century ethnographic fieldwork to more recent exploration in sociolinguistic-related subdisciplines, transcription has proven to be more about theory and interpretation than about mimetic representation. Presently, various methods of transcription ("notation systems") are available to the researcher of oral expression, methods that correspond to different paradigmatic research goals and theoretical and ethical commitments (Duranti 2003, 334).

There are different approaches to transcription according to what sensitivities scholars of speech communication employ (or exclude). As stated by Mannheim and van Vleet (1998, 326), "standard written representations of oral narratives lead inevitably to their being interpreted for their referential content alone." Here again, the tide of the "poetic turn" is evinced, as we are required to deliberate on a variety of paradigmatic issues, extending from epistemology to ethics, and to consider the appropriate representation of tourist narrations.

While the difficulties raised by the transcription of live speech in general are considerable, they are even more acute when ritualistic, highly stylized oral performances are transcribed. Since these live performances are artistic, and since they entail a particularly high degree of involvement on behalf of the participants, a verbatim transcription naturally cannot succeed in conveying the lively exchange. This is why performance researchers interpret the requirement to produce an "accurate" text liberally. As Bauman (1986, x) admits, his choice of representation was "intended to have more expressive than linguistic accuracy." Indeed, Bauman indicates that he has tried to "preserve" in the transcriptions "something of the quality (however vague and impressionistic that term may be) of the oral discourse," which does not necessarily correlate with strict accuracy.

Dealing broadly with the difficulties of transcribing narrative performances, Dennis Tedlock's ideas are appealing. Tedlock contends that "spoken narratives are better understood (and translated) as dramatic poetry than as an oral equivalent of written prose fiction" (1983, 55). Tedlock compellingly promotes the view that the "spoken" facet suggests a different generic rendering of narrative, a term we commonly associate with prose rather than with poetry. In fact, narrative has become the emblem of prose literature in modernity. But performed—embodied, rhythmic, almost tactual—narrativity loses its essential prosaic formal characteristic, and it is in occasions of oral narration that the tensions between prose and poetry are expressed most sharply and dramatically.

Specifically, Tedlock argues that the crucial component missing in transcription and translation of oral performances is that of time: "Of all these realities of oral narrative performance, the plainest and the grossest is the sheer alteration of sound and silence; the resultant lines often show an independence from intonation, from syntax, and even from boundaries of plot structure. . . . It is above all the *when,* or what dramatists call 'timing,' that is missing in printed prose" (1983, 55–56, emphasis in the original). In line with Kirshenblatt-Gimblett's (1998) notions of "extractness" and metonym, the translated/transcribed/extracted representations are hereafter viewed as texts that try to convey something of the original artful occasion. This is carried out by acknowledging the shift in mediums of representation and by employing whatever resources are available for artful expression in print:

namely, space. While the black print on the white page is motionless, the *process* of reading letters, words, and sentences is not. It rests upon motion(s): horizontal and vertical. In the transcriptions in Tedlock's works, end lines mark rhythmic patterns, establishing a correlation between the embodied movement of breathing and eye movement.

It is primarily for this reason that the transcriptions in this book do not require a detailed deciphering system yet are usually not set out in justified or block form. Instead, spatial configurations have been foregrounded, and exact intervals between words were compromised in favor of accessibility and dramatic effect. Throughout the book I freely oscillate between justified and spatially configured textual representation of the pieces, according to the "performance load" (Hymes 1975, 44) and the interpretative aims of their presentation.

In the excerpts cited in this book, *utterances*—units of breath rhythm and content—rather than grammatical sentences are presented. Breath pauses are therefore noted, portrayed by a separation between lines (when an utterance is longer than a line, it continues in the next line). Horizontally, the extracted text begins flush with the left margin and progresses to the right with each breath stop when the context of the same utterance is developed (Briggs 1988). Back-channel cues are parenthesized, aligned to the right on the same line as the utterances to which they refer. The reader may find the layout of words, utterances, and back-channel cues, and their spatial interrelations, confusing and overburdening at times. This should but indicate how in fact highly complex are these stylized occasions of storytelling and how much of the condensed messages and meanings created therein are produced and received unconsciously by the participants.

The following devices are also used:

—	abrupt breaks or stops (in the middle or at the end of a word)
...	a few words left out
[missing words]	words missing in the original transcription and added later
[overlap]	when between adjacent lines, square brackets indicate two speakers talking at once
?	rising intonation at the end of a word or a sentence
(comments)	transcriber's comments
(*italicized*)	transliterated Hebrew original
(1)	a measured pause (in this example one second), when lasting a second or longer
SMALL CAPITALS	noticeably louder speech
"quotation"	quotation marks indicate direct reported speech
aaah	a voiced pause, the length of which is represented by repetition of the vowel

, .   comma and period represent pauses (less than a second long), the first
                    shorter than the second; the comma also marks falling intonation as at
                    the end of a clause, and the period indicates falling intonation as at the end
                    of a sentence

To conclude this section, it is worthwhile to remind and to suggest that through and
beyond this notation system, this book carries and conveys animated voices and will
hopefully be for the reader "a text to read not with eyes alone, but with the ears in
order to hear 'the voices of the pages'" (Tyler 1986, 136).

Arriving at the Destination: No Transcendence

*It's difficult for me to reconstruct and convey the immensity of the expectations I,
a late adolescent shortly released from army service, had before the Great Journey.
These were experiential expectations of the highest order, concerning both the utterly
unique destinations—such as the Everest mountain chain in Nepal or the mysticism
of Indian culture—and myself—existential narratives attesting to transcendent experiences and consequent spiritual growth. No doubt about it: I was deeply enchanted
with the "East."*

*Because I reached Kathmandu from Los Angeles (where I was visiting my cous-
ins), I arrived alone, with no acquaintances, social connections, or recommendations
about where to stay. I soon hooked up with a younger Israeli in a similar predicament. She was about a head shorter than myself, with dark and curly hair. She was
the first Israeli I met on the trip. Together, we ended up in a very cheap guesthouse
run by a kind, chubby Buddhist monk, located at the outskirts of the Thamel quarter
in Kathmandu, a neighborhood where most backpackers lodge and dine.*

*Later on that evening, my new acquaintance announced that she had managed
to get hold of some marijuana and invited me to join her in her room, in which, due
to the low price she had paid, the ceiling was so low we couldn't stand up straight. I
was eagerly looking forward to the experience of "getting high": I had never smoked
marijuana—in fact I had never even touched a regular tobacco cigarette before. But
this was Nepal. This was the Great Journey. I was anticipating transcendent experiences, and the word marijuana had a unique and now attainable aura to it. So
I accepted the invitation, followed her directions, and inhaled deeply—holding the
wheaty smoke in my lungs for a long time. I did so several times. The effect, as you can
imagine, was far from the one desired. I immediately felt a huge headache, my heart
beat quickly and fiercely, I was sweating profusely and was awfully nauseous. I was
so dizzy I could hardly stand up. I thanked her with whatever politeness my receding
consciousness still possessed, and in some miraculous manner found my way back to
my room and to my bed (I think she helped me).*

*At this point a severe rainstorm developed over Kathmandu: the skies were
light, even though it was night, and the sound of the thunder was incredibly loud. To
make things worse, the heavy rain pounding on the old brick building—I could swear*

I felt the building move slightly—was gradually making its way inside; the corners of the walls and the ceiling were getting wetter by the minute. I was sure I was headed for a personal disaster. The last thought I had before fading away into sleep was: "this is no transcendence."

2

Persuasion

"Did you chew coca leaves?" Positioning or Deciding on a Genre

Quite early during the interviews, I noticed that the backpackers asked, offhandedly and repeatedly, whether I myself had participated in the great journey about which I was inquiring. These questions were subtle enough so that I neglected to consider them during the first few interviews, and my laconic replies, documented in magnetic recordings and inky field notes, did not result from any particular sensitivity or appreciation on my part, but from the surprising persistence of these questions.

These inquiries, which sought to position me as an interlocutor and addressee, were coupled with another offhanded suggestion—that I myself should also undertake the great journey and backpack magnificent regions and hike majestic mountains. As these suggestions were usually presented in a humorous fashion and during "small talk," lying in the periphery of the interview conversation, the narrators were able to use heavily suggestive language—"You *should* go travel" and "You *must* go hiking"—without it being obtrusive or even noticeable at the time, and without disturbing the meeting's intimacy and rapport. On the contrary, these remarks seemed friendly and were organic to the developing conversation. They were part of the informal greeting and welcoming routine I encountered upon entering the interviewee's house (where most of the conversations took place). They were both the consequence of the close relationship that emerged quickly between us and their central catalyst.

These warm and close suggestions were also expressed throughout the conversation, which was possible due to the high level of conversational involvement typical of interpersonal patterns of communication among Hebrew-speaking Israelis (Blum-Kulka 1997; Domínguez 1989; Katriel 1986). Yet, in order to avoid answering these questions immediately and still not break the framework of customary politeness, I usually replied I would answer them later—which I did.

Sometime after I had conducted between the twelfth and the fifteenth interview, after listening to the first taped interviews and looking through the corresponding field notes, I decided to make a slight modification in the notes with which I began every interview. I added a remark reminding myself to address the interviewee's question "Were you there?" Only gradually did I realize that these questions represented something whose relevance and importance could hardly be overstated. They reflected the interviewees' need to locate me with regard to their tightly knit social reference group, to position me as an "insider" or "outsider." This indicated that such firm communal boundaries do indeed exist—although, naïvely, I was not initially aware of them—and that they had a pivotal effect on what the backpackers did or did not tell me. Furthermore, the manner in which the interviewees narrated their experiences corresponded with their positioning of me as interlocutor; it had an effect on the *genre* of the informants' narration.

What is more, I felt that most of the stories I had been hearing had a *direction*—that *I* should travel, go on a great journey, and thus become "within": that I should transcend not only geographical distances and boundaries but sociocultural ones as well, and that I should ascend not only topographical heights but also experiential and transformatory ones. During their performances, when I explicitly confessed my feelings to the narrators, noting that the stories indeed aroused within me an "appetite," a deep yearning to travel and participate in such activities as those they recounted, their answers typically reflected satisfaction. They would clap their hands and exclaim, "Then I have succeeded!" This excited metanarration comment suggested that the backpackers were occupied with storytelling competence and with achieving a forceful act, whose persuasive effect was evaluated and validated by my disclosure. They felt that the *aim* of their story, its direction, was to persuade and motivate me to join the practice and share their experience and knowledge. In other words, the stories' words carried and communicated extralinguistic messages, forcefully pointing at realms that are commonly perceived as exiting *beyond language;* as such, these stories managed metapragmatically the relationship between language and that which is construed as nonlingual.

Before elaborating theoretically on the stories' performative pragmatic force and how the backpackers simultaneously create a realm of travelworld (taleworld) and direct the interlocutor into occupying it as a protagonist (Young 1987)—that is, how they protagonize the listener—I would like to turn to a few illustrations. These will address the twofold dialogical issues concerning positioning the listener/audience inside or outside the bounds of the speech community and, consequently, engaging or implicating her or him in the narrative.

The first illustration exemplifies how, in the backpackers' own language—in their own "emic" terms—the experience of which they tell and the genre by which they choose to do so are achieved via positioning the interlocutor. The question at stake is whether I have or have not backpacked, thus undertaking the community's defining practice, and consequently, whether I was endowed with a similar formative experience. Better, the inquiry assumes a present continuous tense, inquiring into whether I am presently a "veteran backpacker," and hence an in-group member, or not.

The excerpt is from the end of my meeting with Noa, who narrates her three-month trip to South America. As we draw near the end of our meeting, I ask Noa whether she has any questions for me. She then introduces the inquiry into my experience in a rationalized manner, appropriate for an "interview" conducted with a "doctoral candidate":

Noa: I have a small question
how did you get into this specific subject? ...
either you have traveled and you wanted
you want to know why people are traveling now
or not necessarily
'cause you haven't traveled and so you want to know why people—
either someone has traveled and 'cause of that it is interesting to him
'cause of his very essence he has traveled
'cause he knows why he has traveled and he wants to
understand why other people travel
what they do while traveling
what they think
what influences their journey ...
on the one hand there is someone who hasn't traveled
he wants to understand why other people travel
why there is something that other people
have done and he hasn't in the same society
two extremes that's all ...
[on the other hand for] someone who has been [traveling]—   (somewhat louder)
it is obvious from the—   (quickly)
all the treks—
if someone was—
then he knows exactly what you are talking about and why
and understands this feeling—
Chaim: Could you give an [example—
Noa: Cuzco is—]
Cuzco is Cuzco   (quickly, as if obvious)
I always remember how before the journey they
explained to me
and all
all the names sounded like CHINESE to me
what is Cuzco?
what is Azangate?[1]
and the minute you are part of it
all these terms seem very clear to you and you are also
speaking in the same language—   (quickly)
if I'm trying to explain to you what [backpackers] feel when they reach the end of the pass
then whoever has experienced it will understand it really
whoever has experienced it will understand it directly

Noa leads with the question probing into how I have arrived at this research, which is to say how did I come to meet her and to attend to her performance of profound travel stories and experiences. More accurately, her question inquires as to *why* I have come to do so—which amounts to an inquiry concerning the interrelationship of both positioning and motivation. What stands behind the inquiry is immediately clear. Noa wishes to know whether I have traveled as she did ("either you have traveled or you haven't traveled") while asking about motivations. The inquiry is an indirect, intellectualized variation of the explicit and straightforward question as to whether I have participated in the practice about which the interviewees narrate. An explicit dichotomous distinction is thus erected between those who have and those who have not traveled ("two extremes," as Noa puts it).

Yet Noa is repeatedly dealing not only with experience but also with motivation ("how did you get into the specific subject?"), which is understood to be the sole consequence of two distinct experiences, both in immediate relation to her own experience and to that of mine: either I have gone through the experience she has or I have not. These two distinct states are of crucial experiential and communicative importance to the performers, to their "essence."

The significance of the experience of "have/haven't traveled" is exemplified in Noa's own words, through addressing the topic repeatedly and through evoking a metalinguistic metaphor ("Chinese"). In fact, Noa does not employ a metaphor, nor even an analogy, as it might initially seem, but rather a homology: it *is* language of which and from which she is speaking. Before experiencing it, the language of backpacking was unknown to her: "What is Cuzco? What is Azangate?" she reiterates, performing her wonder with an unknown, exotic language. Moreover, in the sense that "Chinese" is an idiom, it indexes not only a certain dialect spoken in parts of China, but the Other, that which is ultimately strange, unknown. These words "Cuzco . . . Azangate" were to her as they are now to us, and unless we sojourn on such a trip ourselves they will remain empty signifiers—or secrets—waiting to be unveiled. Once she has participated in the great journey and has gone through the motion, then "Cuzco is Cuzco"! It can only be "explained" to outsiders in a cumbersome manner but never "known" to us directly, in an unmediated fashion. "Cuzco is Cuzco" is an eternal circle that rotates between interchangeable signifier ("Cuzco") and signified (Cuzco). The only way to "know" then, is to *go and travel for ourselves,* which is exactly the core interest of Noa's performance.

This is also apparent when Noa refers, in a tone that says "it is obvious," to "his very essence." This essence is now *dialogical.* Noa indeed changes the "you"—myself—to "him"—general, anonymous ("either someone"), but we should not overlook the fact that the essence is in the here-and-now between performer and audience, between Noa and myself: do I *know* what she is talking about, can I *experience* it, is it of my essence, or does she need to explain it to me—intellectually, verbally, cumbersomely? The way by which one can acquire the esteemed knowledge is presented as direct and immediate, in a word, transformatory. Immediately after Noa mentions words in "Chinese," she evokes time in its instantaneous capacity. She says that "the minute" (or the "instant," *barega*) one joins the community, "Chinese" becomes clear. While the gestalt snaps into place and knowledge is gained instantaneously—the shift from not-knowing to knowing is nothing less than transformatory.

Narrators creatively employ different rhetorical devices by which they may successfully position me with regard to their community. These usually assume the shape of supposedly incidental inquiries. They include inquiring, in an appropriate place in the plot, whether I too have chewed coca leaves, whether I have also suffered from Acute Mountain Sickness (AMS), whether I know what a *Chola* is,[2] whether I have "happened" to be at the height of eighteen thousand feet, and so on. These are more than practical indications: within the context of our meeting they are definitively informative, and answering to any of them positively positions me in the esteemed class of a "veteran backpacker."

Such inquiries, and the positions they imply, also shape the power structures that underlie the interview interaction. Within the backpackers' social hierarchies, veteran backpackers who have traveled long ago are highly esteemed, while those outside the community, or those who are about to travel or have traveled recently, assume a lower status.[3]

In other cases the narrators draw the line between "in" and "out" through various metaphors of inclusion and exclusion. Some (mostly those who traveled in South and Central America) depict the backpackers' frequent congregations in large groups in terms of "families." Traveling, then, amounts to being or becoming a sibling, a term that perhaps indicates the youths' longings for their families far away. Others draw their metaphors from touristic discursive resources, whereby geographical distances are constructed as bearing mythic or symbolic qualities.

Sarit, for instance, tells humorously of backpackers' diversions during the trip to South America, in the form of playing a card game: "[One] MUST know it when you are in South America, otherwise you don't get a visa." Through mentioning both trivial and central practices in which they engage, narrators forcefully perform divisions and inclusions. The "visa" in this case suggests that in a parallel manner to the crossing of national borders, within their rite of passage the backpackers also *cross social borders* and are permitted entrance not only to foreign countries but to sociocultural collectives as well, and to the identities they enfold. Note that what grants this permission are the little things, pastimes the backpackers are well acquainted with.

In another instance when, toward the end of our conversation, I remind Ari of a question he has asked me earlier (at the beginning of our meeting he asked whether I have hiked), he replies: "It's interesting—look, in fact if you were there then you know already all these things," which recalls Noa's use of the word "know." Ari calls his nine-month trip the "most beautiful time in my life." When he continues, it is apparent that what is at stake in his account is not only the described experience but also a derivative, implicit persuasion:

Ari: If you've been there
                          then you already know
                                        that is—
                          you know the atmosphere
                  no need to explain to you
                                        the atmosphere that's there
Chaim: [mmm
Ari: I can] explain to you
                                  the atmosphere
but until you're there
                      you don't understand it
                      you can't feel the atmosphere
                      you can understand what someone else feels   (slowly)
                      you couldn't feel it yourself until YOU'RE THERE ...
                                        until you're there and you see it
                      it's impossible to know
                                  only when I returned did I understand what had happened

Ari reiterates the uniqueness and singularity of the experience of backpacking, suggesting it cannot be wholly captured and represented in language. One has to really be "THERE," in the faraway, remote destination in order to "know," that is to be intimately acquainted with the backpacking experience and to be able to share it ably. Typically, Ari contends that there are no referential, representational shortcuts; there is no way around going through the ritualistic motion in order to arrive at, consume, and experience the ineffable.

The stories the backpackers enthusiastically perform, which are heard as instances of tourists' notorious verbosity, have, in fact, ineffability at their core. They point at an extralinguistic site that exists elsewhere, not in the here-and-now of the interaction. The tellers construct within the occasion of storytelling a place and/or an activity, and a derivative experience, that lie beyond discourse. The stories thus point to what supposedly exists outside the story: the "actual," "literal," bare practice of backpacking. In the words of both Noa and Ari, a true understanding of the experience of which they tell necessitates a *repetition or a citing of the undergoing.* This is the key to how what is told could truly be "known" or "felt" by the audience; it is also the key for the assumption of a sought-after category of authority (agency) and identity.

As Ari's words, akin to Noa's, point to the site where profound experience readily exists, they come closer to prescription than description. Though not yet straightforwardly explicit, Ari's emphatic use of the second person makes it clear that it is the present interaction that he is addressing. In a roundabout way he points the interlocutor (myself) in a certain direction. As he realizes it is his experience that I seek to learn, he draws a dichotomous, hierarchal distinction between the here-and-now and the longed-for taleworld, which his narrative both evokes and points to. He stylistically repeats the words "you are there" (and variations thereof) several times. Toward the end of the strip, however, he stresses these words, and adds the temporal condition "until," suggesting that the possibility of following the steps he has taken is available: more so, it is impending.

The very concluding expression is an evaluation, whereby Ari succinctly makes another important point. Reflexively, he notes that visiting the sites and participating in the activities he has been narrating about does not suffice in and of itself. Rather, one has to *return* in order to make sense of the profound adventures and experiences. Truly "knowing" or "feeling" are not inevitable consequences of participating in the trip. The additional necessary condition is that a circle be completed, which makes for a popular version of the van Gennep (1909/1960)/Turnerian (1967, 1982) threefold phases of rites de passage: departure, liminality, and reaggregation. Only then, from the vantage point of reflexive hindsight, does the experience assume coherency and sensibility, and only then—as Ari implies—is it narratively communicable, tellable.

Such expressions demonstrate how the backpackers seek to locate my position as a researcher: whether I am inside or outside the boundaries of the community. As it is, my presumed location was that of an outsider—an identity that was partly revealed by the very fact that I attended their stories as a passive, albeit enthusiastic, audience and did not collaboratively join in on the narration, sharing my awakened travel experiences. Also, while they demarcate the communal boundaries, they make it clear that there exists a deeper, more "real" and profound level of experience. The center of the community, they imply, has vertical dimensions (it is "deep") in addition to horizontal dimensions (inside/outside, center/periphery). And the best they can do as narrators, they contend, is have their stories point me in a direction, the pursuit of which can endow me with the profound, transcendent (ineffable) experience I seek.

While in these excerpts the narrators do not use explicit persuasive language, they are not far from that. Inasmuch as they construct a necessary experiential divide—that corresponds with and overlaps a geographical distance—over which persuasion can carry one's body, they establish a crucial prerequisite of persuasion: they suggest *somewhere experientially to go to.* By and large, the genre is not downright missionary but more covert and suggestive. This is accounted for by one central reason: the rite of passage these youths undertake, and of which they narrate, is importantly perceived by themselves and by their audiences as "secular." It is the modern touristic incarnation of the premodern religious pilgrimage (Badone and Roseman 2004; Cohen 1992a, 1992b).

Here the global characteristic of tourism conflates with the particular collective identity of the social sectors from which the backpackers originate, which, too, are perceived as "secular." Had they been more downright missionary and openly persuasive, they would have run the risk of being misinterpreted and misplaced within the ideologically suffused politics of identity in Israeli society. Backpackers thus talk and walk a thin line: on the one hand, they are persuasive; on the other

hand, they cannot make free use of divine rhetoric, as do their born-again counterparts and other members of evangelist speech communities is Israel. That said, the
following indicates that persuasive rhetoric is certainly employed, and when the
discursive setting allows for it, such rhetoric is not necessarily covert.

From Intersubjective to Interactive: Experiences and Narration

> We speak only in definite speech genres.
> Mikhail Bakhtin

After the backpackers persistently inquired whether I had participated in the great
journey, the answer to which I postponed to latter parts of the conversation, the
interviewees assumed that I had not traveled—suggestions, directions, advice, and
wholehearted recommendations that I do so soon followed. This was done much in
the same taken-for-granted way that people routinely augment the telling of their
everyday consumption practices with suggestions that their listeners should experience these activities for themselves ("It's a great movie; you must see it").

   When Galit elaborates on the question she has asked me (whether or not I have
traveled), she asserts that a companionship exists among backpackers. Earlier in the
conversation she said that, unlike most Israelis, she did not tell of her experiences
"to too many people," thus singling herself out from the majority through pointing
metadiscursively to her unique and exclusive patterns of communication. Furthermore, Galit's metadiscursive claim does not merely illustrate the case of backpacker
communality, it also generates this sense of community between the hearer and
the teller in situ. By indicating how and to whom information is discreetly disseminated, she makes me a collaborator, an accomplice. Galit therefore tries to further
"lure me" me into the community by granting me access to restricted information
and by confiding to me information regarding the elitist social circles within which
this information travels.

   Additionally, Galit is suggesting that the story, akin to a valuable commodity
that may erode with use, is precious. Too much use, too many storytelling performances, might exhaust the text of its uniqueness and of its performable authenticity.
As Nelson Graburn observed of tourists' recollections, "to share is to lose power"
(1989, 31). Galit is reminded of friends of hers, a couple, who traveled sometime
after she did and to whom she did reveal her feelings:

Galit: There's a fellowship of travelers (ahvat metaylim)[4]
       there's a fellowship of travelers
                        "what—
                              you've been in South America?"
                        "I was also in South America"
                              "really? where?"
          sorta locate the thing
                        "where was I?

in India"

"we've seen the same sights" ...

I also gave them recommendations for the journey

so I kinda sent them with a push

they're the only ones I sent a postcard to

"many people can go without [the trip]

and that's fine

YOU GO TO INDIA"

hmmm

there's a fellowship of travelers all right

Galit both establishes the shared and communal character bonding those who traveled and forcefully illustrates (via metonymically evoking the communicative capacities of the artifact: postcard) how these bonds are created: through persuasion. Interestingly, while the first illustration she supplies indeed indicates the emergence of a shared repertoire of profound experiences ("I was also in South America"), the second illustration, with the postcard, indicates that to some degree the experience of fellowship in fact *precedes* the actual practice. That is, though veteran travelers surely have much to talk about by way of comparing recollections, the fellowship of which Galit speaks is also what enables the narrator to send a postcard to those who have *not yet traveled* to begin with. In this way the postcard—Galit's literally traveling words—validates the venue of communication between sender and addressee, which already existed between acquaintances of the same sociocultural milieu and persuades the latter to join simultaneously.

The participation in the trip and the exceptional experience it bestows are described succinctly with words, which, again, evoke ineffability. Galit contends that the experience is reserved to a few select individuals. Quoting the postcard performatively establishes the borderline between those who do not travel, whose description has a condescending undertone ("that's fine") and those chosen ones who do travel and who materialize their fellowship and gain the cultural capital associated with this form of travel.

The persuasiveness, whether implicit or explicit, silent or voiced, was so compelling for me that I soon came to assume that this was, in fact, the very *motivation* that had drawn the interviewees to this study in such an easy and open manner. Each of them has been more than willing to be interviewed and has let me know this explicitly. (This much was also observed of backpackers by Elsrud 2001 and Riley 1988.)

I recall that while driving home after an evening long with stories, I recorded my own worded feelings, my own experiential account of a conversation, which powerfully echoed and was moved by persuasive performance: "Truly, the impression that what was most powerful, is the—the immensity of the experience that took place there . . . something really, ah, STRONG. that also—something that WORKED. that really communicates in the form of '[I] should travel there.' that I feel the right thing [to do] is to really go there, in order to experience as she did something very,

very deep. something really STRONG, emotionally strong." Although I did not run into a near car accident as a consequence of the pervasive performances—as Susan Harding (1987, 169), whose work I will discuss shortly—did, the stories did, nonetheless, implicate me forcefully; I was certainly hit by the narrators' storied "arrows" (K. Basso 1984). The backpackers created an emotionally charged and heightened interpersonal field and then acted within it. In a way akin to the backpackers, I found myself, too, experiencing something deep and profound, which was difficult—in fact, impossible—to convey in words (as evinced in the use of intensifiers and prosodic features, indicating how raw, huge, and inarticulatable is the feeling—in a word, authentic). To my surprise, I, too, was quoting, already joining the quoting narrative community, trying to articulate—as they do—an amorphous feeling, trying to signify distances: between the here-and-now of driving the car after the interview and the there-and-then of the interview performance, between the here-and-now of the narrative performance of the interview and the there-and-then of the taleworld, between (persuaded) audience and (persuasive) narrators, and so on.

Yet another striking parallel existed between our separate, but resonating, experiences. While backpackers insisted "[I] should travel there," I realized that I did travel, but "*here*" rather than "*there*." My *arrival at the interview*, to meet with, talk with, and listen to the backpackers telling their stories was interpreted by them in the same context or in the same "real situation" sense (Bakhtin 1986, 88) as their own travel. They conceived of my physical attendance of their performances as a minor travel I performed, perhaps a preparatory excursion before the "real" grand journey, perhaps its first step, its foreplay.

The actual or corporeal "meeting of motivations," as Consuelo Corradi (1991, 109) puts it with regard to interview context, indeed "made possible the reconstruction of the story," and with it the metonymic taste of the unique backpacking experience. Corradi contends that the construction of a story is a collaborative achievement in the sense that motivations, or interests, meet. The scene of our meeting was conceived of in similar ways as the journey was and hence was not only analogous but also homologous with the journey and with the backpacking experience. For the backpackers, performing travel narrative was an integral component of the experience-generating practice they were talking about.

In the following excerpt, Shula makes roundabout and covert allusions to the present occasion of the interview and to my position therein. She addressed a seemingly anonymous potential interlocutor who, she suggests, might be "hesitating" about whether to travel.

Shula: I think that it is something that is very mmm important that everyone will do

    I—

       EVERY person who is—

           who hesitates

     I tell him

"GO TRAVEL"

like—

you gotta go and travel to know what it's like ...

I really push'em and tell'em as much as possible so they'll go

Since at this point in our conversation Shula did not know whether I had traveled, she has arguably positioned me as a "hesitator," one whose mind is not (yet) firmly made up and who needs a "push" in the form of narrating persuasively "as much as possible" about her experiences. This, however, is *precisely* what she has been doing in the interview. In a way, in the beginning of the extract she subtly indexes the *current occasion* of the interview and her participation in it when she reveals her persuasion concerning the benefits of participating in the great journey. Hence, her metanarrative comment frames the narration in a persuasive, matter-of-fact framework, suggesting she has abundantly supplied me with prescriptive travel information. Furthermore, it frames the interview meeting itself as a site of resolution. This is where a "hesitator's" mind should be made up, with the help of the emphatic persuasive assertion ("GO TRAVEL"). As we shall later see in more detail, the backpackers manage the requirement to use nondirect evangelist rhetoric by implicating me vis-à-vis quotation in the capacity of an overhearer. Corresponding with the designation of a "hesitator," the narrator proposes that I am a (Goffmanesque) bystander or an eavesdropper, who may accept or reject the role, responsibility, and responsivity (Bakhtin 1986) of a hearer/addressee. This is how the performers hold the stick at both ends: on the one hand, they do employ overt persuasive language; on the other hand, they commonly do not address me directly, so that their performances are not perceived as downright missionary (which, as I mentioned, would have rendered them undesirable to a "secular" audience). This is true of Galit's (re)citing of the postcard she sent to her friends (above): while the overt persuasive language is aimed at her friends, the direct recipients of the message, I am exposed to these messages in the capacity of an overhearer, in a roundabout way.

In other instances, reference is made not to someone in particular but to the occasion of storytelling and storyhearing and to the constitutive effect hearing other backpackers' stories has had on the performers. Such is indicated in the illustration supplied by the following backpacker, who recalls the reason—the motivation—for his travel: "It's the people you meet who come and tell you stories, they stir you up, and you decide to join. you embark." Listening to backpackers' stories, these backpackers reveal, is inspiring and provoking. Recounting the stories they have heard before embarking on the great journey suggests that the stories lead directly to decisions and thence to actions. Perhaps a case of "narrative motivation." The touristic stories "direct you," as the narrators put it, in the strongest sense. The stories indicate what to do, where to look, when to do so, with whom, and moreover, *how to feel* and *how to experience* being a backpacker (Binder 2004; Elsrud 2001; Sørensen 2003). This is consonant with the conceptualization of the rhetoric of persuasion as encompassing a strong construction of reality and of the individual's actions therein (Torronen 2000).

The fact I chose to spend my time with and among backpackers, listening to their narratives, hearing their explanations, and looking together through picture albums should, in itself, "direct" me in a certain direction, on a certain path. I am implicated both within the performance and *over and beyond it.* The con-text suggests an ex-text, which is my own personal story, whose beginning, or Labovian abstract (1972), is being dialogically drafted during the interview, yet to be consummated and embodied.

Harding (1987, 173) points out that while persuasive stories appear to be about "other characters, on the narrative surface," they are, in effect, "on a deep level about the listener: You, too, are a character in these stories; these stories are about you." Akin to my observation of how the backpackers perceived and positioned me, Harding further observes that according to the perception of the born-again Baptists she interviewed, "if you are seriously willing to listen to the gospel, you have begun to convert" (178).

Centripetal Narration: The Suggestive-Persuasive Genre

We can now resume the theoretical discussion while considering not only experience but eventually the genre of dialogic narration that faithfully captures/conveys/ evokes it. Thus the genred utterance is carried out in reference to the *presumed or verified position* of the audience—that is to say, to the shared or unshared experiential state—with the intention of persuading me to join the backpackers, participate in such hikes and journeys, experience their profound uniqueness, and, not the least, join and experience the "fellowship of travelers."

When describing her experiences trying to learn the religious language of born-agains, Harding writes: "[For them] there is no such thing as a neutral 'participant-observation' position, no place for an ethnographer who seeks 'information.' Either you are lost or you are saved. . . . It was inconceivable to them that anyone with appetite for the gospel as great as mine was simply 'gathering information,' was just there 'to write a book.' No, I was 'searching'" (1987, 171). I find the striking parallels of our experiences telling. In both cases the researcher is positioned as a "searcher," an outsider stripped of the reflexive and intellectual "re-" prefix. The researcher is perceived by the backpackers, or by the born-again Christians, as similar to the way *they themselves were prior to their transformative experience* and initiation into their respective communities.

Consequently, since the researcher is presumed to be "searching," she or he is presented with an adequate interpersonal genre—that of suggestion and persuasion—that is relatively mild and implicit in the case of tourists and downright missionary and straightforward in the case of born-again Christians in order to guide the researcher and supply her or him with the "know-how."

Incidentally, note that Harding's text inadvertently expresses tensions that stem from the ideologically suffused encounters she had. Using words such as "neutral," "simply," and "just" reveals the efforts made by the author-*re*searcher to vindicate herself from the implication entailed in being in an emotionally and ideologically heightened field. Dialogically, there is little that is "neutral" about her position when regarded from the perspective of the Baptist performers. In a twofold sense Harding, too, is implicated: first, there is the question concerning what has brought her to "seek" the gospels as her research subject (with "great appetite," as she indicates). Second, and more important, precisely as a researcher, Harding, too, is a member of a tightly knit discursive community. The encounter, then, is an instance of the meeting of two *representatives* of communities, inquiring, positioning, and implicating each other simultaneously. Researchers are no more or less "neutral" than their informants, and the latter are not necessarily more zealous or orthodox than the former; rather, both are involved. It is between both that field-induced emotions and impressions powerfully reverberate.

Note that from born-again evangelists to backpacking tourists, the above observation is particularly true of ideologically charged groups and communities. With regard to tourists (and their operators), Bruner (2005, esp. 1–7) shows how ethically delicate are interactions and interventions of ideological bearing. When suspecting a threat to their underlying ideological metanarratives, tourists and their operators are as fierce as a lioness protecting her cubs.

The persuasive dialogic genre has an extralinguistic direction; its essence is to *move* the audience, as any good story does (and so a good story is, literally, one that *moves* us—here, to join the "family," to "know the language," to "feel the atmosphere," to receive a "visa," and so on, via backpacking). The genre is intersubjective, dynamic, and active, and at its core it *influences* and *manipulates* the hearer via its performative, dialogical operation between the participants in the narration occasion. These effects are not, in fact, by-products of the narration but rather its essential feature. The genre draws its force from the mutual motivations, as we have mentioned earlier, that have initially brought the two participants together in the occurrence of the interview conversation. It is interactive in that it is a mode of enacting upon, influencing, appealing, and compelling—not the story but its raison d'être (Bakhtin 1981).

Within schemes of interpersonal communication, persuasion has been traditionally defined as "the attempt or intention of one participant to change the behavior, feelings, intentions or viewpoint of another by communicative means" (Lakoff 1982, 28).[5] Over and beyond the conceptual difficulties embodied in what are, and what are not, "communicative means," the stress on "action" and on what is "real" is crucial for our discussion. In fact, since backpacking is a practice that entails "real," embodied engagement, the actual participation in the trip is crucial to the definition of persuasion and should be at its crux: "Persuasive speech is a process of *symbolically constructing social reality in a strong sense:* It aims consciously to influence people's perceptions of the surrounding world and the way they should act in accordance with those perceptions.... It motivates the subject, who is *outside the text,* to take action" (Torronen 2000, 81–82; my emphasis). Similar to how backpackers' narratives of risk and adventure are socially constructed (Elsrud 2001; Noy 2004b;

Sørensen 2003), the "strong" type of social construction can be viewed as encompassing persuasion and invitation. That is to say, the dialogically constructed realm is already infused with intention, persuasion, and ideology, and the "information" it supplies (which backpackers often marvel at) is thus more precisely conceptualized as "infosuasion" (Savarese 2000).

Furthermore, the invitation to engage backpacking is not restricted to "going through the motions" and the subsequent "knowing," it is directed at the possibility of communicating this experience once it has been consumed. Sharing the experience with veteran backpackers or persuading soon-to-be or "novice" backpackers (Cain 1991) is a *defining element of the experience itself.* As is true of born-agains as well as a variety of evangelical communities, the role of narrative performance and the evocation of the profound experience therein are as crucial to the experience as "going through" the "actual" act of backpacking. As indicated above, it is an organic part of it, regardless of whether the narration is performed during the trip, as is Galit's assertion on a postcard ("YOU GO TO INDIA!"), or afterward, as Shula's admonition ("GO TRAVEL").

It is the frequent telling and retelling of the stories to available audiences—primarily veteran and potential travelers, but also relatives and acquaintances—that completes and brings to a closure the experience of the great journey and its "knowing." As the concluding chapter 9 shows, it entails the impressive performance of tourist-induced self-transformation.

Persuading the Persuaded: Conarration and the Dialogics of *Hithazkut*

> Once turned around, you must *stay* turned around.
> Ludwig Wittgenstein

Eventually, when it seemed that the conversations were approaching their end, and after stirring stories, rich with adventure and exotica, were performed, I responded to the inquiries with which I had been consistently bombarded and which I had initially refrained from answering: "Were you there?" "Did you travel?" "Did you chew coca leaves?" "Do you know what a Chola is?" I admitted that I, too, had backpacked in Asia, along routes and itineraries that were as common then as they are now. Sometimes I have admitted to a desire that my own travel stories be heard, like those of the youths I was interviewing. I said as much to the backpackers because I felt that my urge to reciprocate was stimulated by the stories that I had just heard.

As expected, the conversations did not come to an end at this point, but rather reopened and became invigorated as the dialogical genre shifted: from a "pedagogical" (Briggs 1988) persuasive genre, which occupied the space between "knower" and "seeker," to a genre marked by warmly sharing and comparing the travel experiences of veterans. From this point in the conversations, both interlocutors could conarrate and share recollections from "inside," having a "visa" and "knowing" what the other is "really" talking about, as the backpackers put it.

Indeed, while tourists are commonly engaged in persuasive discourse, in which an ostensible experiential divide is constructed between performer and audience, they are just as commonly engaged in collaborative storytelling. Whether they have traveled similar itineraries or not, tourists have much to share with one another by way of comparing recollections of sameness and difference (a state that is a result of the routinization of tourists' itineraries [Kirshenblatt-Gimblett 1998, 152]).

On the subject of comparing recollections, Elinor Ochs (1997, 201) observes that "collaborative storytelling helps to create solidarity—for example, a coherent family, institution, or community culture." Admittedly, while performance in any case is based on coparticipation and coordination of audience and performer(s), in the persuasive narration the participation of the former is kept to a minimum, whereas in more reciprocal occasions of storytelling, all parties to the performance contribute equally (at least potentially).

Yet there are more shades to the backpackers' discourse than explicit persuasion, on the one hand, and conarration of the type discussed by Ochs (1997), on the other. Interestingly, persuasion is often performed not only with and with regard to out-group members (yet-to-be backpackers), but also *within the community.* In these cases, the dialogical genres of conarration and persuasion uniquely conflate.

Consider the following rhythmic strip from Tirza's narration, wherein she depicts the impressive number of Israelis with whom she crossed paths during the great journey. Tirza states how frequently Israelis engage in conversational interactions with one another. Of importance to the issue at hand is the narrative frame by which she frames these interactions at the end of the excerpt, suggesting that backpackers continually persuade each other throughout the lengthy trip.

Tirza: All the Israelis—
        it's by word of mouth (mi'pe le'ozen)
       by word of mouth
          simply like that
so simply Israelis went to trek the Azangate
    they had fun
    [they] enjoyed
    [they] passed it on to more Israelis
        more Israelis went
      [more Israelis] ENJOYED
          [and] so on by word of mouth
now simply
    Israelis
    who do they talk with?
       with Israelis
    they don't get to talk with tourists   (slower)
      to persuade tourists   (slower)
          "GO TO THE AZANGATE"   (faster)

Tirza communicates the cyclic (metapragmatic) relationship between persuasive interpersonal interactions (what she calls "word of mouth," or mi'pe le'ozen, "from mouth to ear") and the itinerary collectively pursued by backpackers ("more Israelis went"). It is evident from the last few lines in the excerpt that she is depicting a boundary that demarcates the backpackers as a highly distinct social group, insulated by discourse. Here, however, we find that she does not locate veteran versus novice backpackers at the boundaries, as indicated in the illustrations above. Instead, the boundaries are established between Israelis and foreign backpackers, and, correspondingly, between backpackers and "tourists" (see chapter 5).

Importantly, Tirza makes an assertion (expressed by means of negation) that Israelis *persuade* other Israelis *while* traveling. In other words, the enthusiastic persuasive discourse *does not* terminate when one decides to undertake backpacking and to unite with the community, as might initially have been expected. Rather, it is excitedly intensified. It seems that the lengthy, multisited trip *continually* supplies *forever more activities with regard to which the backpackers can persuade each other to participate.* Within this sociotouristic scene, there is always something—an activity, an attraction, a sight—to persuade and to be persuaded about, and someone with whom one can do so. The founding tourist practice—that is, the trip—and the profound experience it entails metonymically split into multiple minute attractions, which, like small crystals that form a large crystal rock, endlessly provide occasions of intracommunity persuasive narrations (Noy 2005a). The touristic discourses-cum-practices are here at their best, when they abundantly suggest resources for narratives of personal experience of a persuasive character.[6]

Yet, a difference does exist between intracommunity persuasive speech, which inherently rests on the members' shared practices and experiences, and the persuasive speech that I encountered, which has novice, "yet-to-be-born-again" backpackers as its audience. And while persuasive discourse has been extensively researched, conarration, which is no less persuasive, has not received due attention (but see Lerner 1992, 1993; Mandelbaum 1987, 1989).

In attending to this genre, I borrow conceptually from the religious language of contemporary Orthodox "born-again" Jews in Israel (known as *hozrim bitshuva*). I do so in order to describe the heightened discursive activities in which born-again Jews engage *after* assuming an ultra-Orthodox identity and way of life (in various social settings ranging from large-scale highly spirited rallies to small-scale daily congregations). This is in line with the work of Katriel (2004) on emerging genres of dialogical interaction and storytelling in contemporary Israeli society, which deals with the decline of the *dugri* speech style (characterized by directness or matter-of-factness and informality, among other dimensions), and with the work of Blum-Kulka (1997) on polyphonic storytelling dinners in Israel.

The emic term commonly employed to denote persuasive discursive activities that take place in communities of ultra-Orthodox *hozrim bitshuva* is *hithazkut.* The term is derived from the root *h, z, k* (literally, "strong"), which, in this reflexive conjugation, means "becoming stronger," "overcoming," and "asserting oneself." (It is commonly employed in the present form too: *mithazek.*)[7] Hithazkut designates empowerment and is aimed at group members *after* they enter the community and experience a transformation. Since at this point the believer is still vulnerable and is liable to "fall" back into her or his (sinful) previous lifestyle, there is a constant need for discursive work to be performed on one's recently acquired identity. This work, which can be undertaken only after the point of conversion, entails practicing more rituals more carefully and more ardently. The term *hithazkut* succinctly depicts the active, ongoing assertion of individuals in their own eyes and in the eyes of their recent and past social reference group. In line with recent developments promoting the dynamistic quality of the terms *culture* and *identity,* the continual persuasive activities of the type caught in the term *hithazkut* index the ongoing performative *maintenance* of individual and collective (communal) identities.

It is not only that the backpackers share—during the trip and afterward—the collaborative storytelling typical of veterans who are publicly performing their travel narratives, "comparing notes" with fellow narrators, and fine-tuning their versions of the events. It is more than that: the experience they shared, and the shared communal identity it entails, is fortified and deepened through a continual engagement in empowering performances. The state of postconversion or posttransformation entails then a reinvigoration in the form of intracommunity genres of narrative performance aimed at repeatedly crystallizing the community around its (ideological) tenets and empowering one's self through a continual reenactment of the moment of transformation.

This is how the paradox embodied in the title of this section, which suggests that there is room for persuasion among those who are already persuaded, is resolved. Persuasion performances do not take place only on the fringes of the speech community, demarcating in their recital the borders between veteran and yet-to-be-members or between Israeli and non-Israeli backpackers. On the contrary, persuasive storytelling is performed ceaselessly and lies, in fact, at the core of the community. It is a vital part of the process by which backpackers maintain and perform their identity. By persuading others and suggesting that they themselves have done something others have not (yet!) done, the performers demonstrate their esteemed hierarchal position and put into effect the community-creating and community-preserving processes.

We are reminded here of Anthony Giddens's well-known observation—essential to the theory of structuration—stated in terms of social agency and social systems: "The point is that the sustaining of 'being seen as a capable agent' is intrinsic to what agency is, and that the motives which prompt and reinforce this connection as inherent in the reproduction of social practices, are the same as those which order such reproduction itself" (1984, 80). In this chapter, the agentic social practices that are "intrinsic" to the (re)production of the category "backpacker" have been shown to be persuasive interactions. The interactions' primary course is the interview interaction between the performer and the audience. And yet these courses have a shadow or an echo in the form of hithazkut or auto-/intragroup persuasion.

Intermezzo 1: From Persuasion (in)to Quotation

> Every sign, linguistic or nonlinguistic, spoken or written . . . can be *cited,* put between quotation marks; in so doing it can break with every given context, engendering an infinity of new contexts in a manner which is absolutely illimitable.
>
> Jacques Derrida

The stories backpackers repeatedly tell each other, and repeatedly hear, are authored and performed in a vibrating interpersonal space, one that is partly constituted by the very act of telling. We have heard various ways whereby persuasion serves to tighten the interpersonal grip among community members, to centripetally recruit new members, and to homogenize the itineraries of the many who participate in backpacking by cyclically intertwining persuasions with practices. As such, persuasion is a manifestation of the communal knowledge embedded in backpacking. In this vein, the observation made by Amy Shuman (1992, 138) of fight stories among youths holds true for travel narratives among backpackers: "talking about fighting was a part of an ongoing experience; talking was part of fighting, not just a report of it."

Now the inquiry turns to what seems to be a linguistic effect of the recurrence of persuasive genres, namely, the *repetition of certain texts* that are at the center of the persuasive communication and at the very core of the narrative community that it glues together. In the performances this repetition is evinced in the form of quotations and voicings (the foci of chapters 4–8). Indeed, the above illustrations of persuasive speech demonstrate that quotations are repeatedly performed (including in the recording of my own reflections!). This, I argue, is no coincidence.

Our focus now shifts from rhetoric and genre to the recurrent reproduction of constitutive texts within a given communal context. Reproduction of cultural artifacts, oral stories included, immediately entails the stories' (site of) production and the exploration of the dichotomy that is commonly construed between creative and innovative tendencies, on the one hand, and more reproductive ones, on the other hand. If we return momentarily to Tirza's narration above, we can hear that the point Tirza is making concerns repetition. Between the narrative act, described in the words "Israelis went to trek the Azangate," and the authoritative quoted persuasion, "GO TO THE AZANGATE," Tirza refers to and performs various repetitions: repetitions of the practices, of the stories that describe them, and of the interaction between persuasive stories and repetitious practices (itineraries). As observed by anthropologists Smadar Lavie, Kirin Narayan, and Renato Rosaldo (1993, 5), "the healthy perpetuation of cultural traditions requires invention as well as rote repetition." It is clear in this regard that the rite about which the backpackers tell—in the form of the great journey—is simultaneously about preservation and innovation.[8]

At present, what will be taken as "rote repetition" is *quotation,* which is arguably the emblem of what (rote) repetition is: in language, but not only in language (as we are reminded by Derrida in the epigraph above). It is within this social environment of endlessly repetitive storytelling and storyhearing, which corresponds to ceaseless undertakings and manufacturing of "events"—profound, risky, exotic— that the "existence of conditions of creativity" is fulfilled (Lavie, Narayan, and Rosaldo 1993, 5). There, a "mix of tradition and change" takes place in a liminal, ludic touristic space. Consider Meirav's quotation in the epigraph in the "Itinerary," in which she says that they played a game that was "invented on the spot" but at the same time was "also invented before us"!

The move from persuasion to quotation is necessary, then, if we only conceive of the latter as the discursive marks of the former, the discursive "footprints" of the occurrence of dialogical genres of persuasion. Persuasion produces citation in that it is a citing genre, a *way* by which citation is produced. It is at the same time a *condition* for quoting—that is, the social and interpersonal mechanism—and a *result* of there being canonic, authoritative texts that are being quoted (Butler 1993). Persuasive-dialogical performances induce quotation as they evoke it in a recursive chain of intertextuality and interarticulation. Instances of quotation are performative and produce subsequent quotations. What is learned or shared by listening to these performances are both social voices and communal tenets. Complementing these is the communicative fashion by which quotations are produced and reproduced among competent backpacking performers. Stated bluntly, evangelism is about repetitive performance and performative repetition (of authoritative texts). Hence, what is being repeated and the very act of repetition itself are the essence of evangelist ideologies of types, tourist ideologies (or metanarratives) included.

To be sure, there is more to persuasion than quotation, and there is more in quotation than persuasion. Nonetheless, where there are repetitive instances of quotations, persuasion can be safely surmised and vice versa: if persuasive genre(s) are evident, one can just as surely expect to hear quotation. This is particularly true when the quotations add up systematically to the evocation of social voices and of the social tenets they evoke.

Consequently, the question arises whether all "things linguistic" can be quoted to the same degree, or whether there are utterances that are more or less quotable. In Bauman's and Briggs's words (1990, 74), are all utterances equally "prepared-for detachability" and "socio-linguistically transplantable"?

According to French discursivist Dominique Maingueneau, certain types of texts, which he terms "self-constituting discourses," and not others are particularly frequently disseminated. Maingueneau (1999, 191) claims that self-constituting discourses "are ideologically dense, are highly bound with communication facilities." What he brings to the discussion of what is and is not sociolinguistically transplantable is an *ideological quality*, which is an underlying feature of persuasions of sorts, and, in the present case, of the appeal to undertake the practice of backpacking and to consume and subsume the identity it embodies. Quoted texts—which will occupy us in the ensuing chapters (3–8), are commonly imbued with "dense" ideology, granting them their authoritative stature, making them worthy of quotation, and making quoting them worthwhile. Structurally, such texts are citable and reproducible in that they are easily disseminated, as suggested by Maingueneau in his observation that they are "highly bound with communication facilities."

"Inscriptions," Maingueneau (1999, 190) further argues, "are situated in series: resting on words already said, they are, in their turn, virtual supporters of other inscriptions. The genres of self-constituting discourses determine precisely the ways texts take their place in inter-discourse: scientific references are not religious quotations" (cf. Derrida 1988; Nietzsche 1967). For Maingueneau, hegemonic ideologies, which seek to institute norms and to regulate thought and behavior, are detectable by means of the types of repetition and interdiscursiveness they demonstrate.

Thus, although persuasion will henceforth not occupy us explicitly (at least not until chapter 9), we will be considering quotations and voices, which are mimetic illustrations of the efficacy of persuasive performances. The systematic repetition of quotations that are attributed to describable social animators demonstrates the shared knowledge of the community and the competent performance thereof of the individual. As stressed by Carla Bazzanella (1996, 285), performing voices and polyphony are socially achieved through the "repetition of fixed syntagms based on . . . the shared knowledge or 'encyclopedia' of a given community." Quotations and voices, then, illustrate how a powerful sense of community and identity emerges through the repetition of utterances, and how community members can make persuasive use of the shared discursive resources (the "encyclopedia"), which they themselves constantly re-create in praxis.

Consequently, when the corresponding repetitions—of discourse and of practice—are performed, a metapragmatic statement is naturally asserted concerning the unique correspondence between experience and words, on the one hand, and actions and deeds, on the other. In other words, the interrelations between repetitive praxis and repetitive discourse expose aspects of the communal "linguistic ideology" (Silverstein 1979), facets of the metapragmatic foundations of a community's ideology.

SITE II

Quotations and Voices

3

Quotations

Repeating is in every one in every one their being and their feeling and their
way of realizing everything and every one comes out of them in repeating
these.

Gertrude Stein

While listening time and again to the backpackers' excited accounts, I realized
something that I had not and perhaps could not have realized earlier, at the actual
"live" time of the conversations. Being a native Israeli as well as an ex-backpacker,
I was too familiar with such instances to notice and discern the abundance and salience of the oral marks of quotations in the performances. This lay, to use the term
coined by Silverstein (2001), beyond my own (native's) "limits of awareness." I am
not sure at what precise point the observation that the narrators frequently quoted
others' voices and brilliantly and originally embedded them unto their own narrative voices emerged in my research consciousness, bringing together meanings,
texts, and textures. But it was at some point during the work on persuasion and on
the sociointerpersonal origins of the backpackers' stories that this central feature
became salient.

With the acknowledgment of the intertextual role played by quotations in the
stories, I also acknowledged that these possessed tight communal characteristics
and were organically interembedded within a community of voices and stories.
Thus, I emerged from the research hearing the members of the narrative community with an auditory and even acoustic impression: that of fleeting quotations and
multiple ventriloquism. Over and above the intertextual role they played and the
shared (communal) voices they introduced into the narratives, quotations helped
instantiate a performative context. Hence, beyond their referential contribution
(quotations of . . .), they were highly meaningful in and of themselves.

Quotation, or "direct reported speech" (DRS, *oratio recta*, also called direct
speech/quotations/discourse), is defined as an utterance that "evokes the original
speech situation and conveys, or claims to convey, the exact words of the original
speaker in direct discourse" (Florian Coulmas, cited in Holt 1996, 222). Conventionally, it "represents an exact reproduction of a verbal communication" (Banfield 1973, 30), a case in which the "reporting utterance purportedly represents a

speaker's exact words" (Lucy 1993b, 13). It is a linguistic performance with which all competent speakers of all natural human languages are familiar, wherein there appears to be an "original" utterance that was initially uttered in a different context from the here-and-now and is currently being quoted into an ongoing conversation. What is "direct" about this particular type of *direct* reported speech is its supposed exactness: purportedly a clear case of discursive mimesis.

Although there is general agreement on the formal definition of quotation, there is some divergence in perspective and terminology. For one, the mere convergence of "direct," which indexes exactness, with "report," which indexes mediation, is oxymoronic.

In any case, the formal components of a quotation performance include:

1. the alleged original discursive event wherein the quoted utterance was initially presented and from which it is quoted

2. an utterance—a quotative—that is currently being reported and is framed as conveying the exact word-by-word order of the original occasion. The quoted utterance retains the (personal, spatial, and temporal) deixis of the supposed original context, thus retaining the original perspective

3. an animator to whom the utterance is attributed in the original context, and who is usually the original author of the utterance

4. a speech verb (*verbum dicendi*), which marks the fact that what is presently *represented* is *words*. Occasionally, the verb is not a speech verb but a verb of action (such as "goes"), while at other times, the verb is entirely absent. The pronoun (addressing the original animator) and the verb form are sometimes called an "introduction formula." Correspondingly, the end of the quotation is marked by what we will call a "quotation-closing formula," which indicates the return of the voice from the reported context to the present context[1]

5. a present discursive event (occurring in the here-and-now) into which the utterance is being transported

6. an animator who is presently quoting the utterance and performatively framing it as reported speech

7. distinctive prosodic shifts. Oftentimes, when narrators replace their voice with the voice of others, one or more types of prosodic indications occur.[2]

An additional common form of reported speech, which is usually compared to quotation, is *indirect reported speech* (*oratio oblique*, indirect quotation/discourse). In indirect reported speech a voice is reported *without* an indication that these are supposedly the very words that were originally uttered. In this case the other's words are not cited but paraphrased, and the deixis is not aligned or calibrated with the original context but with the present conversation (at least partially). Since there is no emphasis on the directness and imitative nature of the reported utterance, it is commonly not as highlighted or singled out by prosodic markers, and the prosodic nature of the utterance does not indicate quotation marks. Usually there is an indication of subordination (such as the prefix "sh" in Hebrew or "that" in English) that indicates the digetic approximation, rather than mimetic directness, that exists between the report and the supposedly original, authentic utterance.

Let us briefly consider a few of the extracts of persuasive speech presented in the previous chapter, most of which include quotations. In the excerpt from Galit's narration, (pp. 34–35), the narrator demonstrates and enlivens her contention that a "fellowship" of backpackers exists by directly evoking a typical exchange. As expected, the pronominal deixis within the quotation is aligned with the spatiotemporal perspective of the original occasion, and not with the occasion of the interview. Hence, the direct, second-person address in the quotation does not refer to the interviewer ("you've been in South America"), nor does the first-person singular pronoun index Galit. Similarly, the first-personal plural pronoun that appears at the end of the quotation ("we've seen the same sights") does not index Galit and the interviewer. The narrator avoids the use of an explicit speech verb, and the quotation is largely framed from its *interior:* by deictic orientation and by the use of a vocative. The first word of the quotation strip is "what-" (*ma*), which is an exclamation that commonly functions as a vocative and indicates from within the quotation that a direct address has been made. The absence of speech markers is apparent not only in the initial quotation but also throughout the ensuing turn-taking exchange, a fact that requires of the audience a degree of competence in following the dialogue. Overall, the final quoted utterance correlates with and reiterates the contention that "there's a fellowship of travelers," but it does so more "authentically" since it is purportedly drawn *from the very scene that Galit is reporting.* As such, it excitedly conveys the *realization* of the "fellowship" in vivo, or performatively.

In the second instance of quotation in Galit's extract, it could be argued that her mention that she has sent a postcard—which "appears to be [an] unambiguously accurate mode of representation" in tourism (Urry 1999, 76)—amounts to a quotation formula that frames the reported speech to follow. Note that the narrator's prosodic emphasis does not color the entire quotation but is used selectively for highlighting only a few words therein. Interestingly, Galit terminates the quotation by making a sound ("hmmm")—a quotation-closing formula that obviously could have not been written on the postcard (the original discursive context).

Simpler forms of quotation indicate persuasion in the excerpts from Shula's (pp. 36–37) and Tirza's (p. 41) performances in chapter 2. Both narrators improvise using the formal features that construct quotation: in both cases the prosodic shift is performed not only to frame the quotation as such but to emphasize its persuasive importance; in the latter case *two* speech verbs, not one, are simultaneously used ("talk" and "persuade"), suggesting metalinguistically that talking is equivalent to persuading. The termination of the quotation in Shula's narrative is accomplished with the help of a discourse marker ("like-"), which commonly serves as a quotation-closing formula used by narrators to facilitate the shift from highlighted quoted speech to the narrator's evaluation, or from the characters' voices to the narrator's voice (Maschler 2001, 315, 2002b).

These performances show how quotations lively stand out in their quality of exactness and imitativeness. They are employed creatively by the narrators, who mix different formal ingredients to adapt quotation to their aims, thus enhancing their communicative capacity. In the case of persuasion, quotations come in handy: they perform what they are about—the establishing of communication.

The instances of quotations in the backpackers' stories also contribute to the sparse comparative data available on patterns of usage of reported speech in spoken Hebrew. Works dealing with quotations suggest that performers of different cultures employ reported speech in quite different ways (Bauman 2004; Bazzanella 1996; Kirshenblatt-Gimblett 1974; Labov 1972; Tannen 1984). Mary Ott (cited in Tannen 1989, 129), for instance, finds that Brazilian women used more reported speech than women from North America in telling the same story ("Little Red Riding Hood"); furthermore, the findings indicated that Brazilian men used considerably more reported speech than Brazilian women. These and other findings indicate patterns of performances in a given culture, suggesting that what counts as effective performance varies between cultures and genders.

Among Israeli backpackers, the ubiquitous use of quotation is related to broader patterns of social interaction and storytelling among (young) Israelis as well as to the particular social context of persuasion. Although little research has been conducted on the use of reported speech in spoken Hebrew, there are some works that point to an extensive employment of quotation in various discursive contexts (Roeh and Nir 1990; see also Weizman 1998). In addition, research has explored various Hebrew speech communities in which quotations are more extensively employed than others (Landau 1993; Maschler 2001, 2002a; Parker 1999; Schely-Newman 1999). These works indicate that over and beyond such macro terms as "culture," the interaction of specific subcultures with particular modes of communication (interpersonal communication, rabbinical speeches, news, and the like) accounts for the frequent use of reported speech in Hebrew in Israel.

From Repetition to Reflexivity and Performance

> Quotations thus remain the last stronghold of the copy theory of mimesis.
>   Meir Sternberg

A central fact of quotations is that what is indicated within the quotation marks is nothing but language itself. Having linguistic expression as their reference, quotations are cases that indicate both *linguistic repetition* and *reflexivity*. Although the following exploration will discuss repetition and reflexivity separately, it will do so purely for expository reasons, for they are tautologically intertwined. As observed by Valentin Vološhinov (1973, 115), "reported speech is speech within speech, utterance within utterance, and at the same time, also speech about speech, utterance about utterance." From a semanticist's perspective, Donald Davidson (1984, 79) draws attention to this dual quality: "In quotation not only does language turn on itself, but it does so word by word and expression by expression."

Indeed, all *re*ported speech seemingly includes linguistic repetition. This has been pointed out by Meir Sternberg (1982, 112) in his influential work; he observed that "mimesis is surely the crux of quotation." Mimesis, the artful repetition and replication of "reality," which has been pondered upon in the West since antiquity, is confronted with the Homeric notion of *digesis*, which denotes the indirect, interpretative, and reflexive qualities of *re*presentation (Auerbach 1953). While all *re*ported speech may admittedly be viewed as mimetic variation, by conceptualizing quotations in accordance with constructionist hermeneutics we may paraphrase Sternberg and suggest that direct quotations—that is, the convention of seemingly truly imitative utterances—are in fact the crux of mimesis, and not vice versa. Quotations conventionally represent the utterly straightforward "direct" view of reality, a window in the walls of Plato's discourse cave, through which what lies outside is accessible.

According to Bakhtin (1981, 1986) and Vološhinov (1973), meaning making in occasions of speech performance is made possible by creative repetition, which intertwines reproduction with innovation. For both, repetition pervades our (linguistic) lives; it is not a linguistic epiphenomenon or a mere instance *in* language; rather, it is the marrow of live language and the very foundation of a live semantic system of communication (cf. Jakobson 1966; Jakobson and Pomorska, 1983). As argued by Bakhtin, narrator and audience—members of the same speech community—hold vast, albeit mostly tacit, knowledge and skills regarding the "new" use of "old" words to assume ever-new meanings.

Bakhtin (1986, 91) famously observes that "each utterance is filled with the echoes and reverberations of other utterances to which it is related by the communality of the sphere of speech communication . . . [and has] many half-concealed or completely concealed words of others." It is in relation to this observation that a principal question arises addressing how, of the many meanings potentially encapsulated by words, specific meanings are indexed in a narrative community through patterns of repetition and quotation. This inquiry concerns the connection between the performance of reported speech and the "unfinalizability" of linguistic meaning (for example, Bakhtin 1984, 166, and other works), and how shifting meanings become fixed for a narrative instant in storytelling performances.

Along these lines, Davidson (1984, 79) remarks that "language is the instrument it is because the same expression, with semantic features (meaning) unchanged, can serve countless purposes." Alton Becker, rejecting a Chomskyan approach, points out that "prior talk is the real *a priori* of language, not some logical deep structure" (1988, 26). From Bakhtin to Davidson and Becker, it is through repetition that linguistic meaning can be established and communicated; and it is repetition that accounts for the vast semiotic possibilities attained by live language and for its brief restriction and delineation, which, we have said, facilitates meaning.

Indeed, Becker argues that through repetition language assumes its infinitely rich exactness. It is what enables performers to make "you different from you and you different from you" (1988, 28). "Particularity," Becker continues, "is not something we begin with; particularity is something we arrive at, by repeating" (29).

The previous chapter dealt with persuasive discourse as a site of the fervent shaping of shared meanings. What seems to be "pedagogical" (Briggs 1988) about persuasion is not only the teaching of life skills (the backpacking drill, in the present case) but also the teaching of what initially sounded like "Chinese" (as Noa puts it, p. 29). Persuasion achieves this through *stabilizing* some of the "reverberations and echoes" in a certain way that is unique to a specific speech community at a specific moment in time. In Becker's terms, it is repetition of the type inherently typical of missionary performances and the intense interpersonal interaction that can facilitate and sustain it that bring about the sense of precision and particularity suggested by the backpackers' strong sense of exclusively shared meanings. Furthermore, the excerpts point to how fragile and shaky is the art of meaningful verbal communication and indicate how much effort of coordination and feedback between performer and audience is constantly needed in order to sustain it.

Tannen's (1989) work on repetition profitably distinguishes between two forms of repetition, diachronic and synchronic. While the former holds for cases where the quoting context occurs at a different place and/or time from the original utterance, the latter holds for utterances occurring *within* the confines of a particular speech event. Quotations are clearly instances of diachronic repetition. The quotation marks are precisely the *marks of the diachronic:* they refer the listener elsewhere, to a different temporal (and usually also spatial) context from that in which the words are quoted.

A semiotic reliance on the distinction between different contexts is pertinent to the discussion of modern tourism (see the introduction). In the narrative performances of tourists, quotations function somewhat like *touristic souvenirs:* they are "brought back" home from afar, from Elsewhere. Hopefully "intact," they are evoked and performed in their "complete" form by the returning tourists (Kirshenblatt-Gimblett 1998; Stewart 1993). Like souvenirs, direct reported speech marks, but also constructs, the difference between the here-and-now and the there-and-then, between the familiar and the exotic, the Other. Indeed, some authors have suggested that tourists are themselves quotations, that the semiotic relation between tourists and the setting in which they travel is complex, even enigmatic (Lash and Urry 1994; Robertson et al. 1994).

This is why a distinction between synchronic and diachronic repetition that is founded on the notion of context is easily challenged. Arguably, what might be construed as a different discursive context by outsiders (diachronic repetition) might in fact be perceived by the speakers themselves as occurring within the bounds of a communal, homogeneous realm (synchronic repetition). Alternatively—and this is where social construction and linguistic creativity enter the discussion, the differential usages of types of repetition *performatively construct the boundaries* of a designated realm, rather than merely reflect them. Could it not be that through a systematic employment of quotations, the narrating backpackers mark that which is located outside and beyond the boundaries of a given social context, that which is perceived as Elsewhere and Other?

Constructing symbolic boundaries and distances is precisely what the backpackers do, and it is how, through the frequent use of metacommunicative devices (to which we will turn shortly), they performatively stake out the boundaries of their taleworld as the world of their narrative community. In other words, souvenirs—verbal and other—are useful in constructing the experiential divide between the here-and-now and the exotic elsewhere, the ordinary and the *extra*ordinary. Here Vološhinov's (1973, 119) observation comes to mind: "A language may strive to forge hard and fast boundaries for reported speech. In such a case, the patterns and their modifications serve to demarcate the reported speech as clearly as possible."

The clearer the demarcation constructed by narrators between the travelworld/taleworld and the occasion of narration, the more authentically original and souvenirlike are the pieces of discourse carried back by the tourists from the trip. Marking the reported utterance unambiguously crystallizes the narrative voice of the teller. Moreover, when employed communally, it fastens the boundaries of the community, which assumes, in itself, the insular quality of quotation.

The creation of meaning vis-à-vis communication over contextual disparities echoes the Derridian notion of *différence* (Derrida 1976, 1982, 3–27, following Ferdinand de Saussure's work). In order to be discernible as an instance of repetition, something must change. In conversation, what changes is the speakers' roles in the turn-taking moments—the conversation's metronome. Yet in narrative, what changes is the passing of eventful, narrative time (Ricoeur 1984; Young 1987). Through the concept of différence, Derrida points to how the identity of an entity—its recognizable meaning—depends upon the play of similarity and dissimilarity with other entities, including its own recurring manifestations. The thread connecting past and present is metonymic, though: quotation marks, which lie between what is quoted and where it is quoted into, indicate that a transformation, a *différance,* has occurred. This can be conceptualized not only in temporal terms of duration (synchronic versus diachronic repetition, for instance) but also in terms of ontic states. Quotations, which are *signifiers* of something else—that is, of what is presumably the original utterance—carry a different ontic weight (not unrelated to the realm from which they were imported).

As famously pointed out by Derrida (1981, 41), "to deconstruct the opposition, first of all, is to overturn the hierarchy." In this hierarchy the signified is commonly accorded a higher state, as it is perceived to be the "real thing," that which is genuine and authentic, whereas the signifier is viewed as its "mere" replica, a lesser *re*presentation (Benjamin 1968). This is sharply evident in the language of tourists, much of which deals with communicating the vibrant experience of authenticity. And while postmodern trends suggest the deconstruction of these hierarchical binaries, amounting eventually to what Lash and Urry (1994) have termed "the end of tourism," in the romanticist pursuit of the backpackers, the central experience still revolves around the experience of authenticity, which, we shall see, is associated with profound exotic destinations.[3]

"Who's on First?" Linguistic Reflexivity

> The imagination is defined here as a contractile power: like a sensitive plate,
> it retains one case when the other appears.
>
> Gilles Deleuze

Yet quotation is not so much an instance of repetition as it is an instance of an *indication* of repetition. Reported speech embodies and exhibits the *reflexive capacity* of language, whereby the term is used to indicate the general capability of human languages to address not only nonlinguistic, natural objects (object language) but linguistic ones as well. This unique quality amounts to language's constitutive "mirror stage" (Lacan 1977), wherein its users can "see" or "hear" themselves. Indeed, instances of reflexivity permeate language and are essential to its function (Lucy 1993b, 11).

Within types of reflexive language, reported speech—and quotation in particular—constitutes a unique category, as it embodies reflexivity "word by word." Quotation poses a "crucial linguistic and stylistic problem" and plays a "pertinent and indispensable part . . . in the buildup of any human language" (Roman Jakobson, cited in Janssen and van der Wurff 1996, 1). Quotation is "human" not only in the sense that language turns on itself but in the sense that it turns on its users as well: they, too, turn unto themselves. In other words, linguistic reflexivity crucially affords the emergent experience of subjectivity, the persuasive communication of which lies at the core of the backpackers' adventure narratives.

To paraphrase Heraclitus, words, too, cannot enter the same river twice, although linguistic repetition and reflexivity afford them the impression (impersonation) of being "wet," of having dipped twice into the exact place in the stream of experience. Performing quotation evokes the creative—cultural, linguistic—imagination and appeals to what "wetness" comes to mean in respective communities and cultures. Not only is "uttering dialogue in conversation as much a creative act as the creation of dialogue in fiction and drama," to use Tannen's words (1989, 101), this creativity lies at the core of the communal linguistic ideology pertaining to the effects of language. With this notion, and with the idea that the *re-* prefix that seemingly suggests *re*petition in fact amounts to *re*flexivity, *re*trospectivity, and eventually subjectivity, we proceed to an inquiry of the performative aspects of quotation in establishing an intersubjective realm of communication.

Quoting Whom? Performing Voices

In folklore and linguistic anthropology, the performance of voices has received central consideration (which is understandable if we bear in mind the excerpts above). By and large, reported speech is viewed as accomplishing two performative functions: marking (keying or framing) the event of narration as a performance, thus supplying an interpretation of the events recounted, and developing the narrative plot. When employing reported speech in the capacity of a "framing device," metacommunicative and metanarrative functions are performed. These terms indicate the signals by which the audience's interpretation of the narration and involvement therein are guided by the narrator and, conversely, how the performer continuously fashions the narration according to the audience's responses. Metacommunicative expression can thus be conceptualized as a contextualizing mechanism, linking the told with a particular context of its telling (Briggs 1988, 222–24).

In this respect, Bauman has reiterated that different types of reported speech serve metanarratively to bridge the abyss between the taleworld and the storyrealm, between the narrated events and the ongoing event of narration. "Of all the devices by which the fusion of narrated event and narrative event is effected in narrative discourse," Bauman (1986, 54) observes, "reported speech is perhaps the most sociolinguistically interesting."

In reported speech, and particularly in quotation, there is a "reaching out phatically to the audience" (Bauman and Briggs 1990, 69). In its metanarrative function, reported speech is located not only in some (semantic) "distance" from the narrative to which it refers, but also *toward* the interlocutor, as it were. Situated liminally, in between performer and audience, metacommunication is responsible for the coordination of the bidirectional flow of information that constitutes a coordinated event of narration. Quotation and voicing, then, act as intermediaries in events of storytelling, serving as *intersubjective* signals (C. Corradi 1991; Young 1987).

Since performance rests on metacommunicative framing, on contextualization, and on positioning devices, reported speech in general and quotations in particular are means of establishing the very performative character of narration. A profusion of metacommunicative devices within a certain segment of the narrative is an indication of an excessive indexical work on behalf of the storyteller. As put by Hymes (1975, 44), reported speech "may be an index of what might be called 'density of performance,' or the 'performance load' of a discourse."

At the same time, however, quotations also function as narrative events and participate in the construction of the plotline. "Quotativents"—quotations that occupy the role of events in narratives—tend to appear in dramatic episodes as an *organic part of the ensuing plotline*, responsible for the "advancing of action in dialogue" (Tannen 1989, 121). Hence, not only do quotations assume the role of metacommunication, they are also part and parcel of the "flesh" of the story. Further, they are not limited to dialogue. As observed by Buttny (1998, 49), reported speech is "reserved for capturing the most crucial or interesting parts of the narrative," regardless of whether it involves dialogue. "A storyline," Longacre (1994, 125) adds, "may be advanced as much, if not more, by reported speech acts as by the recital of other sorts of happenings." On such occasions verbal expression carries the ontological weight of "real" events and assumes the "marrow" of narrative. This is not entirely surprising, for after all, much of what people talk about is talk, and the world of prior utterances is a *valuable discursive resource* upon which to draw in personal narratives.

The implications of these dual functions of reported speech and quotations are intriguing, as the world of events interfaces and overlaps with the world of language and representation. In their capacity as events in narrative *and* metanarrative framing devices, quotations are acknowledged as bearing expressive and evocative qualities. They are both reference and referred in dramatic moments in narration, in which their function is the signaling of structural and thematic salience. "Direct quotation," Lucy claims (1993a, 118), "effectively conveys its expressive qualities along with its referential and predicational value."

Additionally, while quotations are invariably attributed to animators, the variety of what counts as an "animator" is an illustration of the human narrative imagination. In fact, reported speech can be attributed to any entity—human or nonhuman, such as animals (even fish, whose muteness is renowned!) and even inanimate objects (such as trees or stones). Furthermore, although quotations appear to be specific, the sources of reported voices can be extremely general: the voice of "history" is quoted on occasion, as is the voice of "art," "the people," and the like. In effect, it is the attribution of a voice that constitutes "people" or "fish" as a meaning-generating category, as agents within social life. In more general terms, it is the creativity of the narrator that performatively transforms entities into protagonists who participate in the symbolic social exchange of discourse, and not vice versa.

Hence, exploring quotations inevitably leads to a consideration of social voices, which suggest how *systematic and recurrent attributions of talk can be conceptualized in a sociorhetoric scene.* Specifically, fleshing out both the voices' sources and their quoted contents may point to the embodied tenets, tensions, and preoccupations of people in a given (sub)culture. This certainly holds true of tourists in general, whose social scene is saturated with social encounters, connections, and experiences (Harrison 2003, chap. 2), and of backpackers in particular, who regularly quote certain authoritative social entities, whose words they embed in the heightened field of polyphonic narrations.

The term *voice* is commonly used to articulately convey meaning not previously acknowledged or "heard" (to follow the phonic metaphor) in the public sphere, and which is commonly associated with certain deprived social groups. In this capacity, "voice" is used emancipatorily. To be meaningful and influential (to have agency) is to be heard or to have a voice. This type of use has been promoted largely by feminist inquiries, which pointed to the existence of a repressive "silencing" chauvinist hegemony, previously unacknowledged (from Gilligan 1982 to Butler 1990).

Presently, however, empowering, emancipating qualities are not necessarily a central feature and represent only one of several possible ideological features defining the broad sociolinguistic attributes of voices in the stories of backpackers. The term *voice* stylistically indicates the emergence of a performative mode and summons into the realm of the social agents that act therein. Through the expression of a discernible and authoritative voice, these social agents or entities—the "protagonists," the "narrator," "Israelis," "tourists," "natives," and so on—are discursively constituted. They surface in the polyphonic narratives vis-à-vis the ideological perspectives they express in relation to the events and to each other.

It is through summoning the voices of others and through their positioning that the narrators create an intricate plotline that captures both the social scenes in which they act and the perspectives they themselves hold on the ensuing occurrences. "Ironically," Lucy (1993a, 118–19) remarks, "the very technique of standing back and letting the characters in the story 'speak (and act) for themselves' can be used by narrators to foreground rhetorically what *they* wish to emphasize as the crucial turns in the plot and the larger themes of the story" (emphasis in the original). The one-narrator–many-voices perspective suggests that in referring to the words of another, the text can be enriched by additional, sometimes contradictory, perspectives and evaluations and by the dialogic interplay created between them.

In supplying a plethora of voices, narrative performance suggests a *discursive space* that stretches between acting social agents in the form of multiple dialogues (or "dialogics" [Mannheim and van Vleet 1998]). Indeed, a spatial appreciation of polyphony points to the different distances and positions existing between the various voices: some are "closer" to the narrator's voice, while others "stand even further from the author's ultimate semantic instantiation, still more thoroughly refracting his intentions" (Bakhtin 1981, 299). Such a dialogic-polyphonic web consists of several levels of voices, including the formal level of narrative in an interview setting, the many dialogues embedded within the narrative between the social voices that are evoked and dubbed, and the participants' role resulting from the performative communication and serving as the "pragmatic shadows of the face-to-face event of speaking, evoking multiple interactional frameworks" (Mannheim and van Vleet 1998, 326). These voice-induced sets of distances are enacted in the occasion of narration in the space created between performer and audience. They serve to implicate, web, and position these two parties by interactionally allowing "alterity" (Otherness) in the narrative performance (Wortham 2001, 40). The rest of this section (chapters 4–8) illustrates various alterities of this type and the meanings the performers establish with their help.

Performing the Chorus
and the (Occasional) Emergence of Individual Voices

Groups of various types, from the labor corps and other communes, through
the kibbutz, the youth movement and the cooperative, constitute a melting
pot for the fusion of the private identity into the collective identity.

Haim Hazan

Although the backpackers commonly express their aspiration to travel solo, adhering to the ethos of the lone colonial explorer, during the trip they participate in a dense collective social rite. They do so in the close companionship of fellow Israelis whom they knew before the trip or whom they met during the trip.

Toward the end of our meeting, Dalit hands me a list of twenty or so telephone numbers of backpackers she traveled with (who, judging by the area codes, live in different areas in Israel), suggesting I could contact them for later interviews. She refers to it as the phone list of "the extended family" (*hamishpaha hamurhevet*). She mentions the *reshimat kesher* (list of contacts), which is a kind of list typically used by schools, youth movements, and army units to coordinate parainstitutional social activities. Indeed, she mentions that composing such a list was easy, as she was "used to doing so" from her position in the army, where she took care of the social activities of an infantry platoon.

As mentioned in the introduction, research on Israeli backpackers points to their highly sociable patterns of travel, which habitually leads to travel in large cohesive groups. These patterns, which are "carried over" from the time spent in the army, suggest that social cohesion carries underlying social meanings. During military service, particularly in combat units, social cohesion is not perceived as leisure interaction but is encouraged as a means of coping with, enduring, and surviving rough and hostile conditions. Thus viewed, backpackers construe traveling in groups as not (only) a matter of social recreation and impromptu interactions. Rather, since the youths perceive the destinations—both the peoples and the natural environment—with suspicion, commonly interpreting them as having "hostile or unclear intentions" (Mevorach 1997, 161), they view intense socialization as a serious requisite.

Yet, as the epigraph above makes clear, congregating in cohesive groups is a well-documented pattern of socialization in Sabra culture. And although it surely correlates with military practices, it should also be understood as bearing wider historical and cultural meanings.[1]

Similarly, global backpacking research indicates that traveling in groups in common, amounting to one of the defining features of this form of tourism. Sørensen observes that backpackers "are characterized by impromptu social interaction[s]," whereby "a majority of them spend most of their time in the company of other backpackers" (2003, 850, 854). Hence, local—cultural and militaristic—patterns of socialization seem to accord well with patterns of social interactions sustained by backpacking in general.[2]

The following excerpts illustrate quotations of group and individual (personal) voices in their capacity of vocalizations of social agents in the backpackers' scene. These quoted voices create tensions between the individual and the group which, in turn, creates the social space in which these stories' drama is acted out.

Quotations of the Choral Voice

Shiri commences the telling of an eventful hiking that took place in the scenic and mountainous Azangate region in Peru with the following succinct depiction:

Shiri: And aah

     the guys (*hevre*) gathered—

             I'm not even sure how mmm

                  why ALL OF US got together at more or

  less a time when we hardly knew [each other]

           we came together from all sorts of—

           I and Aviram traveled a little bit together

           I and Mary—

               first of all we were friends

                   and we traveled together

              Aviram joined

              and so did Tali and Neta

              and in Cuzco we met another—

                     Osnat

   and so all of us said

      like

      together

        "[we] want Azangate!"

       we left

In a remarkable depiction, Shiri concisely describes the process by which the "guys" (hevre) got together, a dramatic process that reaches its climax in the quotation. She portrays the process by which the hevre eventually came to recognize themselves and be recognized as such—that is, as comprising a new social entity, which takes the role of a leading protagonist in the narration hereafter. The excerpt begins with a statement regarding the lack of knowledge of and acquaintance with each other, which marks the social baseline wherefrom the ensuing drama of socialization—in the form of crystallization—develops. Shiri describes the creation of a new state of cohesion—hevre: of ultimate, intimate—albeit ad hoc—interpersonal acquaintance captured in quotation. From anonymity the group is collected piece by piece, name by name into identity and social audibility. When the last member ("another—Osnat") joins the group, the group is complete, and the concluding utterance then ends the depiction with a crescendo: the appearance of the group is conveyed through and constructed by its expressive quoted voice "[we] want Azangate!" where narrative accumulation (of names) transforms into action in the form of quotation.

Quoting the voice of the group indicates it *has* a voice, which is to say that such an author—a social actor whose voice transcends the particular, individual voices that comprise it—exists and is effectively operating in the scene. The social whole here is bigger than the sum of the individuals contained in it. The somewhat inexplicable process by which the yet-to-be members of the group gravitate into the group voice ("I'm not even sure how") leads to the end of the strip, where cohesion and intimacy are voicedly achieved.

The group's voice, which is the grouped voice of its members, is commonly the primary protagonist in the backpackers' tales. Typically, the single voices of the members of the group all blur in common social pitch and wave into the group's voice, which represents each and every member as it participates in the unfolding of the narrative.

Such cohesive groups usually consist solely of Israelis and function as a socially extended self, an extended "I." Consequently, the travel accounts are commonly voiced in the plural "we," or "choral" voice (Tannen 1989) rather than in the singular "I."

Not surprisingly, Shiri's excerpt and the following ones are drawn form an early point in the narration, where the narrator lays out the social background against which the protagonists act in the ensuing plot, which will consist of the adventures and paramount experiences the group undergoes *as a team.* However, it is not only the ensuing plot of which Shiri is telling but also the discursive way by which actors—presently, the group or chorus—effectively enter the community's discourse, its shared taleworld.

The function of this short description in Shiri's narrative is evident in the final words: "we left." This concluding statement, which refers to the *actual commencement* of the subsequent activity, is expressed in a factual manner, as if saying after the quotation "Enough with words." The concluding couple of words are posited in interesting relation to the prior quotation. They are located immediately after the choral quote, suggesting that "we left" is a postquotation or quotation-closing formula that establishes a dramatic shift *from quoted speech to the narrated acts.* In terms of the ensuing plot, it is a shift from the conclusion of the preparatory stage to the commencement of the actual excursion.

The quotation-closing formula also serves Shiri in the capacity of "externally" validating the truth value of the groups' voiced assertion. After the latter dramatically declares its will ("[we] want Azangate!"), the narrator informs us that what the group declared had indeed materialized in the realm of acts, as the group was, *already,* on its way. The relationship between quotation and narrative suggests that this kind of quotation functions like an event that cleverly progresses the narrative one event onward.

The group voice in Shiri's story also informs us that the narrative construction of the group is related to motion and occurrence. The group comes into being in and through motion. It is, literally, *going somewhere.* It has a direction, a purpose. Social cohesiveness, at least in the Sabra variation, is not a static state but a matter of purposefulness and dynamics. Task-orientedness, which is a defining feature of Sabra culture, is the condition for cohesion and for the emerging of the hevre category.

In the next illustration the distinct "we" of the chorus voice is apparent right from the onset, after which quotations constantly assume the group's voice. This strip is also taken from an early moment in the conversation and refers to the preparatory phase, before the backpackers engage in hiking the Torres Del Paine route in the Patagonia region of Chile.

Sarit: And then we
       like
            got there and began settling in and that
            and began preparing for the trek in
                     the Torres Del Paine . . .
     we really began thinking how are we going to
                  do it
     we knew that most of the Israelis hike a
              path that is called the "W"
                    it—
                    it takes four days
and you're able to
          see things only partly
         really
        and I really wanted to see the glacier
               there's a
           glacier there [called] Gray . . .
[I wanted] to see it from here
                                (points at picture)
     from the
           mountain pass which is really overlooking it
that's the point—
that's one of the best
        viewpoints there is
            and in order to get there one needs to do the

Round Route that circles the whole mountain and it takes—

it's supposed to take

generally eight days

mmm at least—

that's what it's supposed to [take]

and we didn't know in the beginning whether yes or no

and eventually we decided

"come on (*yalla*)

let's go (*neleh*)

if worse becomes worst

we can always

decide on the way that we don't feel like it and then simply change the plans."

The single voice that is quoted throughout the extract is that of the group, the evocation of which typically marks a pivotal moment in the plot. What precedes the event of quotation and leads up to it is a description, one that amounts to the background against which the group as such has a voice. Preparations and hesitations are indicated as well as a comparison with other Israeli backpackers (who hike a shorter, less demanding route) and an indication that the ultimate attraction, a glacier ("Gray"), can be gazed at uninterruptedly only if the right path is chosen (the Round Route) and the challenging physical demands are met.

As with the previous illustration, the quoted appearance of the group voice impresses us with enthusiasm and its unique affinity to "action." It is not a ponderous, reflexive voice but a declarative one, comprising of the sounds of narrative events themselves. In both extracts the events, which are captured and expressed in quotation, resolve a preceding drama. In Sarit's narrative, the group is described as being perplexed with regard to the route it should choose ("whether yes or no"). This minor drama is resolved in the performance of quotation, which delivers the resolution (framed by the quotation introduction formula: "eventually we decided"). The quotation marks the end of the depiction of the background and the shift into events and action in the form of an excursion (strenuous hiking). It is the sound and seal of an authorized decision.

The relatively long strip of choral quotation ("come on . . . change the plans") conveys both a narrative strip and a disclaimer pertaining to forthcoming events (suggesting they are reversible). The first is accomplished through a short (two words in the original) exclamation, located at the very beginning of the quotation ("come on, let's go"),[3] which voices the decision in the first-person plural (group) voice. The second entails the indication that decisions—that is, the operative mode—are yet open to change. Note that though the narrator indicates that a "change of plans" is possible, actually, what is referred to is a change in the course of action, as the plans are transformed into events in this very instant. Though the quotations encapsulate a resolution, they allow at the same time for vicissitudes and tension in the ensuing plot. Also note that earlier on, a nondirect type of reported chorus thought is exhibited ("how are we going to do it"), which assumes a different temporal conjugation then the surrounding narrative. Although the present focus is with quotations of actual talk, it is nonetheless worthwhile to observe the interrelationship between the two chorus hearings in the construction of narrative: while the former is voiced as thought, the latter is voiced as speech, and while the former's content deals primarily with planning, the latter, expressive and affirmative, deals with (re)solution.

The following excerpt is drawn from a narrative recounted by Ilan, who describes a hike leading to the Everest Base Camp in Nepal. The excerpt reaffirms the affirmative, exclamatory quality of the chorus voice and begins after Ilan mentions "one of the most interesting experiences of the trip":

Ilan: There was some five thousand three hundred feet to climb

and [still] NOT TO MAKE IT TO

THE PASS THAT DAY

but the next day mmm

we said

"well

there are two paths

the one that's recommended

and there's another path that's on the map

we'll take it"

[so we] hiked the path

The decisive choral voice is evoked in a pivotal moment in the story, where it typically resolves a dilemma in the form of reporting that a decision has been reached. At issue here is the timing of the crossing of a high-altitude mountain pass, which is located farther than the distance the group can travel in one day. We hear of the decision inside the quotation. The quotation of the group accomplishes both referential and performative functions: a rationale is supplied and a decision is made. In the last quoted words we hear of the decision: the quotativent that develops the plot. Conjoining or summoning individual members, and the explicit voicing of the choral voice, is the signifier of the event of the decision: "we'll take it" amounts not to a futuristic proclamation but to a present action—the presence of the choral voice reaching/enacting a decision. And while the quotation resolves one drama, that of commencement, it initiates a new one: the path the group chose is the one less traveled.

Marking the closure of the quotation, we hear again that the decision, communicated within quotation, had indeed materialized in the form of a narrative event. Once more, a move from the quotation to the plot is apparent and is accomplished though performing a postquotation comment that repeats the quoted words and links the event of the utterance with the event of the onset of the activity. The quotation-closing utterance, then, *validates the factual authority of the group's voice* ("[so we] hiked the path"). It validates the notion that decisions, in crucial moments along the evolving story, are made by the group.

The stories backpackers tell are voiced and performed through the extended "I" that is formed in the monophonic shape of a group-choral voice. Unlike the Greek chorus, however, the function of the choral voice in the present context is not limited to the background but is rather exhibited in the foreground of the social stage. The "chorus" here does not (only) reflect upon the protagonist, but it is the protagonist of the story, and as such it assumes a dominant, authoritative voice that shapes the plot and advances it.

Socially, the role the group plays in the formation and negotiation of identity vis-à-vis sociality in Israeli society is unique. Hazan (2001b, 61) notes that the group is a social form that has "gained a special hold": "The group's action can be understood in terms of a myth, since it is organized as a series of contrasts which may be reversed, thus allowing the impossible—the metamorphoses of the personal self into the collective self, with a commitment to totally negate the personal, social and physical." Hazan interestingly suggests that the group is a necessary "mediating link" between the personal and the collective, one that "reproduces the collective ethos" (see also Hazan 2001a, 84).

Similarly, Katriel's works on crystallization (1986; Katriel and Nesher 1986) address not the collective ethos as much as well-delineated social groups of the type of a school class, a small military unit, and the like. The collective Zionist ethos rests on central cultural beliefs, she argues, pertaining to "the few against the many" (also described in the term *siege mentality* [Bar-Tal and Antebi 1992; Zerubavel 1995]). The "few" in the present context are the "we," while the "many" will take the shape of the whole of the Israeli collective. Divisions and subdivisions, which distinguish "we" versus "them," are absorbed into the categories they themselves have constructed, as the "we" splits again into "we" versus "them," and so on.

Yet, while usually the group's perspective and voice are presented throughout the narration, in other cases a fracture is apparent in the first-person choral voice, wherefrom the individual or personal voice emerges. Such cases inevitably represent dramatic instances: a drama that emerges between the "we" and the "I," or between the plural self and its social commitments and solidarity, and the self perceived individually, which unfetters itself momentarily from the domineering choral voice.

Quotations of Individual Voices

Though infrequent, quoting single rather than plural/choral voices is not altogether absent from the stories. If the performance of quotation is generally depicted as a rhetorical device reserved for dramatic occasions, then it is indeed uniquely so in cases in which individual voices, which contrast with choral voices, are performed via quotations. The result is that the emergence of individual quotations is a part of a dramatic scene in nearly each and every instance of their employment. Because individual voices are quantitatively scarce and qualitatively "weak" (compared with other authoritative voices), their mere appearance in the stories constitutes occasions that draw attention to a social drama occurring amid dramatic mountainous scenery.

Following are three illustrations that demonstrate the hatching of individual voices from choral voices. The performed individual voice represents instances of one kind or another of *separation: a severance from the chorus.* Against the intense patterns of sociability the backpackers exhibit, all such cases of social severance qualify as highlight moments, regardless of whether it is actual (physical) separation from the traveling group or metaphoric "distances" that accounts for the emergence of the discerned individual quotation.

The first excerpt is taken from the interview with Meirav and Ze'ev, acquaintances who traveled in South America separately for about seven months. (Ze'ev's trip preceded Meirav's by a few months.) In the strip what is actually recounted is a *moral narrative* concerning the "rules" of social cohesion, rules that the narrator, Meirav, indicates she has violated. In the extract, the narrator tells how her individual hiking pace was significantly faster than that of the group's, and how she subsequently found herself physically severed from her companions. The underlying point she makes is moral: backpackers should not isolate themselves from their groups, thus exposing themselves to jeopardy. The following sequence, narrated with a fast pace of speaking, comes after a short pause in the conversation, which took place after Ze'ev lengthily recounted his travel experiences.

Meirav: Now just a minute
　　　I want to tell something about this trek 'cause in this trek I did a slip-up
　　　　　　　　　　　　　　　　a REALLY foolish slip-up ...　　　　　(chuckles)
　　　we began the second day hiking very late 'cause of Sharon's birthday
　　　　　　　　　　　　　　　　　　　and aaah and then
　　　aaah we walked and all
　　　　　　　　and also we stopped along the way
　　　　　　　　　　　　　　　and there at the top of the hill there's
　　　a village where you finish the trek and you're supposed to sleep there in some kind of bakery
　　　according to the trail story that says that the natives supply accommodation　　(quieter)
　　　　　　　　　　　　　　　　　　aaah and that's it
　　　we began ascending
　　　　　　　　and we climbed quite a bit
　　　　　　　　and the hill wasn't really terrible but pretty difficult
　　　　　　　　and I was like already giving up (*nishbarti*)
　　　　　　　　and I saw the night coming down
　　　　　　　　and I began running uphill
　　　　really
　　　　　　　　　not RUNNING but hiking QUICKLY uphill
　　　　　　　　and I was sure they're right behind me
　　　　　　　　　　　　　　a million percent ...

and I simply SPED through that uphill 'cause I really gave up
and at some point I started to stop hearing them
                                          so I waited for them ...
and we also didn't have a trail story at that point
and we didn't have a map to begin with
                                          so we said
                                                         "come on (*yalla*)
                                                         let's climb
                                                         at the end it reaches
                                                         the village"
         and it's really a JUNGLE there
            it's a jungle like THAT
                         like here in the picture   (points at picture)
so okay
         I didn't hear them anymore
                      so I waited for them
                                       and I met with one of them and asked
her where are the rest
                and she said
                      "sure   (as if obvious)
                      they're right here
                      they're coming right now
                      I just simply mmm momentarily [left them]"
                so I said   (slower)
                "okay
                      I'll continue
                                 'cause you guys are right behind me right?"
                "yeah"   (higher)

             so I proceeded
         and at some point AGAIN I stopped hearing them
                                    and it's already
                                               like—twilight
and in the jungle darkness settles in earlier 'cause the light doesn't penetrate the leaves
so
so I simply continued and I said [to myself]
                                 "come on (*yalla*)
                            I'll meet them in the entrance to the village"
         and I really waited for them in the entrance to the village
         and I saw they aren't coming
         and I saw these couple of men approaching in my direction
                                                       like

                                                          in my direction
so I said [to myself]
    "okay"   (fearfully)
              I luckily met there another group of travelers ...
    and it turned out LATER? that afterward they got there an hour later 'cause Michal had
    difficulties climbing ...
    and it was a real mistake
                        'cause I shouldn't have walked alone
                                                    but ah simply ah
Ze'ev: [you] don't separate a hiking group   (slower)

Meirav's kernel story is aimed at conveying a point concerning the relation between
the individual and the group, and hence both choral and individual quotations are
evoked herein, attesting by content and by performance to the tension between
these protagonists. The story commences with a story preface, which frames it in
the author's individual (first-person singular) voice ("I want to tell something"), by
which Meirav enters into the storytelling role in the conversation. However, the
events that shortly unfold typically assume the group's perspective ("we began"),
and it is in relation to this perspective that Meirav indicates her severance, a perspective she retains throughout the story, including its coda (not including a short
flashback episode, assuming the choral voice).

The moral of her story is quite evident, and just in case, it is reiterated explicitly and pedagogically by Ze'ev. The narrative, and the four quotation sequences
therein, supplies an illustration of the social faux pas Meirav has committed—and
incidentally also a glimpse of her unique accomplishments as a (female) backpacker.
The moral rests on the twofold implications the mistake she made bears: first, by
distancing herself from the group, Meirav put herself in danger. It is literally a jungle
out there, she observes, as she mentions how dark and dense it is. (Note that the
threat she describes is not posed by wilderness directly, but indirectly, by two ominous strange men, "natives," who are closing in on her). At dusk, alone, the threat is
at its peak. It is resolved when Meirav temporarily links up with another group of
Israelis and renounces in deeds and words her individual excursion.

Second, when Meirav rejoins the party, she learns her companions were held
back because another (female) companion was not well. Leaving them behind as
she did implies she acted irresponsibly. Over and above endangering *herself*, which
sustained the story's drama, she was wrong also in relation to her companions.

Interestingly, Meirav accounts for her failure with the word *nishbarti* (literally, "I broke down"), which she repeats. The word's connotation relates to one's
strength of will and ability to withstand hardship. Indeed, when backpackers—
mostly women—indicate they were physically exhausted and could not continue
the strenuous activities, the verb *nishbarti* is commonly employed. Meirav employs
the term in reverse, however, which tacitly injects an elitist moral hue into her narrative. She did not break down physically or give up mentally, nor was she even tired

or worn out. To the contrary, she was faster and more able than the rest. What was unbearably difficult for her was the group's slow pace of walking, a difficulty she amplifies by depicting the group's hiking routine: they begun walking "very late" that day, and they were absentminded rather than goal oriented. Meirav was indeed exhausted, but not with the physical demands of hiking; she was exhausted with the impatience of lingering.

In a unique reverse of meaning, the word *nishbarti* addresses not those back-packers who are physically weak and inclined to break down, but those backpack-ers like Meirav and Ze'ev, who are experienced hikers and who are highly capable physically: they, so she advocates, should be aware of different (moral) pits. The responsibility embodied in this morality is of an elitist quality: the issue is about being overcapable and not undercapable. Thus Meirav wisely manages to hold the stick at both ends: on the one hand, she has wronged, a fact that she acknowledges and that serves as the explicit legitimization for her narrative; on the other hand, the very same error aggrandizes her outstanding physical performance as an elite backpacker.[4]

Although the story is framed by Meirav's (individual) perspective, the first in-stance of quotation consists, typically enough, of the evocation of the authoritative choral voice. Through the quoted chorus exclamation ("yalla"), an action is being formulaically declared ("let's climb") as well as the path by which it is to be pursued. Again, we hear the choral voice in the capacity of indicating the group's goal-orient-edness. It is introduced within a short flashback sequence wherein Meirav returns to the commencement of the hike in order to emphasize that the group was impro-vising, which amplifies the risk she took as well as her annoyance with the group's lack of professionalism. Note that although this is the first *direct* quotation, actually, the chorus quotation is the second instance of reported speech, the first being the indirect reported speech of the "trail story" ("that says that the natives supply ac-commodation"; I will return to a discussion of trail stories in chapter 7). This is not insignificant, since a comparison and a connection are made between the second instance of direct quotation and the first instance of indirect quotation, whereby the latter occasion completes and augments the former—it indicates that the group was traveling in an uncharted area, beyond what is mentioned in the "trail story," and thus amplifies the drama even more.

Shortly later, when Meirav departs from the group, a dialogue of *individual voices* is performed. The dialogue occupies a unique social space in which the group is not involved: an extra-group space wherein both (female) conversants commu-nicate without being dubbed by the (male) chorus. Accordingly, the quotations are not authoritative or directive and do not amount to narrative events. Rather, we are made to overhear an ostensibly regular, nondeclarative exchange. Yet the omni-present, threatening jungle in the background suggests that though the exchange is seemingly mundane, such an exchange of individual voices is, in fact, ominous.

In the short dialogue between the hikers, Meirav repeatedly inquires about the proximity of her companions. By way of overhearing she convincingly tells her audience in the storytelling event—Ze'ev and myself—that she has been repeatedly inquiring about the group and has been reassured that the others were "right behind" her in time and place, thus suggesting in a vindicating manner that she did not simply take off and leave them. Consequently, she is also making a point about how one must adhere to the decree of cohesion (or to the taboo of individuality) and not trust anyone in particular, for even if one is so clearly reassured, one might nevertheless find oneself misled and mistaken. The second speaker in this exchange, though also an individual, is nonetheless represented as standing for the group. Meirav addresses her in the words "you guys" and receives a reply in the certified voice of the group.[5]

The next instance is of hypothetical quotation, that of her thought's voice ("I said [to myself]"; see Banfield 1973), wherein she paraphrases the group's assertion quoted earlier. Both quotations commence with the formulaic, exclamatory "yalla," they are both in future tense, and both point to the trail's final destination. Meirav's individual voice, however, mentions the group she has separated from and evokes the village not so much as a destination but as a location of social congregation: it is where Meirav will, hopefully, reunite with her party. Additionally, while the choral quotativents are typically augmented by a postquotation formula indicating that occurrences have indeed unfolded the way the group stated they would, in Meirav's postquotation formula, which includes three successive utterances, she indicates that it is *not* how things turned out. Rather, she indicates that (1) she waited in vain; and (2) the group did not show up ("and I saw they aren't coming"); instead, (3) two male strangers did.

The last quotation in the extract is another instance of an individual direct thought quote, perhaps a "thought act." It is by audibly uttering "okay" to herself that Meirav communicates how she realized the predicament she was in and simultaneously enacted her decision to temporarily join a passing group.

Shortly later, she confesses in a coda to the "real mistake" she has committed, a true moral faux pas that is both reason and excuse—albeit more of the latter—for the short narrative. It is with the postquotation formula, right after the quotation, that the story's plot concludes and does not further unveil. The following few utterances (including the stress on "turned out LATER?") are retrospective and serve to delineate the fact that plot and events have halted. Again, it is with the quotation-closing formula that Meirav is indicating that she returned to the safe bosom of a group (albeit not her original group) and that her narrative actually terminates. The story also illustrates how, as Richards and Wilson (2004c, 259) word it, risk and perceived risk are "recycled into stories" by backpackers. To be sure, the very last words are Ze'ev's—the male collaborator who turns Meirav's concluding personal moral into an impersonal statement, perhaps also taking the opportunity to tacitly reprimand Meirav for breaching a backpacker dictum.

Such instances of individual voices in the backpackers' narratives establish the *dramatic quality* of the undertakings and indicate that these voices are, in and of themselves, unique and exceptional. This occurs not only in moral stories attesting to the wrongdoings of individuals who sever themselves from the group/collective. Following are two shorter segments, to be discussed briefly, that further illustrate how individual voices are evoked within unique social circumstances.

In the first illustration, the narrator's individual voice emerges against an explicitly gendered background touching on the activity of hiking—an activity that is particularly heavily gendered, involving as it does "manly" images of adventures and risks (Elsrud 2001; Noy 2003a). Often women express their disdain for the practice in more or less explicitly gendered terms. In such cases, the expression inevitably digresses from the dominant masculine choral voice and assumes an individual cast. When Inbal recounts her "Chile experiences," she testifies how she and the female friend she traveled with were "conquered" by the notion of "conquering mountain passes." Though she occasionally mentions how hiking was overwhelmingly difficult, she does so almost independently of the narrative she recounts, in which she repeatedly turns to tell of how rewarding were the hiking excursions in which she participated. Such is also evinced in the following excerpt.

Inbal: In Chile I was with—

    in Chile we were with two men (*banim*)

                    they—

               two platoon officers on a short leave from the army with a militaristic

   attitude

                     they had me undergo basic training ah

                         [for] a month

Chaim: wow [wow

Inbal: throughout] Chile we slept in a tent

like once a week I said

        "listen

        I have to wash my head

        take me to ah hotels to wash

               anything   (quieter)

          to bathe in the river"

Chaim: mmm

Inbal: that's what's fun

   that's what's so fun traveling with a car

          you see a nice spot

          you can decide to spend the night there

Inbal evokes the words she had uttered repeatedly during the trip in an individual quotation voiced in explicitly gendered terms. Typically, the narrator's individual voice gains social audibility through quotation, as she distinguishes herself from the masculine chorus. After Inbal succinctly depicts the two male participants (using the common term *banim*, literally, "boys" (see chapter 6, note 6), she addresses them as a group and elaborates explicitly on the group's masculine character: the men are identified only by their military affiliation and position, which they seem to be carrying enthusiastically into the trip. To be sure, Inbal mentions that over and above their institutional affiliation, they held an active "militaristic attitude" (or *rosh tsva'ie,* literally "a militaristic head").[6]

Inbal describes the consequences traveling with the men had on her trip: while in a leisurely touristic practice, she had actually undergone an intense physical experience, poignantly captured in the term "basic training." Her criticism reaches beyond the specific instance she is relating by pointing to the parallel that exists between backpacking and basic training. Insofar as these are socially constructed rites of passage, both practices exert significant cohesive pressure and discipline over the individual and her body.

Against this background Inbal's quotation assumes its saliency. In and through quotation she touches on a central metonym of the feminine body: her hair. She wants to, or better, *has* to wash her body and her hair occasionally. This is where her voice, that of a female backpacker, surfaces and expresses the body's unique needs, which are customarily unrecognized by the group (particularly in the case of the "army boys," who are not allowed to grow long hair, unlike other male backpackers). It emerges within an *illustrative* quotation that exemplifies how ill adapted to women is the masculinist normative practice. Women, therefore, must expressively demand what they need and deserve.

The quotation, which both indicates and occupies a breach between the group and the individual, reflects not a spatial division but a gender one. Inbal addresses the authority of the group, seeking a change in its travel patterns—or even, perhaps, a mere response. That she is not performing a dialogue is exactly what the narrator means when she points out she had to reiterate her request time and again.

Note that overall, the group is comprised of four backpackers: two women and two men. Yet, as her friend is shadowed, Inbal is left alone, outnumbered by the two men and by the masculine discourse they embody. She positions herself as "representatively singular" in the face of men, as Minh-Ha (1994, 15) writes of women travelers.

Soon after she sounds her repeated requests, she breaks with the point her quotation establishes and shifts elsewhere by employing a postquotation utterance. She recalls how she had actually thoroughly enjoyed the trip when it was pursued with a car. Inbal is thus suggesting an alternative mode of travel transportation, one that is far more enjoyable and allows a more gender-sensitive or flexible attention to the body, in which it is not so intensely challenged and disciplined. The contrast shown in Inbal's description calls to mind the observation Harrison makes concerning the discourse of "touristic aesthetics": "The discourse appears to turn a blind eye to the physical discomforts travellers (and their bodies) often endure, choosing to emphasize more positive emotional memories and responses" (2003, 93).

In this short excerpt quotation is typically posited at the narrative's core. Preceded by a description of the events that regularly took place during the trip and followed by an evaluation, which gains its authority and validity from the sense of "directness" evoked in the quotation, the quotation is at the expressive core of Inbal's argument. Moreover, through the introduction formula, which includes a plural vocative ("listen," *tishme'u*), with which the quotation commences formulaically, the narrator positions her individual voice dialogically vis-à-vis the group.

In the last illustration, Uri tells of a relatively minor knee injury he suffered while hiking the snowy Choro trail (Il Choro), near La Paz, Bolivia, which separated him from his companions. A space has thus been created in which his individual voice is performed. Before the extract begins, Uri mentions the company of a relatively large group of Israelis, from which he and two companions decided to part after they lagged behind. He tells that they decided to do so after he pointed out the path they were hiking had no outlets but for the very beginning and end: "whoever begins has to finish. no other alternative."

Uri: By the third night we were approximately half a kilometer
                                        behind the group
   and simply
          we notified them [we were breaking off]
               they knew that they'd be
                         arriving at a certain point
  [and] I said
          "I don't want to go on from here
                   if I continue now I might
  tear the knee ligament and"
Chaim: [really?
Uri: "and] then you'll have to carry me
       I prefer to stop first and rest"
  and though it sounds like all there's left is half a kilometer
                   the path is very
                       very narrow
  one side a wall
  the other a cliff . . .
       and I didn't want to take a chance
              we preferred to stop first

Breaking the taboo of separating a group requires a well-founded rationale, which is the reason behind Uri's explanations and justifications. Unlike Meirav, though, Uri frames his act altruistically, suggesting within the quotation that it is in fact *for the sake of the group* that he should break off ("you'll have to carry me").

Although the quotation is immediately preceded by a speech verb, the quotation formula actually stretches two utterances back and includes "we notified them" (*hoda'anu lahem*). Again, addressing the group is performed formulaically, as though the register is upgraded when addressing an authority. The postquotation formula, too, stretches a few utterances after the end of the quotation and includes the excerpt's closing utterance ("we preferred to stop first"), which reiterates the last quoted utterance ("I prefer to stop first") with a slight modification. This modification embodies the vicissitudes between single and choral perspectives and authorships and brings the narrative back into the realm of action, where the group is the central protagonist.

The narrator employs quotation to indicate and to account for a change in the ensuing plot. In this regard, the quote serves as an event both in its referential capacities—the small group has voicedly (publicly, that is) announced its severance—and in its expressive capacities—it deviates from the plot in both perspective (individual rather than group/plural) and reference (direct quotation rather than narrative). It is at this point, which is a somewhat vulnerable link in the chain of narrative events, that Uri feels most urgently the need to communicate clearly what has lead him to take the decision he has (all the more so because of my short intervention expressing wonder). He implies that his decision is based not on quantitative considerations ("though it sounds like all there's left is half a kilometer") but on existential ones: "one side a wall, the other a cliff."

In varying degrees and manners, these illustrations present the social dramas that allow for the surfacing-into-discourse of quoted individual and choral voices. In the narrations, individual and chorus quotations are inevitably located at the drama's core, which the quotations both embody and express. Amid stories of cohesive congregations, which are authoritatively voiced in and through the choral voice, the individual quotation enacts a tension between the individual and the group, reflected in the tension between the individual voice and that of the chorus. Within the tight and normative context of sociability evinced by Israeli backpackers, incidents in which individual voices hatch out of the chorus are irregular and socially upsetting, and they require a complex performance that includes explanations and justifications. The state of being on one's own, and expressing one's own voice amid unfamiliar surroundings, is a near taboo. At the same time, dramatically transgressing this taboo also makes for a fruitful performative resource.

The ubiquitous performance of the group voice, and the corresponding preciousness of the evocation of the individual voice, is even more striking when we consider the particular genre of the stories. Travel narrative is one of the archgenres of individualism, as portrayed by and pursued in the colonial-romanticist West. That the ethos of the lone traveler/explorer/seeker is inverted, and the travelers are actually hardly left by themselves, indicates the changes that have occurred in backpacking tourism over the last few decades, on the one hand, and the infusion of prevalent themes of a particular culture—Israeli youth—on the other hand.

Further, if we assume that the group does sometimes represent the collective metonymically (Hazan 2001a, 2001b), then tension and severance between individual and group reflexively index the very act of *backpacking outside and away from the homeland.* Indeed, as indicated earlier, the backpackers have to account for their leave, which is criticized by conservative-national viewpoints as recreational and frivolous: in a word, unpatriotic (Noy 2003a).

Whether the protagonist whose voice is directly imported is the group or the individual, the quoted sequences reach into the taleworld and at the same time reach out: to the audience attending the event of storytelling. Quotations are employed in the capacity of evoking negotiation and tension between the group and the individual and suggest that issues of individuality and collectivity are highly significant to the narrators and amount to the stories' morals.

The exchanges between the authoritative and frequent choral voice and the individual voice, as well as the dramatic social space that is created between them, are supplemented by additional sets of interacting voices that produce distinct, multi-leveled dialogues (or "dialogics"; See Mannheim and van Vleet 1998). Such a set of voices includes those that are attributed to *extra*community animators: that is, animators who are non-Hebrew speaking, whom the backpackers refer as "non-Israeli" and "outsiders."

Performing Others' Voices: Quoting Native and Tourist

[Tourists' n]onrepeatable encounters with strangers more easily serve metonymic functions, delivering unambiguous exemplificatory knowledge of "the Frenchmen," "Italy," "the Third World," or even "humanity."
  Judith Adler

While choral and individual voices represent that which is *utterly familiar* to the backpackers—their single and plural selves—we now turn to explore voices imported into the performances from a *foreign exterior*. The following quotations index voices that are attributed to either "native" or "local" (*mekomi*) or "tourist" (*tayar*) animators.[1] Basically, both share a common attribution—namely, being outside the community; they are voices of the Other—that which is alien, whose alienness is both constructed and made discernible against the densely enclaved Israeli polyphony.

Though the evocation of native and tourist voices is infrequent, such voices nonetheless play an inimitable role. As performative resources, they differ from the resources engulfed in voices that correlate with the narrators' selves: individual and group (and, as we will see, collective). By exploring voices that are constructed as emanating from the social space exterior to the community, from the *background* against which travel narratives ensue, light is shed on the construction of the community's borders and thresholds. Additionally, otherness is imported and "translated" into the live discursive communal fabric in the capacity of communicating the *authentic*—profound and foreign—experiences of the great journey.

The evocation of foreign voices in the performances designates the touristic scene depicted in the narratives as multinational and multiracial. While traditionally research had revolved around the "guests–hosts" relationship, recent trends argue that this dichotomous perception is rather simplistic (Bruner 2005; Edensor 1998; Smith 1992). Instead, the various public spaces of tourism engulf various guests and various hosts. The construction of meaning in these heterogeneous spaces is established by multiple and multilayered interactions that take place *among* hosts, *among* guests, and *between* hosts and guests. And although a good deal of the research has been devoted to exploring tourists' perceptions of the Other (following MacCannell 1976), actual encounters with "natives" and representations thereof have been scarcely researched, far less than the theoretical stature would imply.

Further, absent from the literature is analysis of tourists' perceptions of *each other* and the interactions—if and to whatever extent they indeed occur—that take place among different tourists who all share the public spaces of tourism (on national, sociodemographic, and gender grounds). While general patterns of interaction between tourists are occasionally explored (Loker-Murphy and Pearce 1995), the ways in which tourists react to as well as make use of ethnic-national heterogeneity in extra/multinational spaces has hardly been examined. Indeed, recent criticism addresses some of the basic preconceptions among tourism scholars and points to the homologous perception they had of tourists: male and Western/white (Alneng 2002; see also Graburn 1983, 18).

Yet, because borders face two sides at the same time—"interior" and "exterior," "us" and "Other"—by performing Others' voices the backpackers are in fact demarcating the community's borders. Additionally, although native and tourist voices are both foreign to the backpackers, they are performed differently and provide a range of discursive distances and perspectives that narrators may positionally assume. In performative terms, tourist and native voices serve in implicating the audience of the performances differently, and thus amount to creative discursive resources that are unique to the realms of tourism.

With regard to reporting and performing foreigners' voices in interethnic and interracial interactions, Buttny and Williams (2000, 123) observe that "using the words of others can be a valuable resource to understand how out-group members are discursively constructed," which indicates the "discursive constructions of race and interracial contact" (see also Buttny 1997, 1999; Tusting, Crawshaw, and Callen 2002).

Quotations of foreigners are particularly interesting in a linguistic sense, for if the underlying quality of quotations concerns their *accuracy* in conveying the original linguistic expression, a question arises as to the language by which Others' words are delivered. What is the language that Nepalese porters or French mountaineers speak as figures in the backpackers' narratives?

The inquiry becomes still more complicated, even puzzling, when the "natives" themselves *speak Hebrew fluently* (the result of the routinization of backpacking itineraries; see the introduction and Noy 2006a). The backpackers then come upon a conflation of that which is intimately familiar (their mother tongue) and that which is suspiciously foreign. Indeed, backpackers are preoccupied with these instances, which they recount repeatedly, where their very own voice weirdly echoes or bounces back at them from foreign throats.

Lastly, instances of quotation of natives and tourists heavily engulf institutional aspects. As Baynham and Slembrouck (1999, 440) point out, an investigation of reported speech in institutional contexts can bring to the surface the professional-institutional interface, or the "intraprofessional relationship." In the instance of tourism these would concern tourists' interactions that are institutionally "indexical of particular category-based role relationships between representer, representee, and represented voice" (441; see also Holt 1999, 522–28). Performatively exploring the institutional dimensions of reported speech suggests how stories not only reflect backpacking tourism institutional settings but also construct and perform them minute by minute.

Voicing the "Native" and the Case of Illustrative Quotations

Hosts' words are part of a principal touristic theme pertaining to romantic and Orientalist representations of the "Other" (see Bhattacharyya 1997; Bruner 1991; Carter 1998; Cohen 1993; Kirshenblatt-Gimblett 1998; MacCannell 1984; Pratt 1992; van Doorn 1989). Due to the unique features of backpacking—preference for low-budget accommodation and transportation services and a lower level of institutionalization—and in line with the backpackers' romanticist ideologies, the lengthy trip entails quite some contact with local employees of the tourism industry and with local peoples. Hence, their narratives make for a good source of natives' voices, both those who are employed by the industry and those who are solely the objects of the backpackers' gaze.

Of these two groups, the narratives illustrate more instances that echo exchanges between backpackers and local tourist operators. This is not surprising considering that once the backpackers leave urban centers in order to see "exotic peoples," the latter are advertently objectified and hence devoid of agency and of embodied voice. Yet employees of the industry who cater for tourists are more than mere "background"; because their services are essential for a successful trip, they are granted more agency and voice than viewed spectacles (Bruner 2005; van Doorn 1989).

Representations (or avoidance thereof) of natives illustrate the cultural images that thrive in the tourists' home cultures in their preconceptions of and attitudes toward aliens. In present-day public discourse in Israel, representations of the Other emblematically revolve around the image of the Palestinian (and more recently of foreign workers from Asia), which makes for a charged, threatening theme. In Western history, in the history of modern tourism, and in Zionist history, Otherness has consistently been defined by the colonial gaze (Fanon 1986; Pratt 1992; Said 1978). This is why the convergence of the neocolonial features of tourism (Aitchison 2001; Carter 1998; Nash 1989) and Zionist ideology are particularly interesting when examining voices from the "third world" in the backpackers' "Western" narratives (Noy and Cohen 2005a; Stein 2002).

Lastly, by their explicit attribution to *non-Hebrew speakers,* quoted voices suggest a particularly interesting case of the representation of one language within another. Indeed, the definition of foreigners that the backpackers draw centrally revolves around language. Yet, beyond language differences, their distinctions tacitly invoke the problematic, supposedly exclusive unidirectional relationship between Israeli identity and the Hebrew language. The youths perceive Hebrew as a language that is spoken solely by (Jewish) Israelis, hence reflecting the notion of "one nation, one language" (Crawford 1992; Katriel 1990; Lang 1995). In this vein, when they spontaneously make metalinguistic comments concerning their language, they mention *Yisraelit* (Israeli-ish) rather than *Ivrit* (Hebrew). Hence, when listening to quotations of natives, a question arises concerning the degree to which their voices are "translated" (with or without quotation marks) into and heard in backpackers' "Israeli-ish" discourse.

In the first of two excerpts, Ayelet describes a predicament the group she traveled with faced, one that revolved around a decision the group had to take: whether to spend another night on the trail before climbing to the pass or whether to rush and climb to the pass that very day and reach the end of the trail sooner. The discussion is instigated during a description of a lengthy ascent along the path circling the Annapurna mountain chain, north of Pokhara in Nepal. Because one of the companions is not feeling well and is developing, the group suspects, a case of Acute Mountain Disease, the discussion assumes a degree of urgency, and the story a degree of drama.

Ayelet: And we sat
    and we thought what to do
        we said
          [that] maybe we'll stay there another day
          'cause maybe he'll still be able to adjust to the heights
    but our porters didn't agree with this at all
        they said
          "either [going] down or up (*o yordim o olim*)   (quickly)
        staying is very expensive"
          after all
          they paid for their [own]
  accommodation and food

While quotations of the choral voice had previously carried an authoritative quality, in the present illustration it is merely propositional (indicated by such words as "thought" and "maybe"), and it soon encounters an authoritative voice and is rebuffed. The exchange between the tourists and the porters occupies a discursive space to which the narrator neatly leads the audience by employing three consecutive verbs ("sat . . . thought . . . said"), the last of which is a speech verb. Indeed, this progressive succession of verbs with which the narrator commences the description performs a shift from nonverbal events (sitting) through semi- or psuedo-verbal events (thinking) to distinctly explicit verbal events (saying), whereby the exchange unfolds.

The porters who accompany the group are also represented by a plural group voice ("they said"). Although they are certainly not group members, they participate in the exchange and effectively shape it. They do so not by positively deciding what *is* to be done, but rather, their decisive assertion serves to *restrict* available possibilities, excluding the one that the group had leaned toward. In fact, it is not so much that the natives' voice participates in a dialogue as much as it has the effect of a *natural occurrence* that shapes the travelers' choices of paths and itineraries. Akin to an avalanche or a flooding river, the porters' voice here carries a *nonnegotiable* (force majeure) type of authority and is evoked as an independent speech act. Indeed, the exchange that ensues between the group's indirectly reported voice, entailing a suggestion, and the directly reported reply of the porters, entailing a straightforward refusal ("either down or up"), is roundabout and mediated; there is no natural dialogue of which we hear. The figures assume different ontological, exclusive planes. "Voices split," Young (1991, 224) observes of representations of natives' voices in ethnographic texts: meaning is generated but not through direct interaction and dialogue.

Insofar as the porters' voices represent a constraining variable by which the group has to calculate its steps, it suggests a point where the otherwise self-sufficient group "runs into reality," as it were—the discursive representation of which the figures of the porters convey. Accordingly, voices are framed differently: while the group's indirect voice is gradually arrived at, the porters' direct voice is portrayed as a blatant intervention (they "didn't agree with this *at all*").

The first and second quotations are concluded with the narrator's explanations: that is, with metacommunicative, metaquotative comments that supply an interpretation of the words of the group and of the porters. Ayelet repeatedly marks the closure of the reported speech by explaining in a quotation-closing formula what it meant ("'cause maybe he'll still be able . . . after all . . ."). She thus constructs exchanges that are reminiscent of speech interaction in legal (court) settings, where a succession of claims is made whereby each party has a say, which is followed by the narrator's commentary. The closing argument however, is decisive, and the group abides by it.

Thematically, the commentary concluding the quotation relates to an informal institutional contract between suppliers and consumers. Ayelet explains that since the porters have to pay for their own travel expenses, their determined intervention in the course of the activity is legitimate, and hence their argument is stronger than the one presented by the backpackers concerning a companion's illness. Morally, the narrator exonerates herself (and her group) of not pursuing the best and immediate alternative in helping a companion who might be seriously ill. She also resolves a tension concerning the operators' servitude, which seems to have been breached.

Performatively, Young's (1991, 225) critical observation concerning ethnographic narratives holds for backpackers' travel stories: "estrangement from the native permits alignment with the reader." In addition to stressing the utterances' decisive quality, the use of quotations in reporting the voice of the native achieves two aims: (1) of highly distinguishing and marking Others' voices as "nonorganic" components of the discourse; and (2), related to this, of aligning the audience with the narrator through jointly overhearing someone else's voices. The more directly the voice is reported, the more estranged it becomes; and it is estranged, we should note, with regard to the voice of the narrator. As Young (1991, 224) emphasizes, "the narrator's voice remains objective whereas the characters speak in their own voices, subject not only to the constraints of their realm but also to the constitutive disposition of the inscriber. . . . The characters' discourse is captive in the narrator's."

Attending to a query postulated earlier regarding the language expressed within quotations, we hear that the porters are quoted in Hebrew. This is to say that their voice is "thoroughly" translated into colloquial Israeli-ish speech, as evinced for instance in the colloquial expression "either . . . or" ("o . . . o"). Other than the indication that the animators are not Israelis, there are no suggestions that the quoted words were initially uttered in a different language. Though they do not interact directly, the voices of both parties hold the same linguistic floor in the narration and are presented in the narration in precisely the linguistic register typical of the speech style of the community. In fact, porters and guides are commonly quoted as using *idiomatic* Hebrew expressions, which is the case in the next illustration.

Boaz, who backpacked in Asia, illustrates a point he had made shortly before, where he stated that in Nepal he encountered "one of the most beautiful cultures I've ever known. the generosity [there] is exceptional." Boaz then tells of his hiking experiences, specifically of a point along the famous Jomsom Trail (located at the Annapurna Nature Reserve in Nepal) where, due to crowds of backpackers, finding accommodation during the tourist season is notoriously tricky. "Sometimes you can get stuck with no place to sleep," he says worriedly and introduces a drama concerning the operator-tourist relationship.

Boaz: It was our luck that we had a pretty ah
                 a pretty responsible porter—
                             a guide
                   he told us
                     "guys (*hevre*)
                                  I'll walk ahead of you
                                  I'll take your backpack
                                  I'll take your equipment
                                  and I'll leave a
couple of hours ahead of you [in order] to reach the cabin"
it somehow shows you the courtesy of the peo—
                           his responsibility
                           his concern
                                 now
                               now we really knew what it means
     to appreciate him

Typical of quotations of out-group people, the quotations above are of an illustrative type (Holsanova 1998). They "show," as Boaz himself puts it, that the guide exhibited commendable qualities. The illustrative quotation supplies an example of the guide's responsible conduct, one that is stated in operational terms and is evoked from the perspective of the consumers. Boaz suggests that the guide is worthy of the superlatives because he has done outstandingly more than was required of him: he carried all of the belongings of the entire group and left earlier to reserve a room for the next night.

Differing from the account supplied by Ayelet above, and typical of backpackers' depictions of those who supply them with services, the narrative includes explicit evaluative comments on operators' performance. It carries highly evaluative judgments that are either admiring or critical. In some cases, the guide's "fantastic" knowledge of flora and fauna is idealized, while in other cases the downside is emphasized, and the guides' "primitiveness" or "rudeness" is emphasized.

The discursive right to express superlatives, significantly accentuated in tourists' talk, is inherent in the genre of colonial narratives (Pratt 1992). Competent use of a richly superlative language register indicates the *identity* of the narrator, in the sense that she or he possesses the knowledge and occupies the power position necessary for discerning and expressing appreciation (the "entitlement" to do so, in Shuman's words [1992]). In this sense, superlatives are not about the objects they address as much as they are self-referents that position their utterer, establishing his or her right to evaluate others and proclaiming his or her *expertise* in doing so, which distinguish and establish him or her as a competent connoisseur.

In the case of the illustrative quotations, the above applies to "culture" as a whole, which the anonymous native metonymically embodies. Note that shortly after the quote Boaz corrects himself, and instead of addressing "the peo—" (the cultural level), he says "his responsibility," thus turning back to the individual illustration. Indeed, as Buttny observes, voices of out-group members supply a "resource [which] allows the reporting speaker to *epitomize* the group through their characteristic utterances" (1997, 499; emphasis in the original). Indeed, "replicated and reinforced through narrative," such epitomized and stereotyped voices "become part of the . . . language of tourism" (Sturma 1999, 713).

The reported words are conveyed in emphatic "Israeli-ish" terms. This is particularly apparent in the opening address ("hevre," which also occurs in Shiri's words above), which formulaically leads to an extended, stylized utterance. A heritage of the dugri speech style, the term *hevre* (guys) indicates friendship within a cohesive group. It is an address of a type someone from within a group would make, one that establishes that the addressor is both familiar with the jargon and close to the adressee (Almog 2000; Katriel 1986).

Boaz's view of the guide, who is appraised for the skills with which he attends to the group and serves it, is instrumental. The quadruple repetitive structure (beginning each time with "I'll") enhances the guide's portrayed solicitousness, stylistically expanding on the various requirements the guide comprehends he has to fulfill in the aim of serving the tourists optimally. Merely leaving before the group would not suffice. In order to be the commendable guide his depiction portrays, there is also a need to carry the group's gear, which would free the group to travel lightly at its own pace.

Notice that the repetitive structure is that of A, B, B', A'-C, according to which the first and the forth utterances say more or less the same thing (concerning the guide's departure before the group), and so do the two middle utterances (concerning carrying the group's gear). Utterance C adds new information. It bounds the quotation sequence by way of explanation: from C we learn of the intention of the previous recitations, which is ensuring an accommodation facility.

Akin to Ayelet's quotation, the words of the guide are followed by the narrator's metacommunicative comment, which, in addition to its role as quotation-closing formula, serves to explain or justify quoting a native voice. Here, too, the narrator explains or excuses the weaving of quotation in the narration, suggesting it is by way of illustration. In any case, when they are reported, the Other's words are conspicuous and require accounting for.

Remarkably, although the narrator seemingly wishes to establish the guide's commendable behavior, illustrated by his devoted service, Boaz actually does not depict the latter's behavior in any way. That is to say, Boaz does not reveal what the guide has *done* to be proved skillful and worthy. Rather, he illustrates the guide's conduct by addressing his communicative skills. The "it" in the beginning of the metacommunicative comment ("it somehow shows you"), which is the first word that follows the quotation, is meant to address, in effect, *words,* insofar as they indicate conduct or give an example of it. Boaz demonstrates the Nepalese's "concern" (*ihpatiut*) not by a depiction of the latter's actual labor but by conveying as a central component of his commendable service his knowledge of proper communication. Indeed, in relation to the "third world," van Doorn (1989, 77) observes that tourists' concern "is to meet only those people who combine colonial servitude with unbelievable linguistic skills," which are limited to specific domains of service. This tendency may be understood institutionally when observing, as Urry has in a discussion of tourist services, that "the quality of the social interaction is itself part of the service purchased" (1990, 68).

Quotations are employed precisely in order to impress the audience with the guide "objectively." The narrator allows the figure of the guide to occupy the narrative floor in order to express his skills *directly.* This is why natives' quotations here are *illustrative* in the strong sense. In the service of the group, the guide knows exactly what do to and why, and even more important, *how to communicate it competently.* This is why there is hardly need for additional details in order for the listener to know "what it means to appreciate him." With this, the guide's "concern" and, by way of generalization, Nepalese "generosity" are established. Putting the word "hevre" in the mouth of the guide serves to indicate how well suited he is to his job: not only does he carry heavy gear and secure accommodation, he also knows how to address Israelis in their own terms (literally) in a close and warm fashion.

In other instances reported speech makes for exemplary (and illustrative) events that lead to negative—usually condescending and/or suspicious/conspiratorial—evaluations of natives. After one of the narrators reports a dialogue in which a heated dispute arose between the local guide and the group, she generalizes and concludes with regard to all tourists' facilitators: "they're masters of duping (*letah-men*) alright . . . they'll always try to dupe [tourists]." Such cases accord with Buttny's (1997, 500) findings, which attest that most reported speech in interracial interactions serves to criticize or complain about troublesome incidents and to portray out-group members in a negative light. Although quotations of out-group members suggest seemingly particular instances, they nonetheless represent a "prototypical group member" (Buttny 1997, 479; Buttny and Williams 2000, 113). In such cases, in which backpackers evoke locals' words and suggest that they should constantly stand guard against the cunningness of local entrepreneurs, interracial reported speech indeed "seems to be an especially potent device for challenging not only the prepositional content of the quote, but also the source" (Buttny 1997, 492). The evaluation of the reported words travels back, as it were, to their animators, who are then proved, by their own words, to be untrustworthy.

To conclude, local operators who attend to the backpackers are often described through highly evaluative prisms and are either idealized or devalued. This dichotomy, an age-old characteristic of Western Orientalist-romanticist perception, is perpetuated and invigorated in the bourgeois imagination that underlies tourism discourse. Much of the backpackers' illustrations of natives accords closely with Kathleen Stewart's (1996, 119) observations of images of Native Americans in the United States: "People in the hills were friendly and suspicious, talkative and taciturn, fatalist and individualist, religious and antireligious, pathologically dependent and utterly self sufficient, pathetic and heroic, loving and violent." Whether they embody concern and courteousness or deceit and fraud, natives are always more than they actually are. In other words, they are illustrations of this or that quality, of this or that trait. This is why their representations are inevitably imbued with a strong, bipolar split. Communicatively, this is why their words are usually reported in an illustrative capacity; these words stand for some*thing* else.

In these cases, quotations inevitably do not convey the original language. In fact, on a singular occasion in which Spanish words were quoted, their utterer was an *Israeli backpacker,* not the local guide with whom the exchange took place. The foreign words in this case (*todo tiempo* in Spanish) serve to indicate a performative state (in the capacity of being code switchers; Hymes 1975, 24, 66–67) to convey the authenticity of the report and to provoke the audience to either inquire about the meaning of the words or to acknowledge the familiarity of the performers with foreign (natives') tongues.

Israeli Language in Others' Mouths

In a particularly interesting type of quotation, natives' words are presented as initially uttered in Hebrew(!) In these cases narrators enthusiastically stress that the "native" animators they quote *originally* spoke Hebrew, which is to say that they did not translate these words but reported them directly, already translated, as it were.

In itself, this fact should not be surprising: it is a consequence of the processes of institutionalization and routinization whereby regular interaction between tourists and merchants has allowed the latter to acquire the language of the former, sometimes fluently. Yet for the backpackers these instances inevitably amount to a wonder: a linguistic–tourist attraction in and of itself.

When backpackers recount these utterances and stress they were initially uttered in Hebrew, it attests to their further preoccupation with the Other. Particularly, backpackers find bizarre the juxtaposition of utter familiarity (their mother tongue) and utter alienness (spoken by a foreigner). Moreover, because some tourist facilitators learn the languages they know from everyday interactions, the jargon they speak echoes that of the backpackers'. They employ up-to-date idioms, slang, jokes, and recite popular Hebrew songs that are frequently used by and among the backpackers. This enhances the backpackers' wonder at the odd juxtaposition of familiarity and foreignness.

Instances where backpackers' language echoes back at them assume double reflexivity, a double "double-voiced" quality (Bakhtin 1986). In all such cases the backpackers' own language and image of themselves are (re)represented. Others' quotations serve not (only) to suggest a perspective on them but also to ventriloquize a perspective on the Israeli collective itself, which, having been uttered by an outside source, enjoys a higher degree of validity. Hence, performing the Other's voice provides an optimal resource when a need to reflect upon the community as such arises. Enjoying the authority-imbued authenticity, the Other is in an ideal position to be quoted validly: she or he assumes a discursive Archimedean point by which she or he can comment on the community as a whole, seemingly for the outside. In such quotatives *two groups,* rather than one, are epitomized.

The next two sets of quotations correspond with two common themes. In the first set the ubiquitous presence of Israelis in designated destinations (enclaves) is brought to the fore. There, operators and local merchants supply a "sounding board" by which Israelis talk about, perceive, and constitute themselves as a collective. These short episodes, which I term "demographic anecdotes," are particularly stylized and formulaic and present idiomatic forms of quotations (embedded in short humorous personal anecdotes) that circulate among the backpackers. They are commonly told in the first person (singular) and are structured as seemingly spontaneous interactions (see Oring's work on Sabra humor [1981]), thus "purporting to recount a true incident involving real people" (Bauman 1986, 55). Their formulaic structure contributes to their collectivizing—and hence also traditionalizing—effect, which is achieved by the implicit suggestion that there indeed exists such a speech community that shares idioms, jokes, and so on. The focus of the second set of exchanges concerns the knowledge hosts hold of "Israeli" language. Here, a preoccupation with Israelis' collective identity is evinced and with it the impact or impression it has on foreign peoples in touristic scenes.

The following excerpt is taken from the interview with Meirav and Ze'ev. When the conversation turns to address the prominence of Israeli backpackers in certain sites, Meirav recounts an encounter that illustrates an observation she had made earlier, that Israelis have "*a lot* of power there," which, she adds, they use "in a negative way." Ze'ev then adds a similar exchange of his own, which reinforces Meirav's tale but also competes with it.

> Meirav: Once I even asked someone there, "ah tell me, how many people do you think live in Israel?" so he's thinking—thinking, and then he says to me, "25 million" (laughs)
>
> Chaim (quietly): Wow, wow
>
> Ze'ev: I once had something different [happen to me] ah, someone asked me, . . . "how many Israelis [are there]?" I told him "something around 5 million—" he goes, "no, not here in South America, in Israel" (everyone laughs).

The first humorous anecdote commences with an initiative on behalf of Meirav, who tells of approaching an anonymous native ("someone there") and inquiring of him as to the number of Israelis who, in his estimation, live in Israel. The addressee's general/anonymous identity qualifies him as an ideal—"neutral"—out-group animator. The answer Meirav recounts is short, informative, and makes for the amusing point of the short exchange. The person whom she addressed serves as a "scoreboard" pointing to a striking number, at which he has arrived, Meirav implies, by inference from the number of backpackers at the destination. The short sequence concludes with the listener's (myself) expression of wonder. The point Meirav is making is clear: the presence of Israeli backpackers in South America is remarkably high, high enough to lead an impartial observer to deduce that the number of Israelis in Israel in no fewer than 25 million.

Ze'ev, the second narrator, immediately recounts a similar exchange. As he competes with Meirav over the most succinct illustration of the impact Israelis have, he suggests a somewhat more sophisticated variation of the trope. His version includes three exchanges (turns) and not two; the reported dialogue is initiated by a native, and not by the tourists themselves—a fact that grants it a further degree of credibility (it is not an "experiment" but a "naturally" occurring event in which the narrator was inadvertently involved); and lastly, the point Ze'ev makes, which is revealed at the very last words, explicitly goes beyond sheer quantity.

Ze'ev's humorous punch line is communicated through describing a misunderstanding that occurred between host and guest. While Ze'ev took the inquiry concerning the number of Israelis to refer to the population in the home country, it was meant to refer to the number of backpackers visiting the destination. However, Ze'ev's answer ("5 million," depicting the Jewish population in Israel) sounds just right to the foreigner's ears, when what he has in mind is the number of backpackers. Hence the foreigner then reasks Ze'ev for the population size, this time *in Israel*, which reveals the humorous misunderstanding. (Cf. Maoz 2004, 109 for a similar anecdote.)

What is cleverly conveyed in this exchange concerns not only the impact Is-raeli backpackers have and the degree of visibility they evince, but, more astutely, the relationship between the homeland and the "diasporic" backpacking commu-nity. The underlying moral, hinted at in the anonymous native's words, is that the population of Israelis currently residing in Israel is of the exact size of the popula-tion of backpackers. Hence, the exchange is less about numbers than about space, place, and identity. If there are 5 million Israelis, and if they are all presently travel-ing, the question that arises is who, then, is (left behind) in Israel? As in Meirav's illustration, here, too, the anonymous native's impression of the number of Israeli backpackers is high.

The point Meirav makes more implicitly and Ze'ev more explicitly is expressed in various similar "demographic anecdotes" in which the voice of outsiders is dubbed. In all such cases, the relationship between home and destination, country and enclave, permanency and temporality is evoked and explored.

Uri: Natives grab me on the street and ask me

> "tell me
>
> how many are you?
>
> how many are you in the State of Israel?" (*bemedinat Yisrael*)
>
> I say
>
> > "some 5 million"
> >
> > [they say]
> >
> > "and everyone's here?!"

In these exchanges Others' voices are evoked as a part of a heated preoccupation Israelis show as to their presence and acknowledged effect outside the territory of their national identity: that is, in the eyes and ears of Others. Uri describes the homeland by employing the formal term ("State of Israel"), which lexically serves to frame the figure's voice as an outsider and thus imbue it with a degree of neutrality and authenticity. Yet at the same time it is also a part of an intratourist negotiation of identity, which assumes a shape of preoccupation with a web of relationships between the backpackers, the (different indexes of the) homeland—*medinat Yisrael* (the state of Israel), *Eretz Yisrael* (the land of Israel), or simply *Yisrael* or *arets* (liter-ally, "country")—and various representations of Otherness.

Uri asserts not only the sizable number of Israelis, he also evokes a zero-sum type of metaphor: the *place* where Israeli are lively at, or the place where Israeli-ness vibrates, is not the homeland. Instead, it is to be found abroad. Backpacking emerges as pointing to *the* place to be: literally, the "in" place. The enclaves represent not only a tourist *attraction* but an *alternative* as well. A new Israeli frontier has been gradually inaugurated and inhabited, one that is not (only) an extension of the "state of Israel" but experientially an alternative or replacement (Noy and Cohen 2005a).[2]

Metaphorically, Meirav, Ze'ev, and Uri suggest an "evacuation" of the complete (Jewish) Israeli population from the territory of the state of Israel. What they are saying is that the 5 million Israelis are temporary sojourners who "go through the motion" of the backpacking rite of passage. The travelers subsequently become not only backpackers but also citizens of the state of Israel.

A second set of quotations that are attributed to native figures conveys a preoccupation with the *competent knowledge of Hebrew* they hold. Attesting to the knowledge held by natives confirms, in the backpackers' minds, their powerful effect as a (neocolonial) speech community, as it is reported by local people.

When Oshrat discusses the abundance of Israelis in India, she tells of a local textile merchant whose factory backpackers frequent: "The Israelis bring home sheets from Little Bahbah. In the entrance to the place there's a sign, 'Little Bahbah puts Kitan in his little pocket' (*Bahbah Hakatan mahnis et Kitan lakis hakatan*), or 'Little Bhabah's silk is better than Rami and Rita's' (*hameshi shel Bahbah Hakatan yoter tov mishel Rami veRita*) IN HEBREW." Note that while the segment commences with reference to Israelis, the two quotatives are *not* attributed to the backpackers. The point is that by quoting Others' words, the *effect* the Israeli collective ("all the Israelis") has on the local environment is revealed. Because the speech community is linguistically contagious, the voice we directly hear of is in a roundabout fashion actually that of Israelis. It is the vocal stamp left by Israelis on the signs from which the narrator quotes.

The Hebrew written sign atop Little Bahbah's store evinces rhymes and wordplays. In the first quotative, the word "little" (*katan*) rhymes with a name of a well-known Israeli textile manufacturer (Kitan), as well as with a common expression (*bakis hakatan*) referring to the one-upmanship by which the former can figuratively "insert" the latter into his "little pocket." In the second quotative, understanding the wordplay requires knowing that the celebrity couple Rita (a singer), and Rami (a singer and songwriter), have a daughter named Meshi (literally, "silk").

Note that the quotations Oshrat performs do not evoke an *oral* utterance but rather vivify a written commercial sign. Indeed, the shift to the reported speech is abrupt and does not include a speech verb. Rather, indicating there's a sign suggests an inscription space, which is to be filled with quoted words. The quotation-closing formula ("IN HEBREW") is metacommunicative and achieves a quick shift (back) in the narration's perspective. Here it is particularly interesting, for it reiterates the fact that the inside of the quotations was *initially uttered (written) in Hebrew.* Indeed, soon after this strip Oshrat says of the local factory owner, "he speaks HEBREW, like you speak [Hebrew], he speaks Hebrew." In focus here is the fluent Hebrew that those who come in contact with the backpackers possess.

Backpackers are impressed not only by the foreigner's knowledge of their mother tongue but also by its nuanced performance. Hebrew rhymes and allusions to Israeli celebrities strike a welcoming note, as they evoke cultural knowledge shared exclusively by Israelis—they are the only ones who can and who are entitled to judge and evaluate locals' performances.

The last, somewhat surreal, illustration voices local figures who are quoting from a written Hebrew source. Prior to the exchange, Adam alludes to backpackers' "travelers' books" (*siphrei metaylim*; see chapter 7). In these volumes, impressions, recommendations, warnings, tips, and so on are written by backpackers in Hebrew. It is with regard to a travelers' book that Adam recalls an incident that occurred in a northern region of Ethiopia (where he traveled after visiting India and Thailand), by which he illustrates how local merchants introduce themselves effectively to the Israeli tourist.

> Adam: When I traveled in the north in some hole, then a guy came up to
>   us. he told us "I'm Avram fro—from the travelers' book." and then
>   we met this other guy, he tells me, "he's not Avram, he's an IMPOS-
>   TOR. that Avram has gone like—long gone from the town, and this
>   [man] pretends to be the Avram that's in the travelers' book. look,
>   ask him what's his family name and he won't know what to say. I
>   [too] forgot the name that's in the travelers' books" (quickly)
>
> Chaim: Wow, wow

Adam ventriloquizes two local animators, the latter of whom refers to what the former had said. Again, the initial attribution is made to an anonymous animator, to someone—anyone—who represents Otherness or foreignness. The initiative for the exchange is placed with the figure of the outsider, who approaches Adam and addresses him with an implicit commercial aim. In this vein Adam suggests the locals are creatively trying to employ resources by which they can persuasively access their potential clients.

The two quotatives make for a thematically and structurally stylized set. In the first, shorter, instance, someone presumed to be a local introduces himself through referring to the travelers' book, where he says he is mentioned. He presents himself as "your-very-own-traveler-book-Avram." Referring to a highly canonic source, he now owns a name (a Hebrew name) that plucks him out of anonymity. But not for long. Adam has a second quotee untie the association made by the first quotee between signifier and signified. The second animator, who is, again, nameless ("another guy"), erases the discernible identity of the former. He does so by suggesting a fraud has been perpetrated: the original, authentic Avram has left town long ago. The second figure *explicitly* accuses the former of impersonating and suggests a verification test by which the backpacker can find for himself whose words are true and whose are not. Yet the unveiling of the fraud does not lead anywhere, for the real name has been forgotten, and the audience is eventually lost as to the whereabouts of the authentic character of Avram.

This highly mediated, intertextualized report evokes the much-discussed themes of authenticity and representation in tourism through addressing the issues of originality and authority. Authenticity, on which the out-group figures try to anchor themselves, lies within the communal volumes of the backpacking lore:

with the travelers' books. Through making an association with these volumes, the anonymous animators' efforts to gain a high degree of credibility are illustrated. As Adam put it, they present themselves *as figures* from the backpackers' volumes, in perpetual search of a name.

More generally, the above excerpts perform tourists' taleworlds wherein the narrators can conveniently (and in a way that can hardly be challenged in their home countries) assume the role of characters to whom these humorous anecdotes have truly happened (Bauman 1986, 55; Briggs 1988, 171–232). The message that they communicate thus gains a considerable degree of reliability, which only personal (firsthand) knowledge can establish. As far as their referential content is concerned, these anecdotes establish the considerable power of the backpackers' *speech* community and its colonial effect. Performatively, however, they allow the insertion of additional voices into the community's polyphony—in this case Archimedean voices that relate to the community from its exterior; additionally, the audience is made to hear—and more crucially to face and cope with—issues that pertain to collective identity vis-à-vis the Other.

A Visit to the Television Station (September 22, 2003)

I am sitting in the Channel One (national television) broadcasting set with interviewer David Viztum, recording the Saturday morning Globus program. I am participating in a panel of three invited to discuss Israeli backpacking. Occasionally, the conversation halts as short reports about backpackers are broadcasted. In one report, which aired in the early 1990s, young Philippine toddlers are pictured lengthily singing two complete Hebrew songs, which backpackers taught them. One of the songs is monotonic, and its words depict a group of blacks picking cotton amid a white cotton field; the other is either Aviv Geffen's or Arik Einstein's (known Israeli performers). Both are very familiar tunes.

The Philippine toddlers seem very poor. I think there is a young adult figure, maybe the mother, who is hardly noticeable. The scene was shot in a dark hut. The toddlers are reciting more than singing. Some seem to enjoy the attention; others are indifferent.

The experience of watching these toddlers was unexpectedly shocking. The way they monotonously recited the Hebrew songs amounted to an eerie spectacle. Perhaps because I was not protected by the shield I usually had, which was a consequence of meeting the backpackers in Israel and not at the destinations, or perhaps because mass media has a visual way of amplifying emotions, the experience of seeing the consequence of Israeli backpacking tourism was truly disturbing. What was it that came out of the toddlers' mouths? After the report ended and the cameras turned to us again, I just had to comment on the amalgamation of Israelis' expansionist tendencies with an unnatural feeling in the mother tongue, which had brought Israeli backpackers to seek their voices in Others' throats.

It was like a possession. It was expansionist (neocolonial) all right, but with regard to the toddlers' bodies and throats and mouths. The occupation was similar to a phonic rape. Hebrew has been put inside them, scripted inside their bodies, to be performed pornographically. The backpackers had left behind something of their own in Others' mouths. Whether for the amusement of future backpackers, knowing that their predecessors have prepared the amusing spectacle for them, or for eternity: trying to fight the specter of the temporality and uncertainty of their existence (epito-mized in the evanescence of tourism), in Other bodies. Like waste, the voices played from the Philippine (or Nepalese or Peruvian) toddlers' throats were left behind. A mark of abuse.

The spectacle converges two ultimate colonial images: authenticity and in-nocence, "native" and "child." Both pure, both Other—both can be corrupted. Yet it is amusing for Israeli travelers just as long as the us/Other barrier is maintained firmly. It could, however, threaten to undercut the identity of its very consumers and to become horrific in cases where those speaking Hebrew—from Palestinians living in Israel to foreign workers who speak, read, and write Hebrew fluently and possess it as their own. Then the reassuring, amusing divide between "Israeli" and "native" is removed, and menacing issues of identity ("Who is an Israeli?" "Who is a Jew?") surface.

"Tourist" Voices: From Hypothetical Quotations to Pantomime

A second cluster of voices attributed to out-group animators is that of "tourists," with whom backpackers share the public space of tourism. This category of anima-tors complements the category discussed above in that these are animators whose voices are imported—translated from the "outside" into the "inside" of the com-munity. As such, tourists' voices, too, serve to delineate, negotiate, and maintain the borders of the backpacker narrative community. Though the construction of both categories of animators shares an ethnocentric, evaluative perspective, it does so differently, whereby tourists and natives supply different resources for the back-packers' performances and different points of reference in relation to which they may view and position themselves.

While both types of voices are relatively infrequent, tourists' voices are in fact rare (there are seven discernible instances of reporting tourists' voice). This may be accounted for by two reasons: first, structural-institutional interactions do not necessarily include interactions between and among tourists of different groups. In other words, while at least some contact between consumers and suppliers is neces-sary, intratourist interactions are by no means a formal characteristic of tourism.

Second, with particular regard to Israeli backpackers, it can be said that these youths are not at ease among Western peers. The travel-related narrative capital Israelis gain by traveling in the "third world" and gazing at "exotic," "primitive," and "authentic" places and peoples, which positions them as Westerners in their home cultures, is threatened by the existence of other Western backpackers and the way they gaze at Israelis. While traveling in third world countries allows the backpackers a convenient perspective from which a neocolonial gaze may be cast, the presence of European and North American youths problematizes and unsettles the Israelis' gaze. It suggests that they, too, might be its object; that *they themselves might become the attractions (objects rather than subjects) of Westerners' gaze.* This is why, upon meeting Western tourists, their own fragile Westernized identity is at stake.

Indeed, Israelis compare themselves with Western peers and admittedly reach the conclusion that they are "average" travelers, that Western backpackers are equipped better than they are, and that they pursue the goals of backpacking, such as hiking, more devotedly. "Tourists'" conduct is described as more polite than the typical conduct of the "ugly Israeli." Additionally, their limited competence in foreign languages, including English, further enhances Israelis' social insularity and contributes to the perseverance of their monolingual interpersonal communication.

Consider Tirza's metacommunicative observation explored in chapter 2 (p. 41), wherein "Israelis" are categorized as such through a clear opposition with another category—"tourists." When she depicts the patterns of interpersonal communication, Tirza boldly indicates that Israelis actually have no one to "talk with" within the heterogeneous spaces of tourism, and hence, they are socially insulated and gravitate toward each other. She further delineates what she means by interpersonal communication ("talk"): she is explicitly referring to *persuading activities.* As the second chapter showed, at stake here is not only speech activity but the very social process of the bonding of a collective.

Tirza's excerpt sheds light on the reasons that underlie the quantitative scarcity of tourists' voices. While the dichotomized distinction against which the backpackers' identity is discernible commonly opposes them with commercialized, bourgeois, "mass tourists" (Elsrud 2001; Riley 1988; Sørensen 2003), here, "backpackers" signify "Israelis," and "tourists" signify "foreigners." The opposition, which now gains *ethnic-national hues,* establishes the exclusion of Israelis—or, more accurately, of tourists.

Tirza employs illustrative quotations to demonstrate the sounds of "persuasive talk." As with the "native" voice, the quotation epitomizes a group. Yet the illustrative quotation here is hypothetical ("they don't get to talk with tourists"), which is a form by which reported speech is commonly employed to illustrate and enact tensions and oppositions linguistically (Myers 1999). Illustrative quotations do not suggest replication of something that *has* been said, but paradoxically they directly communicate something that *has not* been said. In fact, the performance of hypothetical quotations cleverly illustrates a state of *non*communication—that is, the very words that *could not* have been uttered. The narrator forcibly promotes the notion that patterns of communication overlap with patterns of sociability, which overlap with itineraries and patterns of travel. These intercorrelated patterns converge and amount to a divide of manifolds between "Israelis" and "tourists."

In the next excerpt Rachel accounts in passing for how different tourists are from Israelis and why the two groups do not associate. Hypothetical quotations are performed from the tourists' perspective. The excerpt is taken from a point where, after the narrator recalls the vibrant atmosphere that thrives among Israelis, she inquires whether I backpacked. She then says:

Rachel: If you are traveling with tourists they will never ask you

"WHAT did you (sing.) do in Peru?

WHAT did you (sing.) do in Bolivia?

you (pl.) did the Choro?

you (pl.) did the Pampas?

you (pl.) did this or that?"

there's a kind of a fixed itinerary ...

[but Israelis] they come

"we marked an x   (lower tone, rapidly)

we marked an x   (lower tone, rapidly)

we marked an x^3 (lower tone, rapidly)

great

now we can move on"

If Tirza performs the unuttered voices of Israelis who address tourists, Rachel's repetitive quotation supplies the latter's hypothetical voice: that which "tourists" *did not* and *could not* have uttered. In a complementary fashion we are made to hear the utterances that tourists cannot access. In both cases narrators perform phantom voices. Moreover, if Tirza evoked the enthusiastic, evangelist directions backpackers supply each other with, Rachel supplies the just as enthusiastic detailed inquiries, interrogating as to what individuals and groups have and have not accomplished (in accordance with persuasions and expectations). Thus a tautological loop is created, where persuasion (preexcursion) and interrogation (postexcursion) complement each other and form an overall insulated discourse of experience.

Both persuasive and interrogative utterances demand a reaction, an answer (see Bakhtin's work on "answerability" [1990]), and hence it is not only that tourists do not say these words (Rachel) or that the quoted words are not said to them (Tirza). Rather, in both cases the lack of *mutual commitment* is demonstrated: Israelis do not have to answer to tourists (as they do to fellow Israelis).

Indeed, both narrators are similarly explicit with regard to delineating a clear and persistent discursive borderline ("never ask you"). Through stating what tourists *are not*, Rachel communicates what Israelis *are*. She makes a point concerning the latter's "fixed itinerary" and the fixed discourse along which they pursue the great journey. Tourists are deficient not only in their lack of knowledge of Hebrew, but moreover, they miss the subtle keys and codes that facilitate successful interpersonal interaction: tourists would "never ask" what Rachel suggests Israelis *always* ask.

The structure of the first strip of quotations is that of A-B, A'-B', C, where the second pair of questions reiterates the first pair, adding information in the form of

specificity (the Choro and the Pampas are names of Bolivian trekking paths frequented by Israelis). The final utterance concludes the quotation and reminds the
hearers that it is illustrative. Though C's spatiotemporal deixis are aligned with the
quotation, it is unlikely that the question "you did this or that?" was uttered (it indicates the narrator's tendency to generalize). Rather, we hear the narrator's voice covertly entering into the quotation's end, suggesting *from within* that of importance
here is the general idea and not the specific words—the specific locations, which
were uttered on one or another occasion. Rachel then terminates the fivefold illustrative inquisitive quotations with a concluding postquotation observation ("there's
a kind of a fixed itinerary").

Yet Rachel shortly quotes again. A few words later she introduces a second set
of quotations with a short and affirmative quotation formula that contrasts with
the negative introduction formula that preceded the hypothetical quotation. What
nonmembers of the community never say is opposed to what members commonly
say. And although the second strip is illustrative, too, it is not hypothetical.

Israelis' declarative and authoritative voice is performed with rigorous repetition (A, A, A, B-C), demonstrating how "fixed" their itineraries indeed are: Rachel
performs the repetition of which she tells. The progression within the quotative is
possible once some degree of rote repetition has been established. Only then does
the quoter suggest that Israelis conclude a certain episode satisfactorily ("great"),
and "move on" to accomplish further challenges embodying further repetitions.

Between the two illustrative voices embodied in the two strips of quotations,
a dialogic space may exist, albeit a hypothetical one. The point is that Israelis and
tourists do not interact, and no exchanges between the groups are recorded. Tourists, Rachel implies, would be lost when it comes to the itinerary of Israelis: they
would not know what to ask, and their inquiries will not be accountable (that is,
they would not demand an answer).

Lastly, recall that the quotation sequences are performed shortly after Rachel
alludes to the community's vibrant atmosphere (*havay*), after which she inquires
whether I have backpacked.[4] Asking the question at this point is an attempt to position me with regard to the collective experience that is associated with the intense
havay the travelers share. At stake is the *knowledge* I possess: do I "know" what
she means when she talks about a vibrant havay? This is the kind of knowing that
sharing experiences entails, which is why she inquires whether I backpacked (see
chapter 2). Also at stake is the *evaluative perspective* I hold: do I know what she
means when she talks about the effect that the vibrant Israeli havay has on individual travelers? After all, the extract above conveys not only knowledge of the intense
intrabackpacker manners of travel and interaction but, more important, it conveys
the narrator's critical perspective. In this vein, Rachel is exploring whether I am an
"x"-marking backpacker or, like her, ambivalent or even critical with regard to backpackers' authoritative persuasions and inquiries.

My response, which indicated that my trip was not conducted recently, had
perhaps suggested that I am not well acquainted with the backpackers' intense so-

cial experience or with the havay of which she tells. This can account for her evocation of tourists' voices, which, insofar as they represent an out-group perspective, assists her in the task of communicating the intense experiences of backpacking to an outsider. In a way, Rachel is implying that like the tourists, the interviewer, too, does not know the "right" questions to ask; he is, in a way, a tourist, too. (I will return to this point in chapter 9.)

Hence, here and elsewhere, where the words of tourists are reported, they make for unique discursive resources by which observations "from *outside*" can be competently made and by which hearers of stories, who are not within the backpacking circle or milieu, are positioned as tourists.

Referentially, the multinational spaces in which tourist activities take place afford an encounter with fellow backpackers by which they may view and evaluate themselves and their identities on various intersecting grounds: national, sociodemographic, gender, and others. This is registered in their stories. Performatively, backpackers can summon Others' voices and the external perspectives they embody in order to align with the audience's perspective and incorporate the latter's point of view *within* the story's lively polyphony.

Counter to the backpackers' general tendency to evoke reported speech frequently, in the few accounts of interaction with non-Israeli travelers, the foreigners are mute. This is particularly salient because the comments they make in relation to foreign travelers are often of a metalinguistic type. For instance, one backpacker observes that unlike Israelis, tourists do not actively seek each other's company: "If a Dane will meet a Dane they'll probably speak Danish and will be happy to speak Danish, but they're not— they won't BOND 'cause of being Danish." This is contrasted with a different pattern of socialization and speech interaction: "but the Israeli who'll meet an Israeli, then he'll speak with him like he's his best buddy, he'll bond with him 'cause he's Israeli." Interestingly, the backpacker concludes with the observation that "for them it's weird that we are like that."

Indeed, a critical position can be stated in relation to the community by employing tourists' perspectives. Here, the narrator implies that the isolation of Israelis in a heterogeneous environment is tautological: although Israelis are different to begin with, when they perform this social difference while traveling they are rendered "weird" and are further differentiated and isolated/insulated from their Western peers. The issue here is the relationship between language and sociability, on the one hand, and identity, on the other hand. While the narrator admits that Danes, too, socialize with each other via talk, she observes that speech communication bears deeper meaning for Israelis: while the former communicate, Israelis "bond."

Of the seven instances of quotations of backpackers who are not Israelis, the most elaborate appears in Shiri's narration. Shiri indicates that although tourists are "noticeable," they are "not in such massive quantities as are Israelis." She, too, specifies a particular "Western" nationality (Swiss) when she recalls an exchange that took place in a market in Cuzco.

Shiri: And besides

    I sat and spoke a lot with ah

        I spoke a lot with ah tourists

                who were pretty SHOCKED

              they told me—

      there was this guy I traveled with   (quickly)

              a Swiss

          he said

            "LOOK—"

      I was traveling with him [when] suddenly I saw Israelis

                    immediately I begun talking to

them

      laughs (*tshokim*) and all

             and—

      great and

              he doesn't understand Hebrew but he sees how-

              he says to me

                 "what—

                  you KNOW them from Israel?

                         that's great"

             I told him

                "I've no idea who they are   (quickly)

                I've just met them"   (quickly)

     [The Swiss tourist says] "sure you knew them   (insisting)

            why? how [were you so close with them]?"   (realizing)

     and then he tells me

            "I—

             if I now see a Swiss"

     they don't even ask each other

             "wow

             you're from Switzerland

              from where?

              why?

              how long?"

    also in Switzerland

  he gave me an example

          [people] speak different languages in the different parts

        he says

            "I speak French or he speaks German or"

  they really don't have that connection (*hibur*) among themselves

In this rather elaborate exchange, Shiri quotes the words of a Swiss, who remains throughout the extract identified only via a generic national label, which locates him (not coincidentally) in the heart of Europe. The first significant impression Shiri communicates concerns the genuine surprise her Swiss companion expresses at witnessing the immediacy with which interpersonal closeness is established among Israelis. The three words the narrator emphasizes throughout the extract are correlated: *shocked, look,* and *know.* The Swiss tourist is shocked, and his words ("LOOK") emphatically express his surprise at how immediately Israelis "KNOW" each other (here "know," *makira,* refers to familiarity). Shiri goes a long way in making sure this point is established, and she further has the Swiss explicitly indicate that he naturally assumed these were acquaintances whom she knew from Israel. In fact, she expresses his pleasure with this apparent coincidence ("great"), marveling about variation of the notion of a small world.

When Shiri refutes this assumption, the Swiss expresses skepticism, insisting that what he has witnessed is a manifestation of a long-established acquaintance ("sure you knew them"). Cleverly, the narrator has now the tourist shift from observing Israelis' interpersonal conduct to stating the respective conduct of the Swiss. With this observation and by suggesting that the Swiss speak different languages, which restrains their interpersonal communication, Shiri drives her point home, and again, anOther's view and words are resourcefully employed in regard to one's own group.

The quotation sequence Shiri performs is complicated partly by two self-repair comments in the beginning. First, after she states she often spoke with tourists, she realizes that merely indicating she had communicated with tourists in general will not suffice as a platform on which a credible argument can be presented. Hence, *after* she has already indicated how shocked the tourists were, she moves from general to particular, from reporting to quoting, and adds that she has also traveled with a tourist, which leads to a concrete illustration. Second, after quoting the Swiss ("LOOK—"), she again supplies relevant information, here concerning the sight of Israelis interacting with each other.

The scene that encompasses the encounter with the Israelis is depicted in dramatic hues: the suddenness of meeting unfamiliar backpackers is contrasted with the dramatic immediateness with which the ice dissolves. Talk soon leads to sharing laughs, which is both the process by which intimacy is reached and the indication that this state has been achieved (the word *tshokim,* literally, "laughs," colloquially means enjoying one's self in a social context, having a good time). Shiri affirms this state of immediate social bonding with the word "great" (*yoffi*), which serves to conclude the encounter with the Israelis, to indicate that a cohesive (communitaslike) state has been reached, and to prepare the shift back to the tourist's perspective.

From this point of interpersonal warmth and closeness, the shift to the Swiss's view is sharp: he is ignorant of the language and misunderstands the interaction. (Note that here the audience can appreciate the mistake made by the Swiss and thus align with the narrator, without the narrator suggesting so explicitly). A short he said–I said exchange ensues, which arrives at a crescendo with the observation made by the tourist—which is extended in order to include those whom he can credibly observe (Swiss)—that tourists do not engage in the type of interaction Israelis do. The illustration he supplies is highly reminiscent of the inquisitive utterances mentioned earlier in Rachel's tourist-voice words. Interestingly, here, too, the reported words of the tourist are hypothetical (and the impossibility of their utterance is explicitly stated: "they don't even ask each other"; see Myers 1999).

Note that the voice of the narrator interferes with the Swiss's reported words twice, as Shiri seems to continually direct the scene. For instance, though she could easily have reported his own testimony concerning Swiss avoidance of inquisitively interpersonal communicating, she has *herself* suggesting that amid his words. By doing this, she achieves two aims. First, she assumes that the Swiss's words are understood illustratively (a perspective that might be lost in direct quotation attributed to a specific character). The second aim concerns expressing the narrator's perspective—that of wonder—directly, in her own words.

An intertwinement style of reported speech is established, in which the narrator's words are continually inserted in between those of the characters in her story. The zigzag of voices serves to bridge two conflicting goals: while quotation serves to authenticate and dramatize the telling, the narrator's voice serves to frame these apparently specific instances as illustrative cultural generalizations.

At the end Shiri reiterates the point that tourists are qualitatively different from Israelis and do not share their experiences even remotely. Again, she does so through intertwining her narrating voice with that of the Swiss. We learn that the tourist's country of origin *is by no mean a coincidence.* By converging language, identity, and nationality Shiri illustrates a multilingual state that contrasts with what is familiar to Israelis. Reminiscent of the Babylonian Tower narrative, the words of the Swiss suggest that not only do Swiss not interact with each other as immediately and as closely as Israelis do, they actually *do not even understand each other's languages.* Effectively, and nearly explicitly, Shiri establishes the "one nation, one language" principle, by which Hebrew is perceived as a language that only Israelis speak (Jewish Israelis, that is; see Crawford 1992; Katriel 1990; Lang 1995). The Swiss supplies ideal evidence for unilateral correlation between identity and language. In fact, the "Babylonian principle" is employed to confirm the contention that different languages make different identities. As Buttny (1997, 480) observes, "[u]sing the utterances of others seems to offer material for understanding how members construct a 'portrait' of the other. The notion of 'portrait of the other' is meant to capture how out-group members are presented through reported speech." Yet with tourists (and with natives likewise), the portrait of the Other is evoked in order to portray one's own people from seemingly anOther point of view.

The last illustration tells of an encounter with tourists, Frenchmen in this case, whose voices are *not* heard. It is a vivid illustration of the invisible discursive divide between backpackers and foreigners. Ophir, who describes hiking in Chile, recalls that he asked the porters to buy and carry cold Coca-Cola bottles before the hike. He then illustrates how the group, thirsty and tired from the climb, enjoyed the cold Coke atop a mountain pass. At this point he recalls that they met a group of older

Frenchmen. He describes the Frenchmen's wonder as the Israelis sip cold Coke in a place "where," he stresses, "you are expected to survive only and carry with you [only] the very fundamentals." At this point, one of the Frenchmen approaches the group: "he looked like a pantomimist. Bold, with big lips. He crawled toward the Coke, like begging. It was great" (laughs).

The explicit reference to pantomime conjures a powerful metaphor of sound-less cross-cultural (non)communication (the pantomime metaphor is mentioned in this sense in three other narratives). Ophir implies that when Israelis and tourists interact, verbal communication is either minimal or absent, and meaning is constructed by the gazes both parties exchange from the invisible, soundproof corridors through which they travel. Ophir highlights the mute differences between the groups by indicating that the French are older, by portraying them in a plastic art manner, and by depicting their wonder at the Israelis: compared with European backpackers, and with the colonial ethos of backpacking they fully embody ("you are expected to survive only"), Israelis pursue a more bourgeois—and hence lesser—practice; they enjoy the luxury of drinking cold Coke amid strenuous hiking, something French tourists of an older cohort do not allow themselves.

In several other instances reporting tourists' voices supplies rich resources for (cross-cultural) *gender* representations and comparisons. We mentioned earlier that when the figures of tourists express subversive viewpoints, they do not put the narrator at social risk. This is particularly true with regard to female backpackers, who compare themselves with the performances of their Western counterparts and express disdain with their home society's gender conventions. In several cases, explicit gender observations and evaluations are made solely with regard to women tourists, who are usually depicted as behaving in a less "traditional" manner than Israelis do. European women are depicted as carrying heavier gear, and their appearance and conduct do not adhere to conservative gender stereotypes ("hairy" legs are described as well as "improper" manners of politeness). I will discuss gender more fully in the second part of chapter 6.

The Collective-Canonic Voice: Quoting the Norm (of Quoting)

> In each epoch, in each social circle, in each small world of family, friends,
> acquaintances, and comrades in which a human being grows and lives, there
> are always authoritative utterances that set the tone—artistic, scientific, and
> journalistic works on which one relies, to which one refers, which are cited,
> imitated, and followed.
>
> Mikhail Bakhtin

The most dominant variety of quotations noted in the course of this study has been of a type attributed to a third-person, plural male voice, an attribution that typically included explicit reference to "Israelis" or "Israeli backpackers" as their original animators. This type of quotation indexes *the discursive community itself* and represents both the backpackers' own collectivized voice and the community's authoritative and canonic characteristics.

By characterizing this type of quotation as *dominant*, I address the impression that collective quotations are *louder* than other voices: the authority conveyed in and through their performance and the way they voice the quintessential tenets of the community grant them a type of dominance—a canonic quality. Admittedly, while the choral (group) voice also represents and produces authoritative utterances, the attribution of which is plural, it is clearly distinct from the collective-canonic voice. The utterers of the collective's words are always in the third, and never the first, person, as is the case in the group voice. In addition, animators of collective utterances are *never* mentioned by their name, and their individuality is not specified in any other way. This feature contrasts with the evocation of the choral voice, which conveys the cohesion of a few previously identified individuals. If the choral voice essentially represents an assembly of recognized individual voices, the collective voice qualitatively stands for more than that: it represents the body of the community—a body that transcends its individuals.

Before proceeding to discuss discursive communal authority, it behooves us to consider the following quotation, which nicely illustrates an employment of this voice. In it, Ravit relates her departure from Israel and arrival at Nepal. This took place toward the end of the tourism season, a time that was apparently problematic almost to the point of being taboo.

Ravit: So what was good in Nepal was that we arrived at the very end of the season

the touristic season ...

we arrived right in May   (quieter)

and we arrived at the end of May to   (quieter)

Nepal   (quieter)

and when all the ISRAELIS

heard that we are leaving

now to Nepal   (quicker, louder)

like—

"have you gone crazy?"

and

"there's nothing to do there"

and

"why all of a sudden now?"

and

"[you] can't trek

and [you] can't nothing"

so we said we'll take our chances

they almost blew the wind out of our sails

but we left anyhow

Ravit commences by stating that traveling off-season is potentially beneficial. Indeed, this is a common touristic theme: in order to avoid the "crowded" and "commercialized" high season, tourists seek to travel during off-season periods. Ravit thus employs the discourses of time and seasonality in tourism as a resource of narrative drama, to convey her point (Baum and Lundtorp 2001; Cohen 1986). As she conveys the background information (the story's Labovian orientation [1972]), embedding her story and making resourceful use of themes of backpacking discourse, her words are spoken quietly and slowly, contrasting with the rhythmic and significantly louder tone of the subsequent dramatic words, which include quotations.

The excerpt includes five quoted clauses, contained in four reported utterances, all of which are quoted in the name of "Israelis." Typically, "Israelis" are not specified individually; instead, they are *voicedly represented as simultaneously unanimous and anonymous.* Within the quotations—and, one should note, *only* within them—a critical evaluation is expressed with regard to the timing of the trip's commencement. The impression is that Israelis are not content with the timing of Ravit's great journey. Ravit implies that the decision of the group in which she is traveling does not conform with the norms of the community, at least not with the norms of seasonality.

In the fivefold quotative sequence the first utterance is framed as a question, the second as an exclamation, the third as another question, and the last two as exclamations, thus amounting to a stylized structure of A, B, A', B', B". The structure is that of a double sequence of a question-answer pair, where the questions are rhetorical and the answers are refutative, reprimanding. The answers are typically short and convey an immediate (spontaneous) expression of skepticism, suggesting that there is something unusual in the conduct of the group. The final utterance couples two exclamations, one more specific and the other, concluding the entire exchange, more general, and amounts to the crescendo of the exchange: "can't trek and can't nothing!"[1]

The narrator makes it clear that "Israelis" indeed have a voice, and that their voice is highly opinionated and critical. Backpacking in the month of May is judged harshly: it amounts to no less than being "crazy," to a social abnormality. The decision reached by Ravit's group is depicted as an impulsive act, as an expression of impatience ("all of a sudden"), one that merits criticism.

Though the strip of quotations does not, at first glance, appear to constitute a dialogue, that is precisely what it is. The last directly reported utterance ("can't nothing") is in fact followed by an instance of indirect reported speech. Another voice responds, in a way, to the authoritative statements, expressing a rejection of or opposition to the collective voice. This opposition is performed in the choral voice of Ravit's group ("so we said we'll take our chances"), which is reported *in*directly and amounts to a quotation-closing formula that frames the end of the quoted speech. The dialogue, then, occurs within the social space that lies between the direct collective reprimands and the more intimate (empathic) group voice, which seeks to reject or decline the pronouncements of the collective.

Note that the voiced quality of the social realm constructed by this exchange is in fact evinced earlier. The event immediately preceding the directly reported utterances is the indication that Israelis have "heard"(!) of the group's irregular decision concerning the timing of the trip. By evoking a phonic metaphor, Ravit is situating *social occurrences in a dialogic field*, thus paving the way neatly into the performance of direct dialogue.

Typically, the group voice represents the perspective with which the narrator's empathy lies. Unlike the third-person collective voice, the first-person voice of the group is the extension of one's self. The choral voice, reported indirectly, is less assertive and less animated. In line with Sternberg's (1982, 115) observation that quotation "exhibits the widest and most flexible variability in that it bestrides the whole scale of response, from identification to caricature and condemnation," it is the collective voice that is reported directly and that is being judged.

On the outside of quotation, the group voice adds a crucial brick to the evolving plot and begins the transition from the realm of discourse to the realm of action. The short statement ("we'll take our chances"), somewhat overshadowed by the authoritative quotations, immediately suggests that the collective proclamations are to be refuted. More important, it cleverly lays the *dramatic social infrastructure of the plot* that Ravit is about to unravel. It suggests that the forthcoming travel narrative is dramatic indeed: a "chance" has just been taken. Crucially, it indicates that drama evolves not from the interaction between backpackers and nature, tourists or natives but between the collective and the individual or between the collective and that which is asymptotic to it: the group (Domínguez 1989; Hazan 2001b). Hereafter, itinerary and scenery function as the backdrops against which the backpackers' plots develop and as the resources for the construction of stories of a dramatic social rite of individuation.

By stating that the group had eventually decided to embark ("but we left anyhow"), a succinct opening for an eventful narrative is concluded. Ravit performs a smooth transition from quotation to indirect reported speech to report of action (Urban 1984). Additionally, by employing a group-plural form of the pronoun "you," she establishes and validates the group's social identity vis-à-vis the voice of the collective; the group emerges as the protagonist in the ensuing plot. The exchange concludes with a Labovian type of result or resolution (1972): it is both an ending and an opening, a conclusion and an invitation to the social drama stemming from the actions—rendered provocative—taken by the group.

Through this succinct illustration, some of the qualities and characteristics of the collective-canonic voice can be appreciated. The quotations reveal that the voice is attributed to Israelis (in fact, to "*all* the Israelis"). The voice's authoritativeness is established by perspectives conveyed in and through its performance as direct speech as well as by the themes it addresses. These are augmented—multiplied, as it were—by the voice's inherent plural (collective) attribution, as if the many thousands of Israeli travelers were all uttering the words together.

The fact that the voice is quoted directly allows for its representation as a direct, unmediated source of social authority. The collective that emerges through the voice is highly critical. Its performance authoritatively expresses explicit dos and don'ts concerning how to backpack properly, which is to say how to assume the narrative capital imbued in the backpacking ethos. Furthermore, we shall see that the collective voice is dialogical: it repeatedly enters narratives through a response or a reply, by means of which it addresses social occurrences *heard* within a discursive social space.

The combination of social authority with the collective character suggests that this voice embodies canonic qualities. In this respect, it is a vital discursive asset of the narrative community. As we shall see, the themes and tenets carried by the voice as well as the dialogic positions assumed by the narrators with regard to it grant it an undeniable canonic and hegemonic status in the community.[2]

The social authority of the collective voice rests on and is performed by what Dundes and Arewa (1975) have termed the "impersonal power," inspired by the community of which it is an asset. Speech communities erect oral-linguistic monuments, like proverbs and jokes, that are performed as transcending the social scales of time-space (of individuals and groups). The presence of "so many Israelis" to whom narrators repeatedly refer indicates the traversing of a critical social mass; it amounts qualitatively to a *collective* that is performatively metonymized in collective quotations.

Genres that have the quality of "impersonal" or "generic" communication have been explored mainly by folklorists and linguistic anthropologists (Briggs 1988).

These genres enable the assumption of performative authority—an authority traditionally embodied by the elders, who "ascriptively were the repositories of knowledge, the centers of authority and authoritativeness" (Silverstein 1996, 89).

In the case of the collective voice, it is precisely from the performance of the
utterances that social authority is derived—that is, from the seemingly transcendent (contextually independent) quality it assumes within a highly contextualized
interpersonal communication. It emerges, much as Briggs (1988, 103) has observed
of the rhetorical force of proverbs, "from a subtle and complex use of the pragmatic
functions of language." Collective quotations are performed so as to appear ostensibly decontextualized, and hence acquire the status of familiar proverbs, jokes, puns,
and the like (see the "demographic anecdotes," chapter 5). As Bauman (1986, 75)
remarks of jokes, "insofar as they are known to be in oral tradition they are in a
sense reported out of the abstract collective voice of tradition." It is as though the
"collective" is a discursive well wherein reserves of speech lie, waiting to be pulled
out and performatively put into use by competent narrators who thus endow their
performances with authority.

Yet while most of the folkloristic and (linguistic) anthropological discussion
of narrative authority relates to premodern communities, contemporary tourism
is nested in (post)modern institutional settings. This suggests that what is at stake
is a process of traditionalization—that is, of the retrospective creation of the community's "elders" (who have paved the path along which the community at present
travels)—which, tautologically, indicates the very existence of such a social body
and of its historical roots and continuity (Bauman and Briggs 1990).

In an enlightening discussion of replications and responses, Greg Urban
(1996, 38) notes that in performance, utterances of an impersonal quality are *replicated* rather than *responded to.* Jokes, idioms, and collective quotations do not
comply with the "he said–she said" dialogical stream. These types of utterances are
presented as autonomous, rather than as interpersonal, and their uncontextualized
semblance facilitates the ease of their transportability. Yet as the following will demonstrate, both repetition *and* response (and thus dialogue) are clearly evident in
the travel narratives. While the community's lore is indeed constantly replicated
and reiterated, it is at the same time a prolific resource with and around which the
backpackers perform dialogue in narrative.

To a certain degree, John Lucy's (1993a, 119) constructive account also seems
limited with regard to the performances of backpackers. Lucy contends that an impersonal expression such as "it is said (that)" is a "free particle . . . that does not derive or inflect in any way." Lucy suggests that "paradigmatically it signals, positively,
that the propositional content of what was said is being reproduced (if not the exact
form), or, negatively, that the reporter is not willing to vouch for the veracity or like-
lihood of the reported content because it is only hearsay" (119–20). With regard to
the collective quotations, which are general and anonymous, it could be observed
that far from *reducing* the veracity of their content, their status as hearsay only *in-
stills them with it.* Within this narrative community, sought-after social cohesion

and the experiences of closeness and togetherness are enhanced by hearsay. Hearsay indicates that close and multiple interactions are taking place and that information is being intensely disseminated. This is why backpackers indicate that word of mouth is a highly "authentic," noninstitutional form of communication. With regard both to global backpacking culture and to communication patterns typical of Israeli backpackers, hearsay is an indication of authenticity (Noy 2005).

To conclude, the communally beaten track produces a communally *beaten narrative* (and vice versa), one that is performed by way of repetition and quotation. The footsteps of backpackers could be said to be transportable quotations, a "quotative behavior": they signify how they follow one another and how they are to follow one another with their traveling, interrelating bodies.

Below several uses of collective quotations are arranged and presented according to the degree of hegemony with which their narrators imbue them and according to the different thematic attributes they carry. Although these quoted canonic texts referentially address destinations, accommodations, sights, prices, and so on, the semiotic language of tourism is effectively employed by the backpackers in a symbolic capacity. The quotations amount to a detailed "map" of how one should or should not conduct oneself while backpacking—an authoritative "grid" of how the individual should act in the world and experience it. Hence the following excerpts also portray a social context infused with interactions, dialogues, and controversies of ritualistic intensity.

Performing the Norm and Positioning the Narrator

The social drama revealed by the above extracts conveys two disparate viewpoints that assume the form of social voices: that of the group and that of the collective. Through the intercrossing of multiple evaluative assertions—both negative and positive—a *normative* web is knitted, established in and through the performance of canonic collective quotations. This authoritative norm, with which the narrators are all familiar, bears on communal matters large and small. These may range from what gear one should take to the trip to where to drink water along a certain trail to which countries to visit and in what order and at what times. Normative confirmatory and negative directions make for the invisible discursive walls between which the backpackers journey.

While the narrators are all familiar with the collective norm—a familiarity that constitutes one of the central cultural assets gained during the trip—they express a variety of standpoints toward collective tenets. Some, like Ravit, differ somewhat from the collective norm, while others embrace it wholeheartedly.

Among the latter are Bella and Barak, both of whom perform authoritative collective quotations excitedly. In the first excerpt, Bella recalls how her trip in South America had begun and how she had unexpectedly arrived at itinerary junctions that teemed with Israelis. She alludes to this in an incidental manner, noting that a neighbor had recently visited her and had inquired about her travel (somewhat like me). In the second excerpt, Barak combines collective quotation when he reflects on the difficulties (mainly physical) that he encountered while hiking the Jomsom Trail ("apple pie trail") in Nepal. Shortly before the extracted strip, Barak notes that the many Israelis whose paths one crosses "exchange information with you and you exchange information with them."

> Bella: You see I left for this trip—I reached Ecuador without a name of a hotel, WITHOUT ANYTHING. so I arrived WITHOUT KNOWING ANYTHING (slow, didactically). and simply on the plane? I already met Israelis. they told me: "go to hotel X," and I went to hotel X, and from there I began my trip (faster) . . . For example, in Buenos Aires, we didn't know which hotel to go to (slowly). when we reached Buenos Aires, we met Israelis; they told us: "you know, there's this Israeli hotel X-and-Y, go there." so I went there. at Rio?—I arrived at Rio without knowing what Israeli hotel THERE IS. and Rio's dangerous. it could be VERY frightening. you arrive at a country that—and Brazil is considered dangerous, and you—you don't have a hotel. I got to the station there; I met Israelis: "what hotel is there," "go to X-and-Y," [we're] going to X-and-Y.

Barak: You get many recommendations

whether it's about accommodation   (quickly)

whether it's about what to eat   (quickly)

whether it's about DRINKING ...   (quickly)

you meet people

and they tell you

"here you CAN drink from the water"

"here you CAN'T drink from the water"

"here you have worms in the water"

"here you can—"

like I told you

"here you can eat and here you can't eat"

and you too pass it on

[as] they too pass it on

Both excerpts clearly demonstrate the authoritative voice of "Israelis," which inevitably expresses proclamations, instructions, recommendations, and warnings. In the first case, Bella repeatedly describes her—the protagonist's—state upon arrival at various destinations in terms of the knowledge she lacks. She reiterates that she had no idea what to do or where to go when she left Israel: upon her arrival at every destination she is a tabula rasa, awaiting collective inscriptions. Even during those short transformational periods spent on transportation vehicles, en route to the various destinations, she socializes with Israelis and learns more and more of the communal lore. The initial state of her meager knowledge is quickly amended by her obtaining the communal knowledge, the transmission of which is demonstrated through the collective voice that Bella performs.

Narratively, while in Ravit's words the collective voice generated dramatic tension between the group and the collective, in Bella's stories the collective voice plays an opposite role. "Go to hotel X" celebrates—rather than challenges or criticizes—the collective itinerary of Israelis. As Bella states convincingly, it is only after visiting hotel X, a point where Israelis congregate, that her trip truly commenced. For Bella, the collective proclamations *are* the trail to be followed.

The two sites that Bella mentions after Ecuador—Buenos Aires and Rio de Janeiro—illustrate the same point. Upon each arrival she is in a state of lesser knowledge, which is then remedied by information supplied by other Israelis and by collective quotations. Yet her arrival at new destinations is not described by Bella in terms of (lack of) knowledge per se. Rather, in the third case, "Rio" is depicted as both "frightening" and "dangerous." It seems that there is more at stake for Bella than mere information. In the face of disquieting images, the informative proclamations asserted by Israelis constitute an invaluable resource.

These sentiments are by no means idiosyncratic. As suggested in the introduction, they reflect commonplace perceptions among backpackers (and tourists in general) regarding third world countries to which they choose to travel. Among other factors, the perception of the surroundings as "dangerous" plays a role in the social construction of risk, adventure, and subsequently heroism in the tourists' narrative performances (Elsrud 2001).

What is quite idiosyncratic in Bella's performance is that she does not explicitly mention the names of the hotels to which she is referring. Rather, in line with her *didactic or pedagogic* approach, she supplies illustrations, or generic instances, instead of explicit names of specific sites. In this particular respect, her performance indeed deviates from the performance of others, as she overtly sacrifices knowledge of specificities in favor of delineating a rule concerning the spread of knowledge itself. (It might, of course, be that Bella was not sure about the specific names of these hotels, and hence exchanged them for generic Xs and Ys.) Alternatively, it might well be that Bella wanted to leave me in a state of minimal knowledge, similar to her situation prior to embarking on the trip. If this is the case, rather than supplying specific information, Bella indicates pedagogically how such information is to be attained: through socializing with Israelis. In any case, according to Bella a collective social map is spread over the destinations wherein the signifiers X and Y represent points of reference in the shared itinerary of Israelis.

Finally, an interesting pattern is evinced between the different social voices evoked by Bella when she describes her arrival both at Buenos Aires and at Rio de Janeiro. With regard to the former, the depiction begins with the perspective of the group ("we didn't"), which changes to a collective perspective ("there's this Israeli hotel X-and-Y"), and is immediately followed by an (infrequent) instance of individual perspective ("I arrived at Rio"). In the Rio illustration, the order of perspectives is reversed: Bella commences with the first-person perspective, proceeds with a collective perspective, and concludes with the group's perspective. She is now back at the narrative baseline: the choral voice. Bella thus completes a cycle of social voices wherein she shifts from the group to the collective and from there to the individual, and back from first person to plural-collective to plural-group. In a nutshell, social vicissitudes are illustrated: digressions from the group's voice "upward" to the collective voice and "downward" to the individual.

Much of this holds true for Barak's words as well. Although Barak is preoccupied not with accommodation but with the consumption of foods and beverages, he is similarly engrossed with the relationship between the tourist and the "world": where he can sleep, where and what he can eat and drink, where he should visit, and so on. Within an *incorporative subtext,* exclusion and inclusion hover above Bella's and Barak's words in a reversal: where and how they could be absorbed in enclaves in the destination countries (Bella) and how they should take into themselves these foreign countries and sites (Barak).

Note that Barak does not explicitly mention Israelis but a seemingly more general group: "people." As previously shown, the explicit mention of "Israelis" in association with the collective voice is indeed unnecessary, and the general designation of "people" in fact exclusively designates "Israelis."

The quotations performed by Barak are structured stylistically. They consistently begin with a formula—"here you can('t)" (with a deviation in this formula in one instance, "here you have")—that animates and instantiates the actual presence of the warning. It suggests that there are tourists throughout the path—surveyors, as it would almost seem—who are continually monitoring what should or should not be done (and where and when) and reporting it. The rhetoric is composed of dichotomous distinctions and consists of dos and don'ts with no middle ground. They are reminiscent of the Jewish religious code (*Halaha*), with its rigid binary structure, and of the sanctioning and prohibitory commands therein (*ase* and *al-ta'ase*). Moreover, the content of the collective norm cited by Barak—the restricted consumption of foods—echoes the intricate Jewish dietary laws (the laws of *kashrut*).

The quotations are probably an illustration of the "recommendations" mentioned by Barak at the beginning of this excerpt. However, the frequency of cans and cannots throughout the collective quotation suggests that the "recommendations" do not designate mere touristic tips but instead constitute categorical, commandlike directions and instructions. What is positively (re)commended in Bella's quotations is negatively warned against in Barak's. In both cases, the collective quotations are vehement and are more than suggestive in expressing a norm of proper backpacking conduct.

Finally, in Barak's conclusion he refers to the interpersonal process of dissemination, whereby "recommendations" are spread throughout the community. The two comments he makes are reflexive and metadiscursive, or perhaps more accurately, metaquotative: they refer to how quotations are (to be) cited ("you, too, pass it on"; "they, too, pass it on"). Reverting back to Jewish religious commands, akin to the *Haggada* story, traditionally told on the eve of Passover, when the diners are enjoined to recount the ancient story of the Exodus to subsequent generations time and again, Barak, too, concludes with an allusion to iterative telling (see Blondheim 2005). The pronoun "you," which only a short utterance ago referred to quotations, now has a life of its own within the performance ("like I told you"); it is calibrated differently. Barak, who has been told all this, is *at present* the one who carries on this precious and vital knowledge and who is responsible for its dissemination. He thus indicates his entrance to the collective. By performing the collective-canonic voice in person, Barak joins the community of narrators and assumes responsibility for his narrative performance (Hymes 1975). He becomes a discursive member of the league of (Israeli) backpackers, in whose tradition stories follow footsteps and footsteps follow stories. Barak is becoming a veteran, accomplished backpacker—an "elder."

The excerpts from Bella's and Barak's stories demonstrate that no drama arises from the gap between the normative views engulfed in the collective voice and the voices of the backpackers and their groups. Quite the contrary, the role played by the collective quotations in the narrative is *harmonious.* It resolves (in a Labovian sense) rather than creates a state of drama or conflict. And it does so because it communicates the knowledge essential for the "survival" of the tourists in regions constructed as hostile. The dramatic and potentially threatening states described by the backpackers ("WITHOUT KNOWING ANYTHING," or "you have worms in the water") are mitigated, as the travelers are supplied with a "collective survival kit," with the help of which they can successfully complete the tourist rite.[3]

Regardless of their attitudes toward the authoritative collective voice, the extracts above echo the tourist dialectics—between transition and stay, between foreignness and familiarity—that are so powerfully embodied in the extended, multi-sited backpacking trip. For the backpackers, collective soundings embody and express that which is familiar and constant—namely, the community—amid repetitive transitions that take place in a foreign realm. Whether it is Rio, La Paz, or Pohkara, "here" or "there" (in Boaz's deictic terms), the guiding collective voice establishes a sense of familiarity and sharedness—that is, communality. As the next chapter shows, by evoking collective interactions, the backpackers are engaged in "knitting a continuity of past where there isn't a continuity of place" (Mazali 2001, 33). That there is no chasm or divide between the quoted decrees and the narrative is exactly the point made by these narrators. Both Bella and Barak make it clear that the trip was conducted in close accordance with the authoritative words of the collective. The relationship between narrative and norm, travel and quotations, is mimetic. What is striking about these illustrations is the close degree to which the norm is observed. It assumes here the discursive shape of the relationship between what is voiced—asserted, decreed, proclaimed—and what is then conducted. In fact, Bella repeatedly concludes every canonic quotation with an indication of how completely it was observed. At the end of each and every quotation sequence Bella repeats, or "quotes," the *inside* of the quotations: "'go to hotel X' and I went to hotel X." The narrative, which stands for events in which the quotations are embedded, assures, "word by word and expression by expression" (Davidson 1984, 79), that what is proclaimed *within* quotations is wholly observed and practiced in the *narrative.* There is not even the slightest change or variation; conformity is here piously mimetic.

In other words, there is literally no semiotic space between quotation and extradiscursive—referential, narrative—"reality." By shifting the ear of the listener from quotation to narrative and by repeating the quotation in unquoted discourse—by "undressing" the quotations of their marks—Bella makes a powerful metapragmatic claim concerning the realms of discourse and extradiscourse and the relation between them. For these narrators, quotation is a way to speak reflexively about language, which, otherwise, would be the unreflected-upon act/world.

Hence, the collective norm does not stand only for what is *socially* right or wrong, and consequently for uniformity. Rather, is stands for what "reality" is, and for what is "naturally" healthy, safe, aesthetic, valuable, normal, and so on, in and for the community of tourists who are traveling a great distance from "home" (as a site and marker of familiarity). At stake here is the "world out there" (for tourists it is, indeed, the world *out* there), and adhering to it is presented as more than a privilege or an inclination: it is a necessity, an essential.

However, not all the backpackers embrace the collective norm as wholeheartedly, "quotingly," as Bella and Barak. In the following instances, which I will discuss more briefly, the backpackers convey different viewpoints of the authoritative normative voice that they competently embed in their stories.

The first strip is drawn from Dana's narrative and occurs after the narrator concludes the telling of her group's unique hiking experience in the Azangate mountain region in Peru. She refers, not without self-humor, to the tall tales she has heard about the trails she has hiked. She then says:

Dana: But they enfold (*otfim*) it up in lots and lots of stories
    that is—
        the Azangate was far less than they said it would be
                        it was GREAT
                        and it was WONDERFUL
                        and it was EVERYTHING
     but it wasn't THAT COLD
     and the way wasn't THAT HORRIBLE
     and the night in the hotel wasn't HORRIBLE
     and it's always that way
           that whoever doesn't trek is supposed (*amur*) to feel a little
uneasy with himself
        'cause
          "what—?
          haven't you come to see the landscapes and views of South America?
            you traveled all this way?"
               and I don't think it's right

Although Dana narrates that her participation in hiking activities did endow her with a unique experience, a sense of disappointment is nevertheless evident. She relates that this sense is directed not so much toward the actual sites she had visited as toward the stories in which they were "enfolded." Through the appropriate metaphor of narrative enfoldment or wrapping, Dana makes a metanarrative observation, suggesting that the destinations are heavily mediated by a collective narrative. Participation in some of the core activities of backpacking, the norm asserts, is inevitable.

Through quoting the norm, an expectation is evoked regarding the experiences of traveling and, more generally, regarding the implications of travel. It strongly implies that traveling not for the sake of consumption of "landscapes and views" is almost inconceivable. Yet Dana does not see eye to eye with the collective perspective. Though she has indeed trekked and thus complied with the norm, she nonetheless contends that the requirement to do so is disturbing. She praises the trekking experience but shortly afterward admits it was somewhat disappointing. It seems that in order to be able to pass criticism on the norm, participants must first adhere to it, thus assuming entitlement for storytelling (Shuman 1986, 1992); paradoxically, it is only from *within* the community that one can express a sentiment that is incongruent with the communal norm.

Dana implies that the collective voice robbed the original, authentic sites of what *could* have been their natural charm. The wrapping metaphor conjures up images of flashy gift-wrapping paper, and the collective information is thus criticized as being deceivingly shiny, similarly to commercial touristic brochures. This is particularly interesting since there is no apparent commercial institution to blame for spoiling the experience. It is the community itself, and its efficient network of word of mouth, that replaces some modes of commercial dissemination of tourist images and narratives (a point I elaborate upon in Noy 2005).

Dana inserts the collective quotations into the narrative by means of dialogue, in the typical form of rhetorical, reprimanding inquiries. The three utterances she quotes echo the (double) triple structure that preceded them: three superlatives ("GREAT . . . WONDERFUL . . . EVERYTHING"), followed by their three negative remarks ("wasn't THAT COLD . . . THAT HORRIBLE . . . HORRIBLE"). The entire three-on-three structure comes to an end with the final quotation, when there is a swift shift from collective, dogmatic quotation to an individual voice ("I don't think it's right"). The narrator's position is stated dialogically, though not by way of reported speech. It achieves the aim of forcefully stating her perspective vis-à-vis the direct reported collective questions, while criticizing or "trivializing" it (Radner and Lancer 1993). Note that the word "supposed" (*amur*, literally, "said") appears shortly before the quotations: Dana is *spelling out* the norm, which represents what is supposed/said to be done.

While some backpackers merely convey disappointment, others explicitly express resentfulness toward the norm. Since many do so, a "new" or "counter" collective emerges, one that passes criticism on the "traditional" collective.[4]

In the following excerpt, criticism is expressed toward this "new" collective. While the narrator, Ophir, commends the Israelis who, upon his and his friend's arrival at Quito, Ecuador, directed them to a hotel, he criticizes those who are critical about their fellow backpackers. Ophir describes his and his companion's lack of preparedness when they arrived at the destination and their relief when they met Israelis who told them where to go:

> You walk down the street, and you see Israelis aaah (1) it's simply, simply that's the way it is. it's packed there. and there are people who say (lower tone), "I want to stay away from Israelis, I don't want Israelis." you see, I don't have any problem with Israelis. no problem at all. we didn't have any problem arriving at an "ISRAELI HOTEL," as they call it.

Seemingly of a common type, the collective quotations performed by Ophir are in fact a variation on the collective voice. What he conveys are not normative assertions and decrees but a *reaction* to the collective norm. The quoted assertions express a desire for distance and disengagement, not an embrace of communal authority. Ophir astutely directs our attention to the fact that the voices that criticize the dense congregations of Israelis themselves amount to a collective voice. The narrator implies that collectively criticizing the canon cuts off the very branch on which the claim relies.

The standpoint adopted by Ophir is dialectic and is expressed vis-à-vis the growing, often-heard criticism of this norm (as voiced in earlier excerpts by Ravit and Dana). The final few words of Ophir's excerpt demonstrate that he is well aware of the play of voices within the community. He knows that an "ISRAELI HOTEL" represents not merely a "site" but also a sign, *an expression or an idiom,* and he thus argues that he and his companions are content, both practically and discursively, with the social site and the collective quotation (that converge in the expression) "ISRAELI HOTEL."

The first quoted strip appears immediately after Ophir argues for the prominent presence of Israelis. Instead of (typically) quoting the collective, however, he chooses to perform a countercollective voice, which he then proceeds to ridicule. He depicts the members of the countercollective as arrogant and snobbish. For them, traveling the communally beaten itinerary is "not good enough." The narrator terminates the quotation by shifting to the audience—myself ("you see")—clearly indicating that the reported speech is over (postquotation formula) and conveniently allowing the narrator to criticize it. Such is the case with the latter, shorter quotation, which Ophir terminates by means of a metadiscursive postquotation formula, indicating that "ISRAELI HOTEL" has in fact become an idiom.

The above soundings of collective, normative quotations depict a thematic spectrum concerning areas of practice and experience on which the community's norm bears. While in Ravit's excerpt, the timing was at stake (the touristic season), in Barak's story it was incorporation (that is, edible substances) that was indexed by the collective. In this regard the norm in Bella's story has bearing on similar areas: touristic locations. With regard to Dana, it is not only the sites and the activities that are collectively commended. An experiential quality is pointed toward: rather than places to visit or activities to undertake, particular experiences and impressions are required of the backpackers, which amount to an experiential itinerary.

Performatively, what is of interest is the synergetic convergence of formation and information, or of the categories dichotomously constructed as "content" and "communication" in the performance of collective decrees. As previously mentioned, the social authority and validity assumed by collective quotations rest upon their competent performance, which is not without paradox: the construction and communication of an estranged voice within a narrative of inherently personal experience. In such instances, the interweaving of direct reported speech into the narration allows the quoters not only to position themselves in relation to relevant social decrees and tenets but also to imbue their stories with impersonal, communal authority. The narrators competently make use of the words of others in their efforts to negotiate identity, and, at least as much, to imbue their own narratives with authority and persuasiveness. As observed by Bakhtin:

> The authoritative word demands that we acknowledge it, that we make it our own; it binds us . . . we encounter it with its authority already fused to it. The authoritative word is located in a distanced zone, organically connected with a past that is felt to be hierarchically higher. It is, so to speak, the word of the fathers. Its authority was already *acknowledged* in the past. It is a *prior* discourse. . . . It is given (it sounds) in lofty spheres, not those of familiar contact. Its language is a special (as it were, hieratic) language. (1981, 342, emphasis in the original).

Indeed, performing the collective voice simultaneously constructs and communicates a "distanced zone," which is located temporally and socially in a different, more sovereign, sphere than that of the individual narrators. Reflexively, the quotation marks signal the discourse that is outside the quotative as much as the discourse within it. The construction of "lofty spheres," then, also marks the nonlofty spheres: those of the phenomenologically familiar here-and-now.

Along these lines, the following excerpt demonstrates realms of conduct and experience to which the backpackers' norm relates and demonstrates how these are convincingly performed by means of quotations. In the excerpt, collective quotation is evoked with regard to the experiential value with which sites are normatively imbued. Shortly before the quotation, the narrator, Meirav, who traveled in South America for about seven months, tells of an unexpected delay endured by the group in the Torres Del Paine route in Chile. This wait became all the more dramatic because one of the participants, a religious backpacker, was hurrying back to town before the Sabbath.

Meirav: We began hiking

aaah the first day was

the first day was hiking on a relatively flat strip

all the way there we had terrible doubts whether to do the Round [Trail]   (commenting)

precisely 'cause of that

'cause [people] told us

"what—

it's just rocks out there

it's really not a nice view

it's got to be something really unattractive

nobody even tells about it at all" ...

and actually this place   (points at a picture)

that's the place that they said was rocky (*trashim*) and really unappealing (*mag'il*)

we were so excited there with the flowers

all this yellow here is flowers

it's a STUNNING field of flowers ...

it was simply gorgeous

we were really experiencing elevation

The collective-normative quotations performed by Meirav are intricate and reflexive. First, they typically convey an evaluative, critical perspective. This feature is related to another common feature of the collective quotations—that they are dialogical in the sense that they are *responsive:* the collective voice is set into quotation once the norm is challenged. Hence it assumes its discursive appearance dialogically. According to the normative standpoint evoked by Meirav, the longer trail—the Round Trail in the Torres Del Paine Park in Patagonia, Chile—is not worth pursuing. The group's decision to pursue the longer trail therefore clearly runs counter to the norm, which depicts the trail as "rocky" and consequently as "really unappealing."

Typically, the collective voice commences with the word "what," which is abruptly followed by a triple structure of consecutive negative assertions. These depict the unworthiness of the specific activity at the specific site. This position is rhetorically enhanced by the addition of an irregular fifth utterance ("nobody even tells about it at all"), with which Meirav effectively concludes the quotative assertion.

Second, the quotation is uniquely reflexive since the concluding argument—that the path is "really unappealing"—is explicitly based upon the observation that the path did not make it into the canonic narrative. Somewhat tautologically, the quoted argument that denounces the path has as its rationale the expression itself: what is marginalized and left outside the practice is also left out of the corresponding narrative (and vice versa). More precisely, the validity with which the canonic norm endows sites concerns not the actual description of the site but its *attractiveness* in the eyes and ears of the backpackers.

After a short exchange Meirav shows pictures that she had taken on the longer path (Round Trail), and she informs me that the decision eventually reached by the group contrasted with the collective standpoint. She describes the group's experience with high superlatives that stress how truly beautiful is the site: "it's a STUNNING field of flowers . . . simply gorgeous." It was a peak moment for Meirav and for her group ("we were really experiencing elevation"). Further, when she points at the pictures, as if proving the canon wrong with hard evidence, she stresses, "that's the place that they said was rocky and really unappealing." The narrator thus suggests that the act of not abiding with the collective decree and of violating the canonic, normative itinerary was deeply rewarding. The pictures—full of shiny yellow flowers—serve as documents that validate the narrator's point.[5]

Narratively, the "doubts" Meirav says the group was having, which have bearing upon its conduct as it begins hiking a particular trail, "interfere" in an analogous manner with the ensuing narrative sequence in which the embarking is depicted. After the three narrative utterances with which the extract commences, the group's "doubts" impinge upon the ensuing plot, suggesting that a dilemma requires resolution before the plotline can develop further. The hesitations, then, like a "floating" Labovian evaluation (an utterance that is not tied to the temporal structure of the narrative), are not only nonnarrative but momentarily hinder the development of the plot, thus performatively re-creating within the occasion of narration some of the social drama that accompanied Meirav's hike.

Overall, Meirav's story is effective because its telling is in itself a performance contesting the collective tenet, according to which "nobody even tells about it at all." Thus, the narration amounts to a performance of subversion of the hegemonic narrative and the collectively preferred itinerary. Not only does Meirav "tell it all," but moreover, she tells about how "nobody even tells about it at all."

By quoting the collective voice into their narrations, backpackers like Meirav perform the encompassing thematic spectrum addressed by the social norm. The quotations are part of the lively dialogic dynamics that vibrantly work between individuals and the groups in which they travel, on the one hand, and between the collective identity embodied in an authoritative, collective voice, on the other hand. These are the politics of identity as they are *literally negotiated* between the periphery and center of a culture (or a subculture). As we have heard, these matters concern time and timing, places and activities, and the backpackers' exclusion of and resistance to various cultural perspectives and narratives.

Eih Omrim "Eih Omrim"? Aunt Malka'le and the Search for Collective Authority

I get to talk with Aunt Malka'le several times a week, and sometimes even several times a day. She calls from Tel Aviv, where she has been living for almost forty years, since she left the moshav (agricultural settlement) in the Izrael valley where her parents were pioneers at the beginning of the twentieth century. She moved to the big city after her two older sisters—my mother and Aunt Vered—did so. Indeed, we keep in touch often. That is, Malka'le calls "just to make sure you're okay." She leaves several messages every day on our answering machine, inquiring how my family is doing, complaining that I have not responded to her messages from the day before or from earlier that day (lo, ani lo ko'esset, "no, I'm not angry"), letting us know of her health issues, occasional social interactions, and the like, maintaining an ongoing dialogue with my voice on the answering machine.

Speaking with her, as well as listening to her messages, is a linguistic pleasure. Single throughout her life, with no children and limited social interaction beyond our small family, Malka'le has retained her provincial moshav register of spoken Hebrew, despite the decades spent in the big city. However, in addition to the "rough" Dugri speech, she routinely incorporates neologisms in her talk and does so naturally, as though everyone (myself?) speaks her own register of language. For instance, she makes up plural forms that are not in use in Hebrew but that make a lot of (common)sense, such as pluralizing the word mango in the feminine form mangot or conjugating verbs in idiosyncratic, creative ways.

In our conversations, she frequently uses the somewhat outdated pair of words eih omrim (literally, "how saying" [pl.], meaning "it is said that . . ." or "as people say . . ."), which usually serves as a formulaic "quotation formula" in spoken Hebrew. Eih omrim is usually followed by some common idiom, such as eih omrim: 'sof tov hakol tov' (eih omrim: all's well that ends well). Oddly, however, the words Malka'le quotes after eih omrim are usually a distorted variation of a familiar idiom or words that are not idiomatic to begin with. It is, I think, her naïve and creative neologistic sense, with which she surprises her listeners by not positing well-known expressions where they are expected.

It took me a few years of listening to her talk to realize that the idiom that she does evoke is precisely the pair "eih omrim." It is the metadiscursive quotation formula itself that is formulaically repeated, rather than the acknowledged reported idiom that ought to follow it. In a way, Malka'le reverses the structure in which the quotation formula leads to the performance of a familiar idiom, and by doing so implies that in order to communicate clearly it is crucial that the participants share metacommunication. I believe that Malka'le uses the phrase eih omrim (and its equivalent, kmo she'omrim) frequently because it ties her with a collective—or, in fact, with a lost (imagined) collective. As she becomes in and through her words part of a speaking community (omrim, plural form), using this somewhat outdated collective expression imbues her words and stories with a certain degree of authority and a sense of belonging.

Norms of Gender and Embodiment

> We are here examining, each in her own way, her ability to move. Physically, geographically. Her chin or arm through air. Her steps across a floor or a continent. . . . To propel her self on her own of her own volition. So simple, so basic, so evasive.
>
> Rela Mazali

The hegemonic norm that embodies the community's expressive tenets is by no means gender impartial. Performing the norm by voicing the collective allows narrators—women and men alike—to reflect critically upon vigorous gender codes operating in their home society as these are evident along the great journey's enclaved itineraries. In particular, gender tensions and negotiations reflect the lengthy stint spent by these youths in the army shortly before the trip. More generally, gender preoccupations echo the general militaristic discourses pervading public spheres in Israel.

Gender hues expressed in the voice of the collective norm are inherently associated with the norm's *collective quality* and consequently with *its ensuing authority*. Indeed, as commonly noted by feminist scholars in Israel, gender perceptions and doctrines are successfully camouflaged behind a national-collective façade. When Meira Weiss (1997, 817) addresses gender in contemporary Israeli society, she writes not of gender directly but of intense and oppressive processes of socialization: "the stronghold of collectivism seems to be the necessary price of the crisis-cum-routine pattern . . . 'Israeli individualism' should always be questioned." The ongoing formative processes of social cohesion and crystallization, constructed vis-à-vis an enemy—an Other—revolve around and are nurtured by institutions and discourses of national symbolic stature. These are at the forefront of militaristic chauvinism (Azmon 2001; Kimmerling 2001; Kimmerling and Backer 1985; Sered 2000).

Hence, the tensions between collectivity and individuality are gendered at their crux. In many ways, processes pertaining to collectivization and crystallization lie at the core of the perpetuation of the Zionist variety of chauvinism. Their implications for minorities and marginalized populations are salient characteristics of social and political life in Israel.

The gendering processes of social cohesion and crystallization are also embodied. As shown by recent works, the hegemonic "Israeli body" is a result of an adherence or compliance of the *individual body* to the collective Zionist-Sabra discourse (see the recent surge in research: Ben-Ari and Levi-Schreiber 2000; Hazan 2001a, 2003; Sered 2000). The latter is inscribed in the former in a manner captured by Frank's observation: *"bodies alone have 'tasks.'* Social systems may provide the context in which these tasks are defined, enacted, and evaluated" (1991, 48; emphasis in the original). Indeed, the strenuous and demanding activities in which the backpackers participate under the authority of the collective norm are engendered/embodied "tasks" of the kind imposed by hegemonic institutions. As suggested in the introduction, they are a reincarnation of embodied and engendered cultural preoccupations.

Put differently, the bodily activities in which backpackers are collectively expected to engage amount to a "chapter" in the biography of the individual and of her or his body. They constitute yet another phase of normative progress, addressing the "unfinishedness of human embodiment" (Shilling 1993, 17). They constitute an additional "task" within the continuous rectification of the social state of the body's "incompleteness" (177).

Uniquely, however, this chapter is located "outside" the spaces of everyday life, within and under the institutional and ideological sovereignty of international tourism industries. As feminist tourism scholars have indicated over the past decade, the body plays a fundamental role in shaping the tourist experience and in the ways in which this experience constitutes subjectivity (Aitchison 2001; Johnston 2001; Veijola and Jokinen 1994, 1998). The writing of these and other authors in the field of tourism studies amounts in fact to a critical and embodied ontology of tourism studies.

In performing their travel narratives, backpackers represent and at the same time contest perceptions of and preoccupations with gender power relations within a context that fuses local and global cultural tenets: namely, their home culture's preoccupations with gender, on the one hand, and gender representations embodied in (backpacking) tourism, on the other hand (Noy 2003a, forthcoming). With regard to the latter, research suggests that the backpacking trip is by and large a masculinizing rite. The adventurous practices it promotes and the heroic manner in which these activities are performed supply the narrative capital that can credibly allow the social transformation from youth into adulthood. However, a high price of adherence and compliance is exacted from the performers, and those who wish to assume a coveted position through the process of hierarchization (Sørensen 2003) seem to have to compromise. For women, the price is particularly high. As observed by Susan Blake (1990, 354), in the romantic travel narratives of women there exists a fundamental "split between traveler and lady." Perpetuating romantic worldviews, modern tourism, too, embodies the tenet that "good travel (heroic, educational, scientific, adventurous, ennobling) is something men (should) do. Women are impeded from serious travel" (Clifford 1992, 105). Elsrud (2001, 602) argues with regard to backpackers that "[t]oday's adventure story is still often burdened with predominantly masculine overtones." These masculine features put serious pressure on both male and female performers, who must adhere to or otherwise grapple with hegemonic masculine norms.

This much is echoed in the above excerpts. A gender-sensitive reading would suggest that it is no coincidence that danger and fear are admitted in Bella's narrative (p. 109), nor is it surprising that the bolder, explicit contestations of the norm are expressed by males (see Ophir's narrative above, p. 115). More generally, women expressed considerably more unease with the demands set by the collective, particularly with the poor accommodation facilities in which they had to lodge when participating in outdoor activities, and with the more strenuous backpacking activities. Their stories are concerned with bodily senses, and matters of hygiene are central—two dimensions that are considerably less prominent in the men's narratives.

The travel narratives of female backpackers are typically overridden with the *embodied* dialogue between "self" and "social." Thus, Ruthy describes the considerable physical difficulties and discomforts that she had to endure during various outdoor activities. In the following, she describes the excruciating trail ascending to the Machu-Picchu site in Peru, a prestigious trail with a prominent position on the backpackers' "must do" checklist.

At the beginning of our conversation, when Ruthy describes hiking the four-day trail, she draws in passing a dichotomous distinction between "lazy" backpackers and "combat units veterans," in which the latter engage in a militarized mode of travel, exercising great discipline on their bodies. The story of her hiking and the observations concerning the types of Israelis who participate in it are intertwined.

> Ruthy: Walking was very—it was very nice. except that we arrived late all the time 'cause of me, (chuckles) it was a little—(quickly) VERY difficult for me. it's simply UPHILL all the time, and it's STAIRS, and it's EXHAUSTING, and Peru is HOT, and that region is very hot. so it was very aah difficult (2) (quieter) what else was there—and climbing wasn't easy at all. (quieter) I even nearly gave up (*hitya'ashti*) and wanted to turn back and didn't—they didn't let me, and again—there's that thing that, (louder) "no, why on earth, we—" and it's—more so when you're traveling with aaah male Israelis, it's SUCH a problem, 'cause they never—they're ALWAYS against [hiring] donkeys, and against all those things, and they don't want help from anyone. there's always that thing with (louder) "we're Israelis." they'll always try to do the toughest and the hardest things, so it's clear they'll do the Machu-Picchu trail by foot and won't ask for help from nobody

Ruthy provides a vivid narrative of the events in which she participated as well as offering her perspective on them. Although eventually she expresses her criticism of the norm clearly, she begins in a hesitant manner. As is typical of female backpackers in this study, she does not open with a straightforward contestation of the collective voice or of the practices it promotes. Instead, she says that hiking was "very nice." She chuckles when recalling how late her group had to arrive every evening due to her slow pace of walking (she later mentions that the same is true of early rising: the group would have to wait for her every morning). It is not certain whether it is this recollection, which raised a sense of embarrassment, that energized her to shift her position and to take a stand in the narrative, or whether she intended to follow a formula of politeness by which criticism is conveyed after some words of approval have been expressed ("nice"). In any case, she is performing the norm while being blatantly critical of its tenets. The opening description ("very nice") is soon replaced with a different one, the resonating "VERY difficult." Hence, it is pretty soon in the excerpt that Ruthy demonstrates the tension that arises from friction between the individual and the group vis-à-vis the requirement of sticking together.

Ruthy describes emphatically how hard the walking was for her, an experience in which she had to face a combination of the heat and a steep and lengthy ascent. After this description, which employs a combination of superlatives, intensifiers, and prosodic features, she suggests that climbing was even worse ("wasn't easy at all"). At this point she attests that she nearly broke down in despair. The point, however, is not that she almost broke down, but that she was *not allowed* to break down. Ruthy indicates that behaviors such as breaking down, giving up, and returning ("turn back") are restricted by the group's normative conduct. Her desire to turn back runs counter to the general progressive manner by which hiking and the trip's entire itinerary is to be conducted—incrementally completing and checking off the various "musts." In the masculine-colonial aim of continually moving on and reaching designated spots, ascending and progressing are highly positive engagements, whereas "breaking down" and giving up are viewed as instances of weaknesses of character. Performing the canonic norm is measured in this case against the steep slopes of the hot Machu-Picchu trail.

The argument, we can hear, is utterly embodied. The performance suggests that the text stems from *within* the description of Ruthy's corporeal gendered experiences. The panting, the sweat, and the exhaustion of which we hear, although concretely referring to the conditions of a certain Peruvian region, are *symbolically attributed to the heated friction between the performance of Ruthy's body and the canonic norm* to which it is unable to stand up—or climb up. Wishing to "give up" and leave the rite runs against the colonial-militaristic drives that are constantly directing the participants forward, upward, onward.

Ruthy's body is narrated, then, as stuck—locked, frozen—in the middle, between a rock (the social norm) and a hard place (the personal self). On the one hand, she cannot or does not wish to ascend any further; yet on the other hand, she is prohibited from turning around and descending (*lo natnu li*). (Descent is acceptable and even rewarding only after one reaches the pass, thus consuming the geographical and experiential peak.)

It is at this point that Ruthy performs a typical demonstration of the obstinate collective voice—the first of two demonstrations. The three very abrupt utterances—"no," "why on earth," "we—" (counting altogether seven syllables in Hebrew: *lo, ma pit'om, anahnu*)—hardly seem to qualify as intelligible expressions. Nonetheless, they make for a telegraphic, codelike quotation that conveys a coherent authoritative expression: the first utterance ("no") is an instance of authoritative negation, the second ("why on earth") is an inquisitive, rhetorical reprimand, and the third concluding utterance ("we") is a positive affirmation of the collective, in whose authority the previous two utterances were expressed.

To be more elaborate, the opening negation is the collective's response or reply to the protagonist's previously described predicament. The narrator thus frames the beginning of the quotation as the continuation of an ongoing dialogue, which has now "surfaced" into an audible social exchange. As a commanding speech act, it is the collective verbal stop sign that prevents Ruthy's body from turning around and returning backward, from walking off the collectively beaten track and the tradition it represents. It is both echoed and complemented in the closing miniutterance ("we"), which conveys an affirmative rather than negative preposition. The word *we* asserts a positive direction—that which is aligned with the collective's footsteps, by which the participants in the rite should conduct themselves and their bodies.

In between these two contentions a question is interestingly posed ("why on earth"), reflecting an uncertainty. Ruthy suggests that this doubt is the raison d'être of the canonic norm: that is, the possibility that *individuals would wander off*, bypass with their bodies the collective signposts, thus ignoring authoritative negations and affirmations, warnings and recommendations.

Shortly after the quotation Ruthy stresses that her predicament was exacerbated by her traveling with Israeli men (*banim Yisraelim*).[6] She thus regards gender themes, which were thus far implicit, explicitly. In this spontaneous expression the two words seem to multiply and intensify each other. In many ways her male companions are embodied representatives of the masculine norm. They are described as macho, demonstrating one of the quintessential traits of hegemonic masculinity: a persistent refusal to receive assistance. To refuse to receive help is also to refuse to ask for it, and it is also to avoid *offering* help, as Ruthy well knows. The succinct refutative "no" in the above quotation is expanded into four negative evaluations ("they never—, they're ALWAYS against [hiring] donkeys, and against all those things, and they don't want help from anyone"). These culminate in the second performance of collective quotation ("we're Israelis"), which succinctly encompasses the traits she has depicted in a sequence: identity, assertion, and cohesion.

Ruthy proceeds with a depiction of the conduct and character of the masculine collective as she metonymizes it in the quoted speech-act "we're Israelis." The male youths she portrays are engaged in very strenuous and particularly risky activities. She suggests that their preference for hiking the trail to Machu-Picchu "by foot," rather than enjoying the benefits of the available modes of transportation (such as a scenic train ride), embodies the perception that the body has to endure privations in order for the experience to be truly "authentic" and rewarding.

In the second excerpt, from Na'ama's narrative, the narrator observes metacommunicatively that Israelis "excite" (*malhivim*) one another and consequently participate collectively in rough and perilous undertakings. Na'ama wonders why she herself is not excited this way. When she describes a beach in Colombia that very many Israelis visit, she remarks that due to their conspicuous presence, it was hard for her to resist the collective authority—that is, to refuse to be excited and exhilarated into a male-constructed pursuit of adventure and risk.

Na'ama: You simply aaaaah get dragged along (*nigrar*)

                         what can I tell you

     I too found myself at some point being dragged into all sorts of things

          but you get DRAGGED ALONG

                simply aah

              "what

                   how come [you] haven't

               I did it already

                        it's worth trying   (quieter)

                        it's very aah fun   (quieter)

> it's very aah helpful"   (quieter)
>   like— ...
>
> it was also interesting for me
>   but I DID get dragged along after the guys that travel (*hevre shemetaylim*)
> who told me
>   "listen
>   it's better to do it by foot
>   it's more interesting
>   you see more sights"

Na'ama performs two sets of quotations that illustrate the authority and, more crucially, the persuasiveness of the collective norm. The point she makes in reporting the collective voice concerns one's inability to stand firmly against the communal tidal wave. Indeed, she admits *four* times that she was "dragged," that is, passively drawn into doing things the way they *should* be done, according to the norm and not of her own free will or choice. She illustrates what it means to be, or to become, "excited" by fellow travelers. It is, she demonstrates, irresistible—a social process depriving her of individual agency.

The first quotation typically commences inquisitively. The two hasty inquiries ("what," "how come [you] haven't") are rhetorical and critical. Na'ama has them leading naturally to a confirmatory assertion concerning the anonymous "quotee," who indicates that she or he "did it already." This is followed by an invitation directed at Na'ama to "try it," an invitation validated by the animator's personal experience. The quotation concludes with two seemingly evaluative adjectives ("fun," "helpful") that serve to validate and enhance the invitation made in the previous utterance. Immediately after these evaluations, a discourse marker ("like—") is employed as a brief quotation-closing formula, which indicates a shift back to the narrative. As noted by Yael Maschler (2001, 2002b), since discourse markers (such as *ke'ilu* and *kaze*) are perceived by speakers as unimportant in and of themselves, their juxtaposition with authoritative (highly "important") speech helps to mark it as differing in perspective and register from the core narrative. This is true for instances in which discourse markers serve both as quotation-introduction or quotation-closing formulae.

The two adjectives employed by Na'ama relate to (unspecified) normative activities. While the first ("fun") denotes a recreational value, the value of the second ("helpful") is not as clear: the animator does not elucidate in what way participation in the activity is "helpful" to the backpackers. It is clear, however, that what is at stake is more than mere touristic pleasure and leisure; it is more than "fun."

The second strip of reported speech (which Na'ama performs not without apologetically admitting that she did find the activities she was dragged into "interesting") expresses another central masculine aspect of the norm. The contention embodied in the collective voice is that there is a certain preferred manner of doing things "the backpacker's way." A site located at the top of a mountainous trail *should* be reached "by foot." Here, again, an expression is communicated, one that indicates that a specific *type of embodied engagement* is required of the collective.

The insistence on doing things "by foot" (*baregel*), indicates that the body is discursively disciplined and is not permitted any shortcuts or relief. The *proper* way to progress through the ritualistic movement, embodied in the ascension of a steep trail, is by putting in a decent amount of physical effort, with no aid or relief in the form of transportation (perceived by the backpackers as bourgeois). As Michael Kimmel (1996, 120) observes, "masculinity required proof and proof required serious effort." When this is accomplished, when there is both effort *and* proof of effort (that is, the narrative), the experience to which one is entitled becomes "interesting." Again, what is at stake here is not only the recreational issues. How much one sees of the view ("you see more sights") is correlated not with pleasure and leisure but with a sense of worthiness, self-development, and self-worth. Not gazing at the sights (consuming them) from a particular vantage viewpoint could potentially rob the backpacker of this profound experience. The implied threat is that without this experience, the narrator might not have stories to share that are as interesting as those of her fellow travelers. The existential implication is worse still: she might not be as "interesting" in and of herself.

Though gender is not overt here, it nevertheless pervades Na'ama's words. The collective construction of the backpacking trip as one that follows specific lines of conduct—lines that evince a romanticist-colonial type of body discipline and body work—suggests that the norm is hued with manliness and chauvinism. The one who elects to disregard the norm, to confront it, or in any other way to avoid adhering to it risks high social stakes: she might miss out on much of what others view and (thus) gain; consequently, her experience might be shallow and sour. Ultimately, the narrative resources relating to profundity and transcendence would be pulled out from under her feet. This is a particularly poignant loss in a social context that is highly hierarchical and in which the experiences that one attains are critically evaluated. As observed by Riley (1988, 321), "social recognition in these circles (and often at home as well) is derived from the . . . difficulty of one's modes of getting there. The less traveled route and more difficult way of getting there has a high degree of mystique and status conferral."

By way of conclusion, Rapoport and El-Or's (1997, 579) observation seems appropriate: "feminist research in Israel is preoccupied with the price exacted from women who wish to become part of the collective, to participate in it, in the sense of belonging and being recognized, but also in the sense of changing the collective, resisting its patriarchy." As is evident in the narratives, women's performance, whereby the collective norm and collective tenets are voiced and expressed, embodies several dilemmas stemming from the fact that the norm is explicitly masculine and collectively authoritative. This cohesive oppressive pressure amounts to a painful paradox in a rite of passage that is ostensibly about individual initiation in a liminal space.

In both of the above illustrations, patterns of embodiment are both performed and criticized. Ruthy's body is narrated and constructed as "trapped" between the collective demands and its own capabilities and inclinations; Na'ama's body is "dragged" in a similar vein. Being trapped or dragged are images that convey a glimpse of the embodied masculine effect that the collective-canonic authority places on women's traveling bodies, on the restrictions with which they grapple, and on the price paid by those who choose to participate in the backpacking collective.

From Oral Authority to Written Canon:
Quoting Travelers' Books and Trail Stories

The *siphrei metaylim* there are huge, huge.
as big as encyclopedias.
　Ronni

When speech fails to protect presence, writing becomes necessary. . . .
It diverts the immediate of thought to speech into representation and
the imagination.
　Jacques Derrida

Thus far, evocation of the collective voice has suggested its attribution in and through quotation solely in the realm of speech. The narrators ventriloquized the spoken words of an authoritative social entity—namely, "Israelis"—which they constructed through the very act of voicing it. Quite remarkably, however, some of the backpackers' authoritative quotations are attributed to *written sources.* This suggests that the collective voice, harboring in the vivid realms of word of mouth and hearsay, has also been formalized. It has been put ("raised" in Hebrew) into writing, from where the narrators performatively quote it back into the realms of oral communication and storytelling. They thus demonstrate competence in performing these different discursive sources of social authority. In this capacity, quotations represent a case of intermedium intertextuality, whereby written texts infiltrate oral discourse, from which they originated—all within the semiotic context of tourism.

The documents to which the narrators commonly attribute the inscribed quotations are *siphrei metaylim* (travelers' books). Dozens of such books are found in sites frequented by Israelis, amounting to a library that establishes these spaces as "Israeli." These volumes are usually composed at backpackers' enclaves, junctions along their itineraries, where backpackers meet before and after participating in various excursions. Hence, these sites are ideal for the exchange of information, experience, and stories in both oral and written forms.[1] The volumes are handwritten, consisting of notes, personal anecdotes, impressions, tips, warnings, suggestions, narratives, and the like. The pages of the volumes are cased in nylon and are ordered chronologically in large office folders. This arrangement enables one to read chronologically or to extract specific pages referring to particular activities.

Sippurei dereh (trail stories) are one of the main components—and genres—included in travel books, certainly the one quoted by backpackers most frequently. Trail stories contain detailed depictions of popular activities (such as hiking routes), supplemented by tips, observations, and warnings. As we shall hear, the backpackers attest that these stories are part and parcel of the gear with which they equip themselves when embarking on outdoor activities.

As the travelers' books and their trail stories represent a written mode of the collective voice, they carry the authority assigned to the collective's oral representation. Furthermore, because of their textual nature, travelers' books signify bound canonic authority, *in which the collective voice is physically captured.* The volumes make for a prolific discursive resource, which is materialized through quoting with much the same enthusiasm as the oral collective voice.

The following discussion, in addition to furthering the exploration of the backpackers' authoritative norm and its performance, will touch upon sociocultural processes of entextualization (Silverstein 1996) that facilitate the emergence of this unique genre of written touristic lore.

Yisraelim ze 'am bidrom America: The Collective and the Trail Stories

When evoking the written facet of the collective voice, the backpackers repeatedly point to the existence of vibrant communal interactions in designated, enclaved spaces, much like when evoking its oral facet. In line with the inclination of romanticist tourists to intellection (as noted by Urry 1990, 89), the narrators in fact perceive corporeal textuality as a more formal ("higher" and more prestigious) indication of the community's sociocultural center and knowledge than its oral counterpart. It seems that they take pride in this unique communal creation. It represents for the backpackers a *materialization* of the social norm, which can be created and can thrive only within a vibrant social environment. The collective knowledge embodied in text, contrary to oral assertions, is not fleeting—the sites in which these volumes are written and read, created and consumed, constitute a landmark in the youths' shared itinerary. Travelers' books, in fact, constitute a self-created touristic attraction themselves. Further, while the compilation of the volumes is clearly a consequence of processes of routinization, the backpackers nonetheless conceive of them as authentic evidence of the community's shared history and identity. The pages' chronological order and the contributors' identity as veteran Israeli backpackers suggest that the volumes are an ideal medium for embodying an accessible communal biography. They are, at one and the same time, gates affording access to the collective lore, whereby travelers can "connect" or "hook on to" collective knowledge, and signposts along the vibrant collective itinerary, directing their readers to the next activity, site, enclave, and so on. As one of the backpackers says, "everywhere there are travelers' books. [when] you arrive—you first read a travelers' book. it's in almost every hotel or every town." Travelers' books, like "Israelis," are ubiquitous; functionally, they are as accessible and as rich with information.

In addition, these handwritten compilations constitute the travelers' alternative to commercialized forms of tourist publications. The travelers' books are often mentioned in comparison to commercial touristic publications; in such comparisons, the former are of a unique genre, valued for their "authenticity" and for their up-to-date nature. In the consumer-tourist context, they are valued highly as "handmade" artifacts (Cohen 2000). Furthermore, unlike commercial backpacker guidebooks and backpacker-related literary works, whose writers become "backpacker icons" (Wilson and Richards 2004), the sippurei dereh are a communal production, and in no cases of reference to them or citation from them do the backpackers mention by name any individual contributor. As is the case with the collective-canonic voice, the "icon" is the community itself.

The following extract from Shiri's narrative occurs after I inquired about trail stories (which she had mentioned previously).

Shiri: Israelis it's
          a PEOPLE in South America
    and there are hotels of Israelis
                    actually hotels that all the Israelis go to ...
    and so
    and so there are travelers' books
                    and in these travelers' books [they] write about all sorts of
  routes in the area
               and [they] write a trail story
                      what the route's general features look like (monotonously)
                    is it difficult   (monotonously)
                    how many days—   (monotonously)
                     and in fact a detailed trail story
  like
     "you cross the bridge
            on your left you'll
                see a stream
                   continue straight
                      until you see a
  waterfall after about a quarter of an hour to the right"
                 all kinds of such things
  that's how you walk for four days

Shiri commences her depiction of trail stories with a typical allusion to Israelis' gathering places, which, according to the backpackers, provide the social condition for the creation of this genre of written lore. Shiri points out that in terms of their traveling and socializing along the collectivized itinerary, Israelis amount to "a people" or "a nation" (the Hebrew expression she uses, which appears in the title of this section, is *Yisraelim ze 'am bidrom America*). The notion of a distinct and cohesive group is expressed by the word *'am*, which is in fact a common idiom in colloquial Hebrew used to attribute characteristics to collectives and thus to designate them (for instance, taxi drivers are said to be a "vulgar 'am"). Collective identity is, again, central. What is interesting, however, is that Israelis amount to "a nation" when they are away from Israel. Shiri indicates that Israelis can be distinguished from other peoples (such as "natives" and "tourists;" see chapter 5) who share traveling spaces. It could perhaps be said that Shiri is suggesting that Israeli backpackers differ on two levels: from the Other—the foreigner—but also from Israelis *in their homeland.*

From this opening statement, which presents an overall point of view, Shiri addresses increasingly concrete social units, eventually reaching quotation. She specifies the sites where Israelis-as-people are to be found and heard, where they *become* the people they claim (and are claimed) to be, and where they acquire and perform their social canon. The expression "hotels of Israelis" implies that these tourist sites are appropriated by their visitors, who form and transform themselves therein into a collective.

The third facet into which Shiri's argument naturally evolves consists of the travelers' books and the trail stories they contain, which are located in the above sites. This is how Shiri arrives at the point where she demonstrates what a trail story is, alluding to its crucial quality: its authoritativeness. She describes what a trail story *does* and then demonstrates it by quoting one directly. The quotations are illustrative and hypothetical: the narrator does not imply that she is quoting a specific trail story, but that this is how such a source typically sounds.

The content of the quotation includes detailed instructions, directing the travelers where to go and what to look at. It is rich with spatial and temporal deixis that vivify the protagonists' hypothetical point of view. Note that the evocation of time at the end of the extract from Shiri's narrative ("a quarter of an hour") suggests that there is an ideal pace of progress by which the normative directions are effective and sensible (as with recipes, following these instructions successfully requires a closely synchronized performance). It thus supplies yet another illustration, temporal in this case, of the gripping power of the norm. Akin to instructions, which repeatedly direct the tourists' gaze, the quotations constitute a verbal map that suggests the contours of the everyday reality of backpackers.

The quotation-closing formula ("all kinds of such things") functions like the words "et cetera." It assures the hearer that the reported speech is exemplary and illustrative and shifts the story's perspective back to the voice of the narrator. The extract immediately concludes with an evaluative comment. The utterance "that's how you walk for four days" indicates that quotations are an authentic (mimetic) illustration of how things actually are, how they are actually practiced. A tone of criticism is also discernible: the duration of which Shiri narrates ("four days") contrasts sharply with the temporal interval she mentioned shortly before, within the quotation (only a quarter of an hour). The aside suggests that this type of detailed description guides and controls the travelers and their bodies step-by-step, minutely yet at the same time comprehensively.

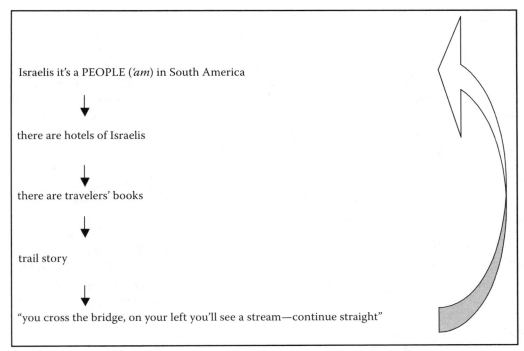

Fig. 1. From *'am* to quotation: Social concretization and objectification

Shiri shifts skillfully between different levels of representation of the collective: she begins with Israelis as "people," moves to the Israelis' "travelers' books," ultimately reaching a "sample" of these people—that is, directly reporting the collective's voice (see fig. 1). This process of *gradual social concretization* begins with a statement of the bird's-eye view and ends with the actual (if hypothetical) metonymic sounds of the "people" and of their "becoming." The boundaries of the description—the opening and concluding observations—link up with one another to form an intelligible, circular illustration, wherein the relations between "Israelis it's a people" and the sounds of quotation ("you cross the bridge") are complementary facets of the same whole. Shiri cannot reply to my inquiry concerning trail stories by referring to a decontextualized genre of written lore. Rather, the query invites a performance concerning the canonic norm and the formation of social authority and identity among backpackers.

Later in the conversation, Shiri recalls her hiking adventures, which she describes as "fascinating." In doing so, she embeds the description with idioms concerning the type of embodied discipline required of the travelers: "And it's really fascinating, to CONQUER THE MOUNTAIN (*lihbosh et hahar*), to do—to navigate, like—by oneself. 'cause it's walking the treks by a trail story (*holhim batrekim lephi sippur dereh*)." Here Shiri evokes common maxims, which she emphasizes by the use of prosody—a louder voice and a lower tone, an emphasis reserved for canonic authoritative codes, or, as in this case, for truisms performed vis-à-vis the collective voice.

After making these declarations, Shiri utters the words "to do—" (*la'asot*), which alludes to the action-oriented character of this discourse. To "conquer" and shortly afterward to "navigate" are the cultural tokens of action and of how a community should ideally pursue and embody action. "To navigate" indexes another masculine-romanticist ideal of the Sabra tradition, that of the lone scout reconnoitering. Hiking is not *an* activity, it is *the* activity: it is *about* action and about adventure. As indicated by the excerpts from Ruthy and Na'ama in chapter 6, performing backpacking means actively engaging in and embodying the merits of this type of actionable lore and engaging in and embodying the forms of authoritative narratives and narrations that it can endow.

In line with the image of the lone scout, Shiri ends the strip by implying that one can orient oneself and hike and travel *by oneself*, because the practical knowledge one needs is entirely supplied by trail stories. An interesting image of the relationship between individuals and the community is evoked: one is by oneself, yet at the same time one has *the (knowledge and voice of one's) collective.* Somewhat akin to hiking with a Walkman, the backpackers can travel by themselves and still hear collective voices.

The next illustration was supplied by Meirav (in chapter 4, pp. 68–70), who, in the course of a narrative sequence, performs quotations from travelers' books, elaborating upon the discursive sociocultural context within which these books are created. In the first instance, Meirav addresses a trail story in a metacommunicative note explaining (to me) why the trek should end at the particular point ("according to the trail story"). This clarification is necessary because the social drama Meirav is about to depict depends upon the fact that the group was "supposed to" reach a certain point at a designated time. The allusion to the trail story, like an allusion to the collective voice, illustrates the normative guidelines according to which the practice of hiking should be conducted as well as highlighting the social tensions that generate the story's underlying drama.

In the second allusion to trail stories, Meirav depicts her predicament. She has inadvertently cut herself off from the group and is now choosing her own path for and by herself. She indicates that the scene took place in an area as yet uncharted by trail stories—in other words, an area that lies beyond the collective's inscribed sovereignty. This fact enhances both the narrative drama—Meirav has no collective map to mark her footsteps—and the potential for her individual gain (in term of cultural capital). Meirav persuasively makes the point that she is exploring uncharted realms, external as well as internal, social as well as individual. Her words intimate that the trail stories hold maplike collective knowledge, against which claims of individuality, and personal choice and change, are made.

The final excerpt is drawn from Ari's narrative. It further demonstrates how the narrators explicitly refer to the *written mode* of the canonic lore—that is, to its materiality. In the excerpt, from the beginning of our conversation, Ari depicts the arrangements made shortly before embarking on a hike. He then mentions that he visited a "hotel of Israelis" in La Paz, Bolivia, which was "full" of Israelis and was "well-known by Israelis in South America in general."

Ari: Everything's written there, written in Hebrew, (quieter) naturally. Israelis who've traveled wrote it. [backpackers] take a trail story, simply read it and write a trail story. (faster and louder) no need for a map or anything like that. it says there, "on the first day you have—you can sleep here and here, there's a ramp there, here there's water, on the way there's a village where you can buy Coke?"

Chaim: Wow

Ari: Coke, by the way, is the one product I found that's not missing anywhere

Chaim: What, [Coke? (surprised)

Ari: Coke], Coca-Cola. you walk, [you see a] village, no-water no-food no-electricity no-nothing. there's Coke, [they are] selling [it]. "wanted to have a bottle of Coke?" (1) aaah so that's it, from there we took a trail story (1).

Ari exemplifies the complete and inclusive nature of the information contained in the travelers' books. With regard to the hiking activity, which he employs illustratively, he assures his audience that "everything's written there." Consequently, since the volumes contain all the practical information one could possibly need, any further assistance (such as local guides) or gear (such as maps and guidebooks) is unnecessary. In Ari's words, there is "no need for a map or anything like that." After saying that these volumes are "naturally" written in Hebrew, an illustrative strip is recited. Typically, it consists of short, prescriptive utterances (second person, male), detailing the dos and don'ts of the praxis of hiking.

Immediately after the quotation, Ari associatively recalls something about what he just quoted, a recollection that neatly demarcates the reported strip. In other words, the narrator terminates the reported sequence by employing a *meta/ postquotation comment* that relates to and repeats the end of the quote (compare similar framing by Ari, below in chapter 8). The content expressed in the quotation seems to have sparked a subject upon which the narrator elaborates and which advances the plot. Indeed, the quotation's unexpected closing formula—"Coke, by the way"—caught me by surprise.

The description of the written norm moves typically enough from the general to the particular: from where the backpackers ought to go to where they ought to sleep and what they ought to drink to the particular instance of where they could purchase a Coca-Cola (see fig. 1 above). The Coke aside accomplishes a sharp shift from the realm of quotation. First, it expresses an individual voice (it is stated in the *first person*) immediately after a collective expression. Second, akin to discursive markers, the incidental quality ("by the way") marks it as being different from the preceding expression, which is canonic and authoritative. This structure of the comment allows the narrator to "hook on to" the voice of the authoritative collective and to align himself effortlessly with normative proclamations. Arguably, the Coke aside is concluded by a quotation, wherein Ari playfully imitates the voice of a local merchant offering a Coke bottle.

Toward the end of the extract, Ari returns to the beginning and mentions, by way of conclusion, from where the group copied the trail story. Akin to hiking gear and traveling provisions, the trail story is presented as a backpacking essential: taking one or more trail stories is part and parcel of the group's preparation for hiking. It is a ritualistic part of the preparations because this discursive (talking) map allows individuals and groups to link to the communal chain.

Reproducing Trail Stories: Replication and Improvisation

> To sign your name, your mark, is to leave a track like any other track of the body; handwriting is to space what the voice is to time.
>   Susan Stewart

The backpackers often stress the *reproduction process* by which the written facet of the collective norm circulates. The terms they use to describe the dissemination of authoritative texts within the community reflect the canonic status of these texts and indicate how they serve as sources for authoritative performances. For example, when narrators mention how they *copied* these texts from travelers' books, they indicate how they reproduced quotations exactly, adhering as closely as mimetically possible to an authentic, "baptismal" original. This is what Ari, for example, does in the previous excerpt, when he conveys that trail stories are copied ("read it and write a trail story"): they are first read and then written, thus assuming a form that the backpackers can carry with them. They become, in Silverstein's (1996, 81–82, esp. n. 1) terms, references to "'originary' entextualization," which create an original, a prototypical referent.

Backpackers often evoke the "check mark" metaphor, suggesting that there are actual records listing activities and sites to be pursued. In one instance, a backpacker observed that "things are written for you in the book, in the travelers' book that you've copied to your notebook, like [sites that] you have to see if you're there." This description points not only toward the authority ingrained in these texts but also toward the reproduction processes, the means by which *communal knowledge* is individually disseminated and then pursued. Like Ari above, the narrator suggests that individual copies are made from the stationary travelers' books (the authentic original), which are then carried around by backpackers. In other words, the texts are copied from public-collective compilations into private-personal diaries (often written by backpackers during the trip) to serve as verbal maps and—after the trip's conclusion—as textual souvenirs. Indeed, a few of the backpackers showed me the dog-eared trail stories by which they had traveled during the trip. They presented them in a way reminiscent of how tourists present authentic souvenirs brought from the destination.

In relating an excursion at "Devil's Tooth" near La Paz, Bolivia, Tova says that "people" laugh at Israelis because "we do everything that's written for us, everything that others do." What she is saying is that the Israelis' adherence to a *written norm* is prevalent enough as to be recognized (and ridiculed) by nonmembers of the community. By regarding the collective norm through the eyes of foreigners, the narrator, who, not surprisingly, is a female, is able to safely critique the mimetic adherence to the written norm and its excluding, insulating consequences.

Michal evokes the issues of the reproduction and dissemination of trail stories in the context of a distinction she makes between leisurely and strenuous modes of travel. She indicates that while trail stories are frequently reproduced, they are constantly being supplemented and modified: "There are simply trail stories, it's people who (1) people who simply did this trek once and sat and wrote what they did. and so it's found in the travelers' book. [people] simply take—a copy and embark on the trail according to what it says. and every time people modify it, like—ah if someone sees that something's wrong [he] adds [something] of his own or writes a new addition, or simply an altogether new [story]." Michal fleetingly fantasizes the emic "historiography" of the genre of written trail stories. Through the preservation of written documents, Michal and other backpackers hear what their fore-travelers once did and, through a lively chain of constant reproductions, additions, and modifications, establish an ever-changing linear narrative.

After describing how the volumes were created, Michal recounts how they are modified and updated. The second part of her explanation depicts not only how the past is communally extended into the present but also how the collective voice retains its livelihood and relevance—in a word, its *authority.* Despite the fact that the volumes are written, and in this sense are essentially static, they are nonetheless perceived as a flexible medium, a truly adaptable verbal mirror or map of "backpacker reality." If "something's wrong," Michal assures me—that is, if an incongruence between "text" and "reality" occurs—directions are promptly modified so that they will precisely reflect the "reality" on which they "have a command" (to borrow from Goffman 1981, 187). Hence, the canonic texts are not merely reproduced—quoted from stationary collective volumes into personal, portable inscription devices—they are also creatively modified and, if necessary, replaced completely.

Backpackers place high value upon traveling with and according to trail stories, compared to alternatives such as tourist guides or commercial guidebooks. First, avoiding commercial touristic services is perceived as a *more individual manner of traveling.* With only the trail stories to guide them, backpackers view themselves as more independent and self-sufficient in sustaining themselves in outdoor spaces. They prefer their kin's guidebooks to commercial services and publications—although it is something of a paradox that in their "independence" they are actually traveling a collectively beaten path. In addition, since the stories are perceived as

tantamount to gear, adhering to them also reinforces the masculine ethos of the explorer, who manages to operate equipment purposefully, or, in this case, to employ
and effectively "read" portable extracts from travel books.

Second, traveling in the footsteps of "elders" carries a positive value *in and of
itself.* Semiotically, it charges the trip with additional layers of meaning and ritual.
Through the great journey backpackers relate to and form a link with a collective
chain. Their engagement in backpacking is not perceived as merely frivolous or
"touristic." Instead, it is an existential and "authentic" endeavor, wherein the youths
add their own bodies and footsteps to the chain of Israeli wanderers and explorers
who have traveled these particular routes for decades.

Travelers' books represent more than merely an inscribed, bound form of social authority. Performatively, narrators point out that the volumes function *interactionally*—that is, they are "open-ended" and there is no formal point at which
they are declared "complete." As expressed by one backpacker, "it's books the guys
wrote, and anyone who's got anything to add can add it with time." Hence the volumes are continually being written and continually being "used" or quoted. By using the colloquial word "guys" (hevre), narrators stress that even though the books
have a canonic value, they do not embody "high culture" and are not restricted
to an exclusive elite. Rather, they are the product of casual contributions made by
"ordinary" members of the community. They are simultaneously "encyclopedic" (as
observed by Ronni in the epigraph above) and personal. As observed by another
backpacker, "travelers' books are a sort of diary (*yomanim*) in which everyone adds
from his experiences." Again, by using the term "diaries," narrators convey that these
volumes are akin to public notebooks, on the pages of which personal impressions
are written. They serve as social inscription surfaces where the individual (the personal) and the collective (the public) overlap and merge.

Indeed, those who read through these dialogical and interactive volumes before embarking on a particular touristic activity, are—potentially at least—those
who write (in) them, upon their return. Reading and quoting them is a meeting
of self and canon. Community members who write in these volumes become gen-
erative members of the community. The comments, observations, and stories they
write constitute their creative contribution to a lasting collective autobiography.
Through returning after the excursion and commenting on them and writing their
own personal travel accounts, backpackers are cyclically transformed from readers
to writers, from quoters to those quoted. This is how they literally inscribe themselves in the canon.

Although everyone can potentially update a trail story or create a new one,
several backpackers hinted that the type of knowledge that is required suggests that
modifying trail stories is in fact an elitist right. Yet all in all, it seems that a community of trail-story users emerges, wherein backpackers copy, modify, exchange with,
and recommend to each other trail stories.

Like Michal, Ophir, too, evokes an improvisational and subversive view of the
written norm. Toward the end of our meeting Ophir mentions trail stories while

recounting what he and his companions used to talk about during the cold evenings of the Santa Cruz trek in Peru.

Ophir: There's what's called a trail story (1)

                         it's usually found in hotels of Israelis [where] there are books

       and about the trek itself it's written   (higher, quicker)

             "okay   (lower, monotonously)

               [you are] walking—

               getting to this trail (*shvil*)

               getting to the trail is the beginning of the trek (*trek*)

               [you are] walking half an hour on the trail

                       the trail after

half an hour splits

        aah right and left

          [then you are] taking a left

                  keeping going on the trail until

the first bridge

        at the first bridge cross the river to the right bank of the—"

                    and so in detail   (higher)

                    and so you walk the trek (1)

   today it's not like the first-first travelers who had [to do] everything for themselves and

perhaps even take maps and navigate

  today everything's arranged [and] the parents worry here for nothing

     EVERYTHING'S ARRANGED

           TO THE SMALLEST DETAIL

so we laughed about it

I remember we laughed about it

         we said we'll write a trail story about the Santa Cruz

        we'll write a new trail story

           "[you (pl.) are] walking

five minutes until it begins to rain (1)

         when it begins to rain [you are] turning right

                continuing

to walk until Gai's knee hurts

      when Gai's knee hurts [you are] taking a break and resting for fifteen minutes

               after fifteen minutes

climbing further up the hill

       until a German couple is approaching in your direction and

continuing in the opposite direction

      after passing the couple—" (1)

something cynical of this sort about the treks' trail stories   (quicker, smiles)

eventually we didn't write it   (chuckles)

     but aah (1)

      it's what we talked about

Typically, Ophir first contextualizes travel stories ("it's usually found in hotels of Israelis") and then goes on to demonstrate in detail how one sounds and operates (see fig. 1 above). The lower and monotonous tone brings to mind a reading (or dictating) performance, and it is clear that a shift between communication media is being performed. The first quotation, which is illustrative and hypothetical, is a typical evocation of the directional, recipelike genre of collective lore. It commences by demarcating the very boundaries of the touristic attraction, which are demonstrated by the transition from a mere "trail" or "path" to the touristic "trek," from the Hebrew word *shvil* to the tourist lingua franca word *trek* (pronounced thus in Hebrew). Note that unlike Ari's quotations, in which the verbs are in the second person singular (male), Ophir makes use of plural (male) conjugations to construct a more indirect (implied) and impersonal directive rhetoric.

After Ophir explicitly notes the detailed nature of the trail story, he reaches the point he has been getting at (through the elaborate quotation): the routinization and formalization of backpacker routes. This point, which is where his prosodic emphasis lies ("EVERYTHING'S ARRANGED, TO THE SMALLEST DETAIL"), provides the background against which he can perform the ensuing improvisation. Like Michal above, he alludes to "pioneer" backpackers, those "first-first" Israeli wanderers who paved the narrative for later backpackers. In Ophir's comparison between present-day backpackers and their fore-travelers, he colors the former in pale shades. They are but mere echoes of their predecessors, less adventurous, less individualistic, and therefore less heroic. Those pioneers were not trapped in the web of collectivized itineraries; they had to find their way, literally, on their own, relying on technical equipment rather than, and in contrast to, a social norm. The pioneers, Ophir assures his audience through his imagery, were *true explorers*, traveling to as yet uncharted regions. The narrator thus succinctly alludes to the backpackers' legacy, which engulfs the touristic variety of nostalgic discourses (Cohen 1986; Dann 1996, 218–28).

As Ophir expresses his critique he conveys a sense of the "backpacker angst" (Wilson and Richards, 2004), whereby present-day backpackers lament the changes taking place in backpacking tourism. Accordingly, one of the important categories by which backpackers nowadays distinguish themselves is that of "anti-backpacker," whereby it is less frequently tourists against which backpackers position themselves in the spaces of tourism and more often backpackers, whose patterns of travel are claimed to have been institutionalized and massified (Welk 2004, 8).

In order to exemplify the process of institutionalization, Ophir recalls the youths' concerned parents and points out that their worries are actually unfounded. The mention of the backpackers' parents is a reminder that most of the backpackers are still youths; the figures of their parents (even if only in the background) play an important role in the construction of the adventurous trip as a rite of separation and initiation into young adulthood (Haviv 2005).

Along this developmental line, the unprecedented distance from parents and family is mitigated by the immediacy and security of an embracing collective norm.

Indeed, the pedagogical qualities of the collective voice clearly assume a parental hue. In this sense, parents indeed need not worry about their offspring, Ophir assures us, for the parental function is substituted by a different authoritative and pedagogical social agent, that of the collective of (experienced) peers.

At this point Ophir performs yet another illustrative and hypothetical set of quotations, which echoes yet at the same time contests the previous set. The differences between the normative and improvised forms he performs are illuminating, and by way of contrast they shed light on written trail stories. First, Ophir suggests a trail story that is temporal. It is sensitive, rather than indifferent, to the lapse of time. Temporality does not refer merely to the measurement of time (collective quotations also refer to time—for instance, how long traveling from one point to another should take) but to the improvisational and spontaneous ways in which time, measured by social events, is drawn into the account. This transforms the trail story from a static recipe into a processual narrative embedded in felt time. The timing of the rain, of the sore knee, and of crossing paths with other travelers suggests instances of unexpected narrative unfolding.

Second, not only time but the body—its experiences, pains, and fatigue—invades and enlivens the directional, sterile canonic norm, transforming it into an embodied text. We now hear, for the first time, of sore limbs. In a masculine and disembodied text, the body is either absent or is purely functional—it accomplishes excruciating—and rewarding—physical goals. It is the object of the prescription, rather than the subject of the story. The improvisational mode, however, is constructed on subjective, embodied experiences; it is closer to description than to prescription. Bodily pain is admitted in the narrative, and with it bodily needs (rest and recuperation). If, as observed by Young (1991, 221), "bodily withdrawal from the realm of events or disembodiment in it are the marks of objectivity," then what is at stake in Ophir's illustration is not the authority of the objective and factual (normative, canonic authority) but subversion vis-à-vis the subjective and experiential.

Third, not coincidentally, there is a consideration of other tourists—or, in other words, of the changing human landscape along the trails. This suggests that the route is part of a "heterogeneous touristic space," one that is shared by many tourists (and locals) and is not exclusively Israeli (Edensor 1998). Although in a static, predetermined map, tourists are not mentioned/seen (but only flora and fauna), a narrative trail story conveys a crossing of ways and perhaps interaction with fellow travelers.

At the conclusion of the reported improvisation, Ophir frames his group's perspective with regard to the collective canon in one word: "cynical." The above differences between the canonic trail stories and the group's trail stories instantiate the group's critical view. Generally, in order for the narrator to be critical of—or even creative about—the norm, she or he needs to be a competent backpacking storyteller and story quoter (Babcock 1993). As observed by Bakhtin (1986, 80), "genres need to be fully mastered in order to be manipulated freely." This accounts for Ophir's commencing with a detailed, quoted account of a normative trail story (the first set of quotations). It is not only that he wishes to introduce the genre to the audience or to create a dramatic effect by juxtaposing the two instances of quotations, he also wishes to establish his competence in expert improvisation. Only from this stance—from the competent knowledge of a member of the community—can he viably criticize the norm.

Indeed, at the very end Ophir returns to my initial inquiry concerning what he and his friends were talking about while hiking the Santa Cruz trek. He notes that the innovative trail story has remained within the sphere of orality and has not been inscribed or transcribed into travelers' books. This, he reminds me, is what they were *talking* about. The group voice is associated with the oral, improvisational, embodied, and contesting mode, while the collective is associated with the written, fixed, authoritative-conservative (and perhaps commercial) mode. While adhering to the norm in praxis, the group playfully contemplates its position vis-à-vis the norm and its perspective on it. Yet, by indicating that the subversive trail story he has told is framed as mere spoken words, the narrator ensures that this carnivalesque appreciation of the norm is contained and does not truly threaten the canon.

In any case, the *written* norm is something to *talk* about. And as trail stories are exchanged, compared, and improvised upon within the community—much like recipes are (Theophano 2002)—they function as both directions that shape social reality in a strong sense and discursive resources that allow backpackers to reflect upon this process and to strengthen communal ties.

Walking the Collective Walk: *Simun Shvilim* Maps

> One can possess only the "visible" whereas that which is only audible is already past in the moment of its present and provides no "property."
>
> Georg Simmel

The exploration that concludes this chapter concerns the evocation of a particular type of hiking maps, commonly called *simun shvilim* maps (literally, "trail-marking maps"), which are popular among hikers in Israel.[2] The discussion of these unique maps concerns inscription and signification in several ways and illustrates an adherence to the written (collective) lore. The evocation of trail-marking maps sheds light upon why trail stories and travelers' books are so frequently quoted, why they are so desirable, and implicitly, upon the mimetic meaning of quotations in the community.

In the following excerpt Shahar expresses a strong opinion in favor of inscription of the communal lore. He does so incidentally. While narrating his adventurous engagements in the Takisi area in Bolivia, Shahar notes that the trek he pursued was not well known among the Israelis there, and one had only partial trail stories and topographical maps to use when hiking it. This is when Shahar evokes the simun shvilim system of demarcation: "Now, trail marking like in Israel is something that doesn't really exist [anywhere], and if it does exist then pretty defectively. I think that the trail marking in Israel is INGENIOUS, really, I haven't seen anywhere in the world such a SIMPLE SIGN that tells you SO CLEARLY where you need to go. it's really good." Although only five narrators made explicit reference to the system of trail marking, its evocation is not surprising. Since most of the backpackers with whom I met participated in youth movements and in various hiking clubs prior to their service in the army, their acquaintance with popular hiking practices is not surprising and neither is its spontaneous evocation in the context of outdoor activities during the trip.

Shahar enthusiastically expresses his deep appreciation of the efficiency of the simun shvilim system of demarcation (a perspective reinforced by the second backpacker in the interview, who shortly later admitted, "it's also maintained very well in Israel"). Its efficiency, Shahar contends, is an outcome of the close correlation between the plain, easy-to-spot signified mark—a colored dash on a stone—and a corresponding signifier—a colored mark (of the same color) on the map. In Israel, he continues, it is deployed ingeniously, unlike "anywhere in the world."

What is indicated in the extract is that outdoor space in Israel, which these maps colorfully signify, is thoroughly marked. As a consequence of the system's effectiveness, it is almost impossible for anyone to get "lost" in the space in Israel—to transcend the system and hike in uncharted areas. This, of course, makes a strong case for Shahar's point: in South America he trekked genuinely uncharted areas of utter wilderness, where there was no marking system, no signification. Real backpackers, he implies, travel away from the homeland in order to travel beyond charted collective sovereignty.

The evocation of the comprehensive system of simun shvilim implicitly touches upon the authority of the collective and on quotation. The effect of the trail-marking system is based upon engraving a mark in the wilderness. Unlike standard topographical maps, in trail-marking editions the signified marks are not natural objects (or man-made objects, such as a road or an electricity post, created independently of maps). Instead, the signified is a mark of a correspondingly colored sign, which was marked precisely in order to correspond with the sign in the map. The semiotic implication is that there is a unique link between the backpackers and their predecessors: there was *someone who marked the signs to begin with.* Acknowledging the marks means acknowledging that there was someone there before who has left a sign specifically meant to be followed, to be quoted. As we are reminded by the comment of the second narrator, since then there have been hikers who have *continuously maintained these signs* (refreshing their colors, making sure they are highly visible, and so on).

This being the case, the connection or connotation between the collective, normative trail stories and the system of trail marking employed by the Society for Protection of Nature in Israel becomes clearer.[3] It is passionately evoked by Shahar and other backpackers in the context of backpacking because it corresponds with the collectivized routes that are inscribed in and promoted by trail stories. Although the latter do not include systematic (institutional) demarcations on the trails themselves,[4] they resemble the trail-marking system of signification in that the information they encode, unlike the information conveyed by regular topographical maps, is of a *collective and directive* nature. Trail stories indicate where to walk and what trails to follow, and, more important, they imply Israeli backpackers have walked these trails before and are continuously walking them and amending their directions regularly. In a way, these are uniquely coded tourist "recommendations" that pertain to the correct and successful pursuit of the activity at hand.

Hence, traveling according to a trail story is not so much about geographical movement and orientation as it is about social movement. It is about traveling in, and possibly improvising upon, the footsteps of previous backpackers and the signs they left behind; it is about quoting the collective norm and abiding by it.

Furthermore, akin to trail stories, the simun shvilim system of demarcation has a written mode of communication. The signs are not fleeting, as are collective oral assertions. The backpackers who hike and travel according to these signs do more than passively progress according to the directions with which they are supplied. Because they can potentially add to the trail stories, modify them, or suggest entirely new stories, they are in effect actively *maintaining the narrative*. Their performances—as both hikers and storytellers—are imbued with additional layers of meanings pertaining to communal knowledge, to identity, and to the means by which they are embodied and communicated.

Thorong La Pass: At 5,416 Meters

When I now look through the journal I kept during the Great Journey I realize that most of what I wrote was during the three-week trek I took on the Annapurna Circuit Trail in Nepal. Although the trek was certainly one of the greatest experiences of the trip, I'm surprised to see that I reserved nearly all my personal space of inscription to the trek's experiences, and not to the many other endeavors and adventures I had.

Regardless of the experiences, emotions, and insights that are described therein, the intensity is clearly manifest graphically (see below). The complete consumption of the space of inscription—in this case by a description of a wild vulture that landed 4–5 meters away from me and then collapsed, dying—reflects a state of being overwhelmed. The large pages of the notepad, like my mind, are hardly able to contain the impressions of the experience, which threaten to overflow. This intensity, I now understand, was part of the once-in-a-lifetime experience of traveling and trekking in Nepal and India.

In an entry written on April 22, 1991, I wrote:

> The fateful day.
> I'm lying on a stone that's cushioned with my down coat. At my side there's snow and the sun is shining fiercely, and I'm at Thorong La Pass. No more, no less: 5,416 meters. I've never written anything at this altitude. We are really fortunate to enjoy great weather. There's still no wind

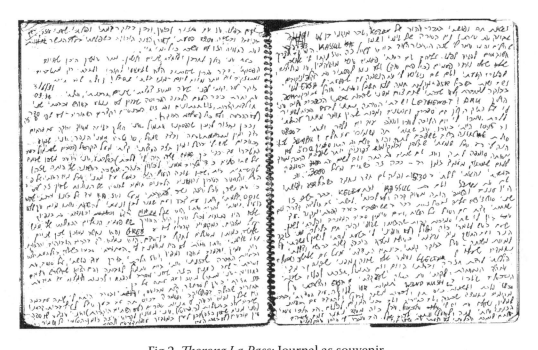

Fig 2. *Thorong La Pass:* Journal as souvenir

(the time is 10:00) and the snow is not too high, and this is why I (and everyone here around me) can take off my coat and lie about leisurely, as if teasing the universe of snow and ice around us.

I realize that the tourist-produced text is a souvenir no less than any other item I brought with me (extracted) from the trip. Unlike commonplace views of language, which hold that it is essentially descriptive and hence reflects and creates an ontic gap between the description (and the describer) and the described, my trekking journal enjoys the esteemed ontic state of an authentic fabric produced in situ. It is an organic, albeit self-created, part and parcel of the backpacking attraction itself.

From Speech Community to Vocal Identity:
The Sound of Quotations

This is really what a Nepalese told me:
  "how do you recognize an Israeli?
  you hear him before you see him"!
    Uri

Every sense delivers contributions characteristic of its individual nature to
the construction of sociated existence; peculiarities of the social existence
correspond to the nuancing of is impressions.
    Georg Simmel

The impressive evocation of quotations in the backpackers' performances plays an additional exciting role. This role is not encompassed in the meaning or function commonly attributed to reported speech per se, that stemming from the infusion of rhetoric and content. Rather, quotations are intriguing because they are more than *illustrations* of social voices. Due to their highly performative and dramatic nature, instances of quotations typically present in speech a prosodic, paralinguistic deviation from the narrative voice of the speaker. In other words, quotations are about not only voices but about human sounds. The live performance of quotations amounts to the Wittgensteinian "hurly-burly" of social interaction. It is the discursive epitome of those familiar "human noises," evoked in a vocal, polyphonic narrative collage.

As I attended the performances, it gradually became clear that *listening* to the prosodically suffused narrations was a *literal* matter. Stories were made meaningful and communicative through *sounds:* not only the sounds of the particular occasion of narration but also the overall sounds of a speaking speech community, which emerged in the performance as a lively and humming community. Thence, as we near the conclusion of the exploration of backpackers' performances of quotations and voices, it will be observed that the narrators represent not only "entexted voices" but also "voiced texts," and that they make for a community of animators who possess and are possessed by social and cultural sounds as much as by texts.

By "sounds" the literal, rather than metaphorical, meaning of the word *voice* is addressed in an exploration that refers to the vocal consequence of the oft-quoted voices. The present aim, however, is not the minute prosodic analysis of the production of quotations and social voices—pitch, stress, intonation, and the like—but rather *how the narrators construe their vocal community and how they interpret its sonorous variety of social voices.* In other words, the emphasis is not on an "etic" perspective but on a reflexive "emic" one, a perspective that is metadiscursive or, more accurately, metaprosodic. The crucial issue is the perspective of the members themselves on their vocal community and how *they* recognize social sounds and imbue them with meaning.

This investigation counters the commonplace assumption that sound does not have intrinsic meaning. It is generally assumed that sound acts solely as a perceivable physical signal (means/medium) by which meaning can be communicated (ends). At stake is an instance of yet another enduring Western-Cartesian dichotomy, one that dismembers the whole entity of lively social language into two elements—meaning and sound—elevating and emphasizing the former (Derrida 1976). Indeed, explorations of prosodic features of speech performance and of how these are taken to grant meaning are relatively scarce, indicating the deafness and disembodied nature of mainstream language-related social sciences.

In linguistic anthropology, Dennis Tedlock, among others, researched the constitutive role played by verbal expression in social lives. "Let us try to ignore, for the moment, what our story says," he appealingly urges, "and consider it purely as an acoustic signal, a signal to be measured rather than a code to be deciphered" (1983, 197). This is an inquiry into communal paralinguistics (and metalinguistics) and into the social and personal meaning voices carry and convey. Following Tedlock, Bauman and Briggs call, yet again, for research into sounds and voices in oral performances, which amount in speech communities to no less than "a primary locus of meaning" (1990, 65; see also E. Basso 1985; Feld 1982; Seeger 1987). Such inquiries explore the semiotics of the "grain" of language in an attempt to resist the hegemony of modern logocentric worldviews and to deconstruct and undermine its presupposed metaphysics (Barthes 1986; Corradi 1995; Derrida 1976).

Indeed, explorations into prosodic features and other vocal characteristics of speech demonstrate that these are highly expressive. Among others, Levelt's work on speech production suggests that "the intonations that underlie speech acts (as well as some other acts of communication) are of a special kind . . . [and convey] *communicative intentions*" (1989, 59; emphasis in the original). Moreover, Gumperz's (1992, 1995) inquiry indicates that prosodic phenomena—among other nonverbal signs—function not only in an expressive capacity but as contextualization cues, evoking "the interpretative frames in terms of which constituent messages are interpreted" (Gumperz 1995, 104).

An illustration of this is provided by Ochs (1997, 187), who observes that in the "shift from descriptive prose to direct quotation," narrators "transform the reader into an (over)hearer." Through its appreciation of a performance, the audience not only *hears* but also *overhears.* What is aimed at here is not (only) a literary metaphor of a phonic dimension but the production of an actual prosodic-phonic

Fig. 3. Israeli tourists: Sounds and sights (Amos Biderman, *Ha'aretz*, December 4, 2002. Copyright © "Ha'aretz" Daily Newspaper Ltd.)

performance. By overhearing or eavesdropping, a phonic position is created and an acoustic space is implied—both metaphorically and physically.

Lastly, Georg Simmel's (1997b) early sociological explorations of sensory sensitivity, which have drawn attention to the modern hermeneutics of sound in and of society, are of particular salience for the present exploration. Simmel, illustrating the distinction between the public and the private spheres, centrally noted that "both sound and the sense of hearing can be counted amongst the most potent mediating agents between both spheres" (qtd. in Fortuna 2001, 77). Simmel's notion of "impermeability" (1997a) of the private and the public spheres has bearing upon the voiced/vocal negotiation of identity in the backpackers' community. It corresponds with Ochs's notion of quotation as metadiscursively signaling "overhearing," since what is overheard in the public sphere sometimes enters the biographical sphere, and, in turn, "private" oral performance may assume or constitute public events.

As noted (heard) in previous chapters, an array of animators is audibly quoted in the performances, a fact that underscores the backpackers' claim concerning their community's conspicuous vocality. This polyphonically induced vocality is used by the backpackers to mark the presence of Israelis at designated sites, to demonstrate the accumulation of individual sounds to create a collective humming, and to demarcate acoustic enclaves of identity.

The newspaper caricature (fig. 3) astutely captures the interplay of sound and sight in the context of Israeli tourists (albeit not relating specifically to backpackers in the third world). The three figures in the caricature *look* Israeli and color-fully occupy the foreground of a familiar tourist scene, which implies that they are "tourists" (in the grayish background, London's Tower Bridge and the city's skyline are visible; two gray figures are visible closer, one walking a dog—suggesting that these figures are "locals"). The tourists' bodies themselves become the subject of the gaze of the viewers of the caricature. The shirts worn by the three bear Hebrew inscriptions: two names and icons of infantry military brigades (Golani [leftmost] and Paratroopers [center]) as well as a well-known Jerusalem soccer team (Beitar [right-most]). While the shirts supply visual signs and symbols of "Israeliness"—a juxta-position of military identity with a lower socioeconomic class (stereotypically associated with Beitar's notoriously violent and racist fans)—the Hebrew voice, which is *visual* in the caricature, is metadiscursive: "Guys, don't talk Hebrew." The Israeli tourists, who typically congregate and form a group (and are, not coincidentally, all men), are preoccupied with and reflect upon how they sound. The poignancy of the scene and its humor are attained through the discrepancy and tension between visual and auditory signs.

As indicated by Uri's quotation opening this chapter, the noisiness of Israelis is notorious. It complicates the common tourist scene in which "the realm of the audible is transfixed by the realm of the visible" (Young 1991, 223). As observed by Simmel, the contrast between sight and sound as modes of sociability is meaningful: "where only the sense of sight exploits proximity, more of a feeling of general-conceptual and unspecific unity or of a mechanical concurrence will result, whereas the possibility of speaking and hearing will produce individual, animated, organic feelings of unity" (Simmel 1997a, 155). Hence, any exploration into the social sounds of the speech community of the backpackers must take into consideration the dominance of vision in the context of late modern tourism (Urry 1990).

While the backpackers do not reflect or comment on how frequently they quote, which is quite natural (the act of quoting lying outside the speakers' "limits of awareness" [Silverstein 2001]), they often mention how *loud they sound.* Of the forty-four narrators interviewed, nearly half (a total of nineteen) *explicitly* mentioned of their own accord how "loud," "noisy," and "boisterous" Israelis are. They demonstrate this repeatedly with the help of quotations that evoke the sounds of the voices and their unique social vocality. The speakers perceive themselves, the groups in which they travel (that is, the choral voice), and their community in meta-discursive terms, as a *vocal collective.* The typical attributions they make conjure up the collective voice, which is evident in expressions such as "Israelis are the noisiest" and "Israelis are simply loud." The narrators' perception of "Israelis" as a community that is characterized vocally—it is first and foremost *loud*—has to do with their perception of themselves as a voiced collective and with their perception of what defines them as such, demarcating their spatial communal enclaves (Anteby-Yemini et al. 2005).

The metadiscursive observations of the backpackers touch upon a few features that clearly manifest their community's prominent vocal quality. First, they stress that regardless of the source of their loudness, it is particularly evident in a *transnational soundscape* that is not solely occupied by speakers of "Israeli-ish." The language they speak is heard noisily within a unique tourist discursive space; there, too, it establishes the auditory boundaries of the community. As attested by Uri in the epigraph above, in order to hear one's self, an Other ("a Nepalese" or the two Londoners whose silhouettes are seen in the caricature) must be present.

Second, the tourist context effects the construction of soundscapes in relation to the different senses. While tourism relies upon and fuels the modern primacy of vision over other senses, the construction of soundscapes relies upon voice and audibility. A Simmelian line of thought suggests that while tourists are by and large attracted to and can gaze upon (and take pictures of) attractions in an equal degree of accessibility, sound enclaves are limited in both physical and cultural dimensions: one needs to be physically close to the emitting source and to be familiar with the language in order for the soundscape to assume meaning. As observed by Simmel, while vision "provides such an identity of impression for a great number of people" (1997a, 117), hearing involves discerning and interpretation, which generate differences and nuances. Whereas the objects of the tourist gaze are there for all to look at and consume in a seemingly democratic fashion (or, in Simmel's words, "[t]here is almost no secret that could be transmitted exclusively by the eyes" [116]), the stories shared by a community live within the fleeting, restricted realm of linguistic sounds, hearings, and meanings.

"Israelis, they love making noise": Voiced Identity

The following excerpts illustrate the backpackers' reflection upon and evocation of the loud sounds produced in order to discern and signify the presence of Israelis. These reflections are concerned with what, in fact, qualifies as "Israeli." In doing so, narrators perform quotations, thus instantiating not only the authoritative content of the norm but also the *sound of the community*. In Gal's description of the travel preferences of Israeli backpackers, he uses a comparison with travelers from other countries. Specifically, he observes that the German tourists whom he met were older and conducted a more bourgeois type of travel (cf. Shiri's description of Swiss tourists in chapter 5, p. 99). After observing critically that their meals were brought to their tent, he concludes that the Germans' trip "is pretty sterile." From this culinary sterility he returns to Israelis and to the voices they sound.

Gal: Israelis are much noisier (*ra'ashanim*)

Chaim: Noisier?

Gal: Much more, much more. you—you, like, the minute you arrive you can immediately recognize (*lezahot*) the Israelis. they love making noise . . . they are much more obtrusive. you recognize the Israelis straight away . . . noise, like, shouts and (louder) "my man, what's

happening (*ahi, ma hamatsav*)?" (quieter) and music . . . Israelis,
you recognize them straight away.

Contrary to the "sterile" German tourists, Israelis are "much noisier." From this
contrastive juxtaposition noisiness emerges not only as a general characteristic of
Israelis but also as a higher state of authenticity: while in the context of tourism
sterility connotes unembodied, commercialized conduct, noisiness evokes sponta-
neity and "roughing it." The latter image echoes exotic images of Otherness as well
as of adventurousness.[1] Furthermore, noisiness is a social quality by which Israelis
are "recognized" or "identified" by others as well as by themselves. According to Gal,
this quality grants the collective its unique salience in a multinational, multilingual
space. "Noise, like, shouts," are semiotically more and less than signifiers—they are
symbols but also physical codes or signals that are "immediately," almost biologi-
cally, deciphered by their hearers.

As soon as Gal makes these metadiscursive observations, he uses noise-creat-
ing voices to illustrate how Israelis come to "recognize" each other. Gal thus performatively allows the listener—myself—to overhear these noises and thus to attend
to them directly during the narration. In a way, the phonic community assumes its
voice within the performance, a voice that is accessed by the audience. The short
string of direct reported speech is a good example. It consists of a familiar, succinct unit of "address and inquiry," which demonstrates the social sounds of Israelis
meeting and mingling ("what's happening?"). The quotation-closing utterance (the
quieter words "and music") indicates an additional channel of shared sounds, which
is mechanically mediated (it cannot be quoted) and thus effectively functions as a
postquotation formula.

Shortly afterward, Gal quotes again, when he notes that novice backpackers
inevitably gravitate toward experienced ones because of a considerable language
barrier with the other (non-Israeli) tourists:

Gal: When you arrive in the beginning you don't know the language

you don't know—

you don't even know how to—

when you don't know the language then—

like

you don't know ANYTHING

and they don't speak English

ABSOLUTELY

like

nobody speaks English

nothing ...

and it's very hard in the beginning

so you're pretty much counting on (*someh*) other Israelis that

"where's there a telephone here?"   (quickly)

and
   "what do you do?"   (quickly)
and
   "where—how do you send mail?"   (quickly)
and
   "how much does it cost?"   (quickly)
and
   "how do you get there?"   (quickly)
         you're pretty dependent (*taluy*) on Israelis

Gal emphasizes the experience of not knowing the language, which serves to justify the emergence of insulated enclaves. He uses the words "counting on" and "dependent" to describe a gradual process of inevitable, powerful social gravitation (cf. Bella and Na'ama in chapter 6, p. 109 and pp. 124–25). Israelis initially rely upon one another for travel information and very soon they find themselves dependent upon one another, immersed within sonorous communal enclaves. Gal demonstrates how this impelling social cohesiveness *sounds* by supplying a sequence of illustrative quotations.

The reported inquiries convey a degree of anxiety, which assumes a form of hasty verbosity: underlying the pragmatic and heroic backpacker ethos is an urgent need to be in constant touch with families and fellow travelers. Soundwise, backpackers extend their voice, searching for recognition and for belonging. As mentioned earlier, these evocations illustrate how peer travelers, and the collective authority they constitute, symbolically replace one's family.

Gal communicates the anxiety and dependency of novice backpackers by quoting hasty inquires that go unanswered. The repetitive sequence stylistically echoes the repetitive negations that precede it: it demonstrates how the assertion "you don't know the language" sounds and feels. The accumulation of five unreturned inquires (interrupted by the word "and" followed by a short pause), indicates how *dialogically oriented and dependent* the backpackers are: how it feels when urgent questions are not satisfied and are left unanswered. Note that the inquiries are urgent because the tourists are anxious—a fact that accords with the regressive and completely dependent state into which they (institutionally) enter upon traveling (Dann 1996).

Similarly, Ari (below) observes that "the Israeli temperament (*ophi*) is noisier and impolite." The characteristic that Gal describes as "sterile" is captured by the word "polite" in Ari's narrative, touching upon the perception and performance of politeness in Israeli culture (Blum-Kulka 1992; Maschler 2002a, 2003). Ari validates this observation by pointing out the intense persuasive sociability among Israelis.

Ari: I was here
   [I] had a good time
   I'm going to meet another FIVE HUNDRED Israelis on the way

I'll tell 'em

"look

you're going there?

go here

I enjoyed it here

there's a good hotel here"

so places are created that sort of belong to Israelis ...

also Israelis communicate among themselves more ...

immediately [when] you see an Israeli

you immediately have something to talk about

he's Israeli too

"where were you in the army?"   (quicker)

"what did you do?"   (quicker)

"where are you from?"   (quicker)

"GEE, YOU'RE MY NEIGHBOR"   (quicker)

he lives right here this guy   (quicker)

people meet their neighbors abroad

Ari performs the persuasive power of intense interpersonal communication in person, in his role of an agent/protagonist who participates in the dissemination of communal knowledge with missionary enthusiasm. The power of his words, he implies, is charismatically exponential: he can deflect hundreds of travelers off their expected routes onto new routes. The equation he depicts accounts for how enclaved soundscapes are interpersonally, ecstatically established. The progressive sequence moves from the narrator's personal experience (where he visited: "I was here") to impressions ("[I] had a good time") to a burning desire to share the experience with friends, which, finally, assumes the sound of direct reported speech ("look . . .").

Ari supplies quotations to perform the voice through which persuasiveness spreads. The framing of the first strip of reported talk by the first postquotation comment ("so places are created") indicates that Ari perceives the impressive quantity of Israelis as a qualitative factor. His words imply that numbers make for presence, which makes for noise, which in turn translates into spatial sovereignty. In this case, zeal is colonizing by means of the sound it generates. (Recall the point made in chapter 5 concerning the notion of "one nation, one language," according to which if you understand Hebrew you are an Israeli.)

If Gal previously assumed the role of the novice traveler bursting with questions, Ari assumes the complementary role of an accomplished traveler who knows all the answers and is well aware of their social value ("go here, I enjoyed it here"). The quotations are typically dialogic and frequently employ spatial deictic pronouns, establishing the existence of a sought-after location, generically referred to as "here." Approval correlates with physical proximity: what is "here" is valued and recommended, what is "there" is disapproved of.

Israelis, it seems, have nobody but themselves to talk with, talk about, and listen to. In line with Simmel's (1997b) observations, a typical transition occurs here between the senses: the utterance "you see an Israeli" (vision) is transformatively followed by the utterance "you have something to talk about" (sound), which is then followed by reported speech ("look").

The second strip of reported speech does not illustrate persuasive discourse, aiming at what the collective will share in the future. Rather, it indicates what the community *already* shares: the individuals' common experience. The quotations illustrate inquiries into earlier points in life. They are structured stylistically: the first two utterances probe into occupational roles—service in the military ("where were you in the army? what did you do?")—and the other two utterances are of a local geographical type, dealing with places of living ("where are you from? YOU'RE MY NEIGHBOR"). While the first two utterances are presented in the form of interrogations, the other pair presents a sequence of a question and a surprising exclamation, responding to an answer that we did not hear (given in reply to the inquiry "where are you from?").

Hence, two complementary genres are performed by Ari vis-à-vis reported speech. Both persuasion and biographical inquiries amount to an emic account of why Israelis are so noisy. After all, these reported strips are evoked while performing the vocality of the community, to which Ari referred in his earlier suggestion that boisterousness is part of the Israeli "temperament."

Ari concludes the quotation strip with a unique postquotation formula. Toward the end of the quotation he "skips" an utterance and does not report the reply of a silent speaker.[2] Yet he himself did hear the reply, and we are left with his excited response (the realization: "GEE, YOU'RE MY NEIGHBOR"). Ari closes and frames the quotations while shifting surprisingly *from the collective (and hypothetical) voice to the personal (and concrete) voice,* establishing a link between them and between the spheres they represent—a link that, in turn, affirms and validates the two. He accomplishes this by a sharp deictic shift from the there-and-then of the quoted dialogue to the hear-and-now of the conversation (see Ari's "Coca-Cola" aside in chapter 7, p. 135). He exits the quotation by instantly indicating a change of deictic pronouns and verbs of time and space, while nevertheless maintaining the excited hue of the quotations. There is no marked prosodic shift. It is as though the excitement, which was ignited within the reported exchange, spilled over beyond the boundaries of the report. The narrator skillfully performs a prosodic "carryover" effect, which, through a contrast with the deictic change, creates drama.

The excitement evident in the last utterance suggests that the general (collective) questions that are commonly exchanged among backpackers and that make for routine interactional ritual can in fact touch upon *each and every traveling individual.* These recurring interrogations, Ari implies, illustrate that the population of the community is limited and that, at least potentially, anyone can know anyone. Accordingly, the travelers are engaged either in zealous persuasion or in eagerly seeking acquaintances and establishing social ties—in which, Ari states, they are eventually successful (Almog 2000; Katriel 1986). The quotation sequence evocatively suggests that the cliché "it's a small world" is valid in the backpacking context. For those who choose to participate in this social rite, it is indeed a small and cohesive world, the diameter of which is made by "Israeli" sounds and voices.

Ari communicates genuine surprise as he makes the cliché evident to our listening ears. Having illustrated his point, he returns in his conclusion to the general contention made earlier—namely, that contrary to mere probability, one of the wonders of the great journey is that one can expect to meet one's close(st) neighbors in remote locations and to get to know them even better than before. Collective, impersonal resources are again personalized: although the inquiries make for a cloud of impersonal teeming noises, there is, in fact, an anchor to which one can fasten oneself.

In her discussion of voices and identity, Deborah Kapchan (2002) points out how, upon arriving in a new town as slaves, Moroccan slaves used to sing, and their words would travel through space and inform of their arrival. Describing this as a way of summoning acquaintances, she notes that the songs served "as auditory icons of identity, as sound 'links.'" By extending their voice, groups would identify themselves and at the same time establish links with their kin. Public spaces are composed of a matrix of interrelationships between embodied voices and performances of identity. In various spatial social settings, identity, sociality, gender, and authority are constituted in and through the extension and expansion of individual and group voices (Delph-Janiurek 1999; Markus and Cameron 2001).

Like moving bodies, expanding voices colonize, create hierarchies, and imbue spaces with meaning. As noted by Simmel (1997a, 1997b), acoustic expansion of voice affords selective accessibility and exclusive interpretation by individuals or groups in relation to sights observed by all. Consequently, a sense of commonality is established by means of the ways sounds and voices are shared, performed, and interpreted.

Bargaining Loudly: Competing for Authenticity

Another major factor to which the narrators attributed their community's prominent vocality engenders transcommunal discursive activity in which *speech with foreigners is performed.* In other words, in addition to heightened patterns of intra-community interactions, social noise was created at the periphery of the community as well. In particular, backpackers depicted how Israelis bargain noisily for the "best deal" with local merchants. In this way they construct the phonic borders of the speech community.

The frequent evocation of the discourse of bargaining is not in itself surprising. Like other types of tourists, backpackers frequently engage in haggling over prices of merchandise and services, an activity inherent in the consumer culture of tourism. The factor that leads to this bargaining mode is the consumer construction of prices of both products and services as *negotiable* (Kharraki 2001). In this, Orientalist and colonial perceptions play a role in relation to "peripheral" destinations. Shopping in Oriental(ized) "exotic" bazaars is hardly understandable—and surely not as rewarding—without the accompanying activity of haggling: it is part and parcel of the attraction itself. The negotiability of prices is a part of the social construction of a radical difference between home and destination, between Occident and Orient. The former is perceived as conforming to modern forms of discipline, whereby prices—as well as much of everyday life—are quantified, ordered, and regimented. The latter, in contrast, is constructed as exotic and carnivalesque.

Furthermore, backpackers indicate that they engage in bargaining in relation to "foreign" tourists. Thus, they distinguish themselves simultaneously both from local merchants—by enthusiastically engaging in bargaining, an activity that marks the consumer and the seller as inhabiting different sides of the Oriental barrier—and from "tourists," who are viewed by the Israelis as bargaining less passionately, persistently, and successfully than they do. Israelis construct a collective category by comparing themselves with other tourists, the image of the local merchant or haggler serving as a measuring scale.

Sharon observes that when it comes to bargaining, European tourists, unlike Israelis, are "nerds" and "squares" (*nahnahim* and *laflafim* are the words commonly used, cf. Gal's depiction of German tourists above, pp. 151–52, and chapter 5). Sharon continues, "Israelis are very prominent because of the noise they make . . . this should be said against us. Israelis are disliked VERY VERY much in the East. VERY much. they make noise and do damage." At the same time, Sharon indicates that Israelis enjoy a positive reputation for not being "easily fooled" by sly merchants. They are not "suckers," but instead bargain persistently and do not sway. The vocal prominence she notes is a result of an uncompromising manner of bargaining. The discursive activity grants the travelers the sought-after qualities of *toughness* (they do not compromise) and *authenticity* (unlike "bourgeois tourists," they are not suckers; they pay the "real" price). As observed by Sørensen (2003) and Binder (2004, 103), prices symbolize authenticity: if backpackers are cheated in the prices they pay, they might well be cheated out of authenticity elsewhere.

Odit locates the source of the social sonority in the conspicuous voice created by groups while fervently engaged in bargaining: "[Groups] make a lot—it's the NOISE, everything's noisy." Immediately after addressing the noisiness of the choral voice, she changes the subject, offering what constitutes an explanation, focusing on the "sucker phobia."

Odit: And another thing that really bothered me sometimes

[is] the sucker principle (*element hafreier*)

like—the Israeli?

what's important for him is not to be a sucker

in the East he bargains for money

"A PRICE ISN'T A PRICE
(quicker)

YOU NEED TO SORTA LOWER IT"
(quicker)

so the Israeli bargains to the end

and something the merchants in India know

                              they know that if they do business with an Israeli then

they'll naturally reduce the prices more than they would've with Brits or Japanese

    for instance ...

    the minute you get somewhere

          you come—

        you meet an Israeli [and] ask him

and he'll tell you	(quickly)
"I was here	(quickly)
I ate here"	(quickly)
what dish is best to order	(quickly)
what hotel	(quickly)
what room	(quickly)
"where I shopped—	(quickly)
did shopping	(quickly)
how much did I spend shopping"	(quickly)
	all the time
	all the time

Odit's description of the noise generated by groups of Israelis carries her associatively to recall a second, related feature accounting for their loudness: the unique role of bargaining, which is related to the image of the *freier*, the sucker. By framing this collective quality in a formulaic phrase ("the sucker principle"), the narrator communicates that saving face is crucial for the creation of social distinction and hierarchy. Indeed, it is no less than a social "principle." Various destinations, and particularly the "East," emerge as *touristic practice zones,* where constant bargaining for the "real" value is the medium through which the status of "not being a sucker" is pursued. Prices in this "exotic" region are not only negotiable but challenging. It is essential for them to be reduced considerably: the more the better. As Pamela Riley (1988, 323) points out humorously about backpackers, "how humiliating it is to pay more than others are paying!"

Indeed, bargaining enables backpackers to "find ego enhancement from getting the 'best value'" (Riley 1988, 320). Social hierarchies are repeatedly established through the performance of bargaining: one's high position on the social ladder is validated by comparing how effectively one has bargained, which amounts to, as Riley says, an "important yardstick for measuring success." Indeed, this is expressed in the first reported utterance, in which Odit performs a dictum that asserts that things are presented differently for tourists than they actually are. "A price isn't a price" means: a representation is not real (or true or authentic) unless effort is exercised to uncover whatever underlies it.

Sørensen similarly points to the central role of bargaining in establishing one's "road status." The backpackers' heated pursuit of bargaining is linked, according to Sørensen, with their preoccupation with hierarchies: "No fixed mechanism can convey the individual's road status and no continuous social relations can confirm and transmit previous ascertainments of it. It has to be communicated in every social encounter" (2003, 857). This continuous exchange, Sørensen adds, "is the key method by means of which the numerous brief encounters with other backpackers are systematized and embedded with meaning." Expectedly, the query "How much did you pay?" routinely opens social interactions.

Hierarchization within the community is discursively accomplished by engaging in transtourist discourse of the genre of bargaining as well as by intratourist discourse of the genre of boasting and comparing quantified results with fellow travelers. Furthermore, because bargaining is a *quantifiable social activity,* conveniently yielding a number (akin to hiking at a certain pace to a certain height, taking a certain number of pictures during the trip, and so on), it conveniently enables the location of one's performances on a competitive social score chart.

As previously mentioned, a comparison is also drawn with tourists of other nationalities (see note 1 in this chapter). Though Brits and Japanese are mentioned in this case as particularly gullible consumers, they provide an illustration of "Westerners" in general (or, more accurately, of tourists from affluent societies), who are not as reputed among merchants as Israelis and with whom a retail honor agreement has not been established. From the Israeli backpackers' point of view, non-Israeli backpackers lack the knowledge and/or the stamina to bargain properly ("to the end"), or even to bargain at all.

Odit turns to a familiar illustration of the precise, detailed, and (therefore) conclusive nature of the information circulated by word of mouth (certain dishes in certain restaurants) and of its accessibility and immediacy ("the minute you get somewhere"). In this sequence, she oscillates between quoting and mentioning, thus evoking the noisiness created by groups by depicting the fervency of their comparing their performances with one another. The rapid sequence terminates with a repetitive quotation-closing formula ("all the time, all the time") which, familiarly, attests to the unremitting and intense nature of the abrupt interactions she performs.

The most common word employed to capture the image against which Israeli backpackers' road status is pursued is *freier.* The word is a popular key symbol borrowed from Yiddish into Hebrew (Bloch 1998, 2003; Maschler 2001). It connotes gullibility, someone who is easily fooled. It came into popular use at the demise of the Sabra epoch and reflected dramatic changes in the relationship between the individual and the collective, a period when the sacrifice of personal resources for the benefit of the collective with no guarantee of a substantial return—the ultimate ideal of the Zionist-socialist imagination—was deemed negative, even embarrassing (Roniger and Feige 1992, 283). Conversely, taking care of one's own interests, well-being, and material comfort not only lost its shamefulness but became (and still remains) a source of pride and a subject for boasting.

The image of the freier, which touches upon personal honor, competitiveness, and avoiding loss of face as well as upon gender-related connotations of bravery, is frequently evoked in the backpackers' stories. "The freier concept," Bloch (2003, 133) observes, "is so central a part of daily life [in Israel], so deeply rooted, and so taken for granted as premise for interaction, that it is used as a motivational appeal in various types and at different levels of persuasion." The issues with regard to which the concept is traditionally employed suggest, yet again, that when the backpackers are engaged in a transcommunity discursive activity, they are in fact negotiating identity. As mentioned earlier, the Other—nature, native, and, in this case, local merchants and tourist operators—provides a seemingly interactive backdrop against which speakers perform and affirm their identities in the ears of their peers.

Parenthetically, the discourse of bargaining echoes more traditional modes of conversational interaction among Jews of eastern European origin, in which argumentation is a salient feature (Kirshenblatt-Gimblett 1974; Myerhoff 1978; Schiffrin 1984; Tannen 1984). Although these features have been successfully suppressed by Sabra discourse and ideology, some of them have resurfaced in various forms in different discursive sites and settings in contemporary Israeli society (Blum-Kulka 1997).

According to the underlying rules of bargaining discourse, *not* being a freier is perceived by narrators (mostly by women) as being obnoxiously loud. Gender-related aspects of the freier symbol juxtapose saving face with manly-Sabra boisterousness. In the present context, it evokes the powerful romantic dichotomy that equates women with nature and serenity and juxtaposes them with manliness, technology, and the noise they generate.[3]

Hearing Range: Traveling in and out of Acoustic Enclaves

The counterpart of loud, animated performances is performances of *listening*—a fact that, if not fully acknowledged, leaves live language in the public and private domains "limited, reduced-by-half" (Corradi 1995, 2). Of concern here are soundscapes, or social hearing ranges, beyond which there is either silence or foreign/Other voices. When backpackers evoke communal voices, they performatively *re*create a fraction of that soundscape. They metonymically give their audience access to the communal voices of which they intensely speak.

Bella, for instance, comments metadiscursively on the social audibility of backpackers by indicating, in a typical manner, that they congregate in "Israeli hotels," where the presence of "tourists" is rare. There, she asserts, *sound,* and the knowledge it engulfs, travel selectively.

Bella: I often traveled with the tourists
> I asked them
>> "did you do the Azangate trek?
>>> "no
>>>> we haven't heard (*lo shama'anu*) of it"
> that means people almost never hear about it

almost only Israelis do it

                   that specific trek

      tourists hardly do it ...

it's all about who hears it

        and who doesn't

              and the tourists

they're the ones who never hear about it

  and the Israelis do hear about it

Bella repeatedly refers to the phonic dimension of interpersonal dissemination of knowledge. She constructs a hierarchical linguistic barrier between "tourists" and "Israelis." The five instances of the word "hear" are employed in an attempt to explain how exclusivity is achieved via sound: an understanding of "Israeli" language as well as physical proximity to its animating sources. Although not comprehending the language is a sure disqualifier, comprehension is in itself not a sufficient factor: one needs to be located *within* the soundscape and have *access* to its emitting sources.

Sure enough, Bella performs quotations in order to demonstrate that she had personally inquired of tourists whether they had participated in certain activities and visited certain sites frequented by Israelis. In their reported voices, tourists persuasively demonstrate how hearing—or rather not hearing—is an excluding factor. Under the supposition that "hearing" is a prerequisite of "doing," the underlying maxim promoted by Bella is: if you do not hear (of) it, you cannot do it.

But Bella achieves even more. As indicated by the second half of the excerpt, she is explicit (reflexive, one might say) about the constitutive fashion in which she uses sounds and voices ("it's all about who hears it"). She concludes with a generalization that establishes the centrality of voices and soundscapes in the construction of communality. Her conclusion implies that the two groups are *defined* by what they do or do not *hear:* "tourists," and more generally "people," are those who routinely do not hear ("never hear"), whereas "Israelis" are those who routinely do hear. While being out-of-sound is constitutive in a negative way—it leads *elsewhere,* away from the beaten track of the collective itinerary, being inside the sound/voice range literally means following each other's sound-steps. It seems that it is not storytelling rights that are at stake here, but their complementary halves: *hearing rights*—that is, physical proximity to collective sounding.

Narrators allude to the "commotion" that typically takes place in backpackers' enclaves. These cacophonic communicative spaces are akin to halls or living rooms through which Israelis travel. Tourists do not frequent these spaces because, as the narrators argue, "they don't like this commotion." One backpacker describes a Dutch traveler who was supposed to join her group for a certain activity. She observes that "the Dutch was shocked when he heard about it, he didn't know what it is. he heard about something different from his friend in London, which is something we didn't hear of at all. you see, it's different paths, unless they [tourists] connect tightly with Israelis and follow them." Different paths or sound-paths make for different itineraries of identity. Unless foreigners choose to follow Israelis sufficiently close as to (physically) hear them, follow their communal voice, and acknowledge its authority, the paths followed by "Israelis" and "tourists" remain irreconcilable.

Since the collective soundscape is under the sovereignty of the collective voice and of the authoritative norm it promotes, traveling *beyond* the hearing range is viewed unfavorably. This is evinced when backpackers indicate they have found themselves—seemingly inadvertently—beyond the soundscape of familiar voices. While the narrators at times celebrate quietness, equating it with the sought-after experience of tranquility, in other cases they express concern over the dramatic predicament. In Meirav's excerpt in chapter 4, for example (see pp. 68–70), the narrator accounts for how she found herself separated from the group. She mentions that on three separate occasions she did not hear the choral voice ("I didn't hear them anymore"), and on each of these it was an alarming experience.

Meirav's impatience and impulsivity lead her to hike at a considerably faster pace than that of the group, which, she admits, was improper conduct. As she insists on repeatedly evoking *sound* rather than sight with regard to intracommunity communication, vision is reserved in her account for depicting and constructing the Other, whether nature or native. Indeed, Meirav opposes the triple references of losing her companions' voices ("AGAIN I stopped hearing them") to the evocations of vision, which are related to two dubious and frightening (male) strangers and to the ominous, darkening scenery ("the jungle darkness settles in earlier . . . I saw these couple of men approaching in my direction"). Positioning herself beyond the hearing range of the choral voice is nothing short of dangerous. What lies beyond the hearing range—what is *visible but not audible or hearable*—is utterly foreign and frightening: the moment that Meirav finds herself beyond the choral soundscape is precisely the moment at which twilight becomes visually apparent with a menacing air. This effectively infuses the narrative with drama.

Transcending the range of the group voice means traveling beyond the possibility of calling for help and beyond the discursive range of quoting. It is a "no-quoting land," a space in which the physical, as well as the symbolic, connection with backpackers is momentarily severed.

The repeated evocations of loudness are complemented by references to the quality of quietness. This type of reference contributes to the construction of exclusive, insular soundscapes where an acoustic void is experienced, one that is located beyond the physical-vocal range of the gushing sonorous enclaves. Such spaces assume the "feminine" half of a romantic dichotomy, in which verbosity and loudness are associated with machismo performance. Indeed, the commonplace tourist perception concerning rural, remote, and exotic locations encompasses serenity and quietness as central features. These are components of sublime primitiveness and remoteness, constructed on the basis of their distance and difference from the noise produced by modern machinery in industrialized urban centers (Bijsterveld 2001; Dann 1996, 102; Fortuna 2001).

In the narratives, tranquility and quietness are presented as experiences attained by traveling *away* from the noisy Israeli collective. They endow the backpackers with a unique sense of singularity. As Nadav says with exhilaration, outdoor activities are done in "UTTER silence . . . utter silence, alone, and clear clear air. it's a wonderful feeling." Orly mentions that one of the peak experiences she had was when she bathed in a river not far from Kathmandu: "there were no Israelis there and it was awfully quiet."

Quietness is commonly associated with images of the Other. For instance, Vered recalls several instances in which she experienced quietness joyfully. In one case, she mentions a porter hired by the group who aided her and carried her heavy backpack while she was touring the northern Indian state of Himachel Pradesh. She speaks of him admiringly, observing that he did "everything so quietly. without saying a word. and without—usually if you're with Israelis, it's always a lot of noise, a lot of jabbering (*kishkushim*) . . . no one offers you help without it being heard."

These illustrations demonstrate the association of outdoor spaces and Other peoples with quietness. Alone in the wilderness, not being within group and collective hiving soundscapes endows a unique, particularly rewarding experience. For Vered, the help offered by a local porter is a gentlemanly—albeit servile—gesture, which she found far more pleasing than the boisterous manner characteristic of the help-giving behavior of her male cohort.

Odit's description of men as being particularly loud and obnoxious, thus generating a marked contrast with the experience of pure, serene nature, is evident in the following, in which she conflates noise and machinery (motorcycles) with masculinity. These two, she suggests, intrude in conjunction on otherwise pastoral, idyllic sceneries. When Odit describes how she and her female group companions bathed in the river one morning in the midst of a trek in northern India, she observes: "It was very primal . . . I simply felt like I'm in a painting from the Middle Ages (1) where you see women bathing, very primal, very beautiful, in the nature, with nothing . . . the ultimate quietness. it's a large part of trekking—ultimate quietness . . . to wash our clothes in the river like in the paintings. really, to feel like in a painting (1) with the horses, the horses near the lake. in my eyes it's picturesque." Odit depicts conservative feminine imagery, which is intimately associated with nature, through the evocation of vision (gaze). She establishes a relation between sight, epitomized in her evocation of a "Middle Ages" painting, and the utter lack of sound. Indeed, paintings are absolutely devoid of sound. The image is mute, and its muteness, combined with a nostalgic (romantic) sentiment, adds all the more to its serene and sublime detachment from noisy everyday life in Israel and from its reproduction in backpackers' enclaves. As expected, Odit does not perform quotations, for it is precisely her aim to keep these descriptions *mute*.

Shortly afterward Odit alludes to noisy gatherings of Israelis that intrude upon the aforementioned pastoral setting: "You see a gang of five Israeli men ah arriving loudly and declaratively on motorcycles[4] . . . it's very very noticeable . . . they make a whole lot of noise. we have this character. if you're somewhere that's not here

[Israel] you'll understand it . . . you understand—ah our character, where we come from—that is, I realized why we founded a state (we laugh)."

The previously described pastoral and feminine scenery is intruded upon by the arrival of a loud motorized "gang" or "bunch" (*havura*) of Israeli men. Loudness, congregation in large groups, and unwillingness to relinquish technology, even temporarily, are clustered into a succinct description of the macho nature of Israeli men and how masculinity invades and contaminates (feminine) nature through sound.

The observation made by Odit transcends the loud group of motorcyclists per se to consider the fundamental nature of their boisterousness and vulgarity and the contribution of these traits to the identity of the masculine Israeli collective. The connection she draws extends to the entire Zionist enterprise. Loudness, Odit argues, captures both the sounds of the activities of "organizing and congregating" and some inherent trait of Jews that could account for their national congregation.

Sound(scapes) and Identity Back Home: A Phonic Digression

The frequent metadiscursive references to collective and choral vocalities and to the soundscapes they generate, vivified by prosodic performances, echo cultural patterns of interaction in Israel (see note 4 above). The narrators emphasize the role of vocality and acoustics, of sound and soundscapes, in assuming meaning and constructing identities, commonly attributing this fact to the "Israeli nature." Hence, a digression "back home," to Israel, is worthwhile in order to examine how language sounds and how soundscapes establish sovereignty and map identity. After all, it is at "home" that the youths initially internalize the play of voices and identities that they later incorporate in a polyphonic touristic theater. We commence, therefore, with a depiction of informal interpersonal interactions in Israel and gradually ascend toward more—much more—hegemonic constructions of identity vis-à-vis sonorities and soundscapes in public spheres.

The prevalence of noisiness in the Israeli public sphere has often been acknowledged. In researching Sabra culture, Almog (1997, 373), reminds us that the most common greeting in Hebrew—*ma nishma?*—literally means "what is (being) heard?" This suggests that common patterns of interpersonal communication are closely linked to hearsay, to word of mouth, and perhaps to gossip. Furthermore, ma nishma and other such terms are status symbols, indicating, as Almog notes, "proximity to actions and wide social networks." As noted elsewhere (Noy 2005a), within these semiotics of interpersonal communication, a message heard is of higher value than a message read; the listening ear supersedes the reading eye, for the former is perceived as being closer to the realm of action and events (consider words such as *hitrahshut,* meaning "occurrence," the root of which—*r, h, sh*—means "sizzle" or "rustle," placing the phonic realm at the very core of the cultural signification of "action").

Katriel's depiction of the dugri speech style (1986, 2004) implies a range of prosodic performances: from toughness, authority, and decisiveness to a pragmatic matter-of-factness. Interestingly, another underlying feature of dugri speech suggested by Katriel is the "spirit of communitas." Consequently, the loud and assertive prosody of this speech style has everything to do with the creation of a speech/sound community, the boundaries of which are constructed acoustically. Assertiveness, together with the state of interpersonal interaction in Israel, which is a "verbally aggressive society in which people frequently express themselves with vehemence" (Bloch 2000a, 54), amounts to a collective prosody.

The overwhelming noisiness of urban traffic, coupled with drivers' argumentative exchange of shouts and horn blows, are commonly noted by observers and visitors to Israel. This public sphere is seen as particularly loud, aggressive, and vulgar. For instance, in an article in a weekend supplement of *Ha'aretz* (September 14, 2001) titled "Vulgar Country," columnist Uriah Shavit notes that the road is an emblem space of vulgarity, where "the most decent citizens become ugly monsters" and which "hosts the entire variety of vulgar conduct in Israel" (36).[5]

As suggested by research on bumper stickers, public spaces of automobility are highly communicative (Bloch 2000a, 2000b; Salamon 2001). Political/ideological and other bumper stickers are extremely prevalent in Israel and appear to be used by car owners to perform their collective identity publicly.

Incidentally, public performance of collective identity is also evident in the excessive use of cellular phones in the country (Raz and Shapira 1994). The heightened patterns of the use of cellular communication indicate and are partly sustained by the unique interface of private and public (or mezzo-public) spheres in everyday culture.

At the uppermost, hegemonic level—that of the state—the activation of a countrywide net of thunderous war sirens creates and sustains a sovereign soundscape through which sounds and spaces fuse into meaning and identity. The last activation of the penetrating, sinusoidal roar in wartime was during the Gulf War in 1991 (when Israel was targeted by missiles launched by Saddam Hussein's Iraq).[6] Yet, the infrastructure of the war sirens is activated on a regular basis, not only during war. The sirens operate thrice a year, in a flat, rather than sinusoidal, blow (an "all clear" signal) in order to signify national commemoration. The three instances occur on National Memorial Day (twice) and a week later on Holocaust Memorial Day (a single activation).

During their commemorative peacetime activation, when the sirens' call is heard mechanically throughout Israel (and is broadcast electronically on all public channels), citizens are all expected to stand still. These three occasions, which powerfully conflate the memory of those who perished in the Holocaust and of Israeli Defense Forces (IDF) soldiers who were killed in action, on the one hand, and the performance of commemoration through the activation of the war alarm, on the other hand, are chilling experiences for Israelis. They draw the "landscapes of national sacrifice" (Handelman and Shamgar-Handelman 1997, 89). The sirens' roar, epitomizing the state's supreme authority and command, does more than create a mesmerizing soundfield. The sirens' commanding emission suppresses other—

everyday—urban sounds (such as motor engines), with the effect of sustaining a hegemonic, uniform *soundfield* rather than a heterogeneous, polyphonic *soundscape* (Rodaway 1994).

Compared with interpersonal interaction in public spheres (whether direct or mediated), war/commemoration sirens do not entail dialogue. One can hardly talk (back) or honk (back) at the sirens' roar. The authoritative voice of the state is one-sided, monologuist, during whose expression all else is still—dialogue and discourse included. Paraphrasing Fiske (1989), it could be said that the siren amounts to "national speech act," connoting and commemorating the sound of a collective grieving roar. Performatively, these immense sounds of memorialization make use of a roar, expanding in space to fill, physically and symbolically, the absence—or the "unconsolable presence" (Handelman and Shamgar-Handelman 1997, 114)—of the dead.

Other soundscapes vibrantly exist alongside the national hegemonic soundscape. Muslim soundscapes, for instance, are constructed and extended in villages and cities via the muezzins' calls for prayer. The convergence of Jewish and Muslim soundscapes in mixed cities yields interesting variations on the hegemony of the nation-state. For instance, during the Jewish Day of Atonement (Yom Kippur), when public and private transportation has been stilled, the muezzins' calls for prayer are significantly more audible. On the eve of Yom Kippur (October 5, 2003), the *Ma'ariv* newspaper described Jewish-Arab tension in the cities of Tel Aviv and Jaffa: "In an exhibition of coexistence between the peoples, the leaders of the Muslim population in Jaffa agreed to be considerate with regard to the Jewish population during the holiday, and to operate the muezzins' loudspeakers on a relatively low volume" (16). The article quotes the head of the Islamic Movement in Jaffa as saying: "The Arabs in Jaffa respect the feelings of the Jews, and on Yom Kippur close the shops and do not drive on the streets. I promise that whoever visits Jaffa during the day will think he has reached Bnei-Brak [an ultra-Orthodox Jewish city]"(!)

On an interpersonal level of communication, too, cultural differences within Israeli society can be conceptualized in terms of sound and noise. While the Sabra dugri speech style connotes spontaneous, argumentative, and loud interactions, Katriel (2004) points out that the Arab *Musayara* contrastively represents a compliant, intricate, intentionally slow and soft-spoken manner of interaction.

To conclude, the above phonic and sonic spheres illustrate the Simmelian (1997a) notion of "impermeability" of the private and the public spheres vis-à-vis the emission and consumption of voices and noises. They demonstrate how in different, albeit connected, planes, the constitution and negotiation of meaning, identity, and cohesion are achieved by means of sounds and soundscapes in public spaces in Israeli culture. In this light, the backpackers' extranational enclaves echo a familiar play of sounds both within the community and at its fringes—in the zones of vocal contact with the Other. This play of sounds establishes the spaces of national identity through the extension of a physical voice that embodies a dominant collective authority.

INTERMEZZO 2: FROM QUOTATION TO SELF-TRANSFORMATION

Travel to Medieval Europe and find . . . yourself.
Tourist advertisement

Previous chapters have shown how quotations and voices facilitate a performative, constitutive mode of storytelling. Reported words supply the association or link between the dual performances of the backpackers: traveling and narrating. The point is that in order for speech to be *reported,* a taleworld needs to exist from which speech can be drawn into the present. Travel—monopolized, commercialized, and institutionalized by the modern industry of global tourism—supplies precisely that: an instant ("ready-made") and "authentic" taleworld. In the case of backpacking tourism, the great journey supplies an animated social scene, a vibrant social strip in the travelers' biography, crowded with words, voices, and events.

Previous chapters have also shown how narrators conclude strips of reported speech by framing them in evaluative, postquotation conclusion formulae. These serve to mark the termination of the reported utterance and—like Labovian (1972) codas—to bring the taleworld up to the here-and-now of the telling. The concluding of quotations marks the advancement of the plot and the changing of the narrative. Hence, quotations in narratives—"quotativents"—play a determinant role in the progression and development of personal narratives (Buttny 1998).

The next chapter argues that this holds true for narrative identity in general, in which events constitute the substance (the "matter") from which identity is artfully carved. In this sense, tourist practices in general, and the great journey in particular, supply occurrences and adventures in abundance that serve in the construction of identity. When the backpackers conclude their trip and return home, they symbolically *emerge from quotation* and construct the travel in hindsight as a formative episode in their lives.

Akin to quotation, the trip becomes a bound semiotic unit, a fragment knitted into the biography of the backpacker. Once the youths return home to the sphere of everyday life from which they departed months earlier, the phenomenological Turnerian cycle (based on van Gennep's triadic model of rites de passage from 1909)—departure, liminality, reaggregation—is complete: their narratives attest that something unique within them has changed. In their biographies, the trip amounts to a Labovian "complicating act" (1972), which propels a dramatic sense of self-change.

Tourists render liminality as a state associated not only with "action" but also with "authenticity" (see chapter 1). As a result, they performatively carry with them the commodity of authenticity from the taleworld into the storyrealm, or from the destinations into their daily lives. By visiting "authentic" sites and consuming authenticity, the backpackers themselves become endowed with and touched by authenticity, which then permeates the narrating as well as the traveling. This permeation, which lends to the narrations some of the unique awe of the trip itself, is established performatively by means of quotation, which communicates "a more *authentic* piece of information than an indirect quote" (Holmes 1986, 16, my emphasis).

The notion of departing from an original context rests—like quotations—upon romanticist phenomenology, which provides the "glue" between persuasion (see chapter 2), reported speech, and the performance of self-change. Discussing "romanticist linguistics," Vološhinov (1973, 119) remarks that the use of reported speech stresses individualization and "maintain[s] its integrity and authenticity." A causal connection is established between travel, language, and personal change, between "outer" and "inner" transitions and changes.

Accordingly, what can be said about quotations may also be said about the self. The relationship between the well-delineated reported speech and its context makes for a strong textual metaphor of the correlation between self (internal) and environment (external; see Gergen 1991). Indeed, if tourists were to be construed as quotations (Rojek and Urry 1997), they would be embodiments (souvenirs) of authenticity.

No wonder, therefore, that tourist commercials of the type quoted above are common. These commercials indicate that the discourse of self-change is not merely a consequence of contemporary touristic endeavors, it is their raison d'être. The discourses of romanticist tourism, which are particularly dominant in the case of backpacking, perpetuate the mutual autonomy of part (quotative/individual) and whole (context) as they touch upon the poetics of difference. With the evangelist spread of psychotherapeutic discourses in Western and Westernizing societies (Gubrium and Holstein 2000, 2001), corporate tourism, too, has joined in and enjoyed the lucrative discursive resource of identity and self-change. The augmentative fusion of the discourses and the practices evinced in tourism provides an experiential, epistemological, and communicational syntax by means of which the construction of identity is credibly accomplished. Nowadays, tourists are expected to frame their travel experiences in terms of identity, which in turn serves to evaluate and validate their experiences. Indeed, as we shall shortly see, by admitting the profound change they underwent, backpackers acknowledge and verify their unique experience.

An animated and animating set of social voices is a prerequisite for an inner sense of selfhood and self-change (Handelman 2002, 283). Addressing the subject of religiously inspired self-change, anthropologist Don Handelman contends that "the self must interact socially with itself, within itself, in order for the person to exist socially in the world" (239). It is by means of this new array of social voices that were acquired during the great journey and by means of these voices' polyphonic narrative web of exchanges that accomplished backpackers performatively bestow upon themselves and upon their audiences a compelling sense of inner change.

Further, through evoking polyphony, a mode of dialogical and intersubjective communication is established, essential for the performance of self-change: this mode interactionally draws the audience into the taleworld, positioning the audience as a character sustaining a sense of inner change. In order to achieve this sense in an authoritative manner, narrators rely on authoritative texts, such as quotations.

As Bauman and Briggs argue, following Bakhtin (1990, 77), "an authoritative text, by definition, is one that is maximally protected from compromising transformation." Hence, quotations assist in performatively constructing a sense of selfhood that is imbued with authority.

Finally, the experience of self-change brings to closure the rhetoric of persuasion in a satisfying manner (see chapter 2). It suggests that backpackers undergo *transformation in attendance:* from hearers to speakers, from audience to performer, from layperson to accomplished backpacker. Persuasion and self-change are thus complementary facets in the backpacking narrative community. With performance as their common denominator, the dialogical genres of persuasion and self-change together establish the narrators' identity and sense of belonging, two accomplishments that together constitute a contextualized rhetoric achievement (Keane 1997; Lee and Roth 2004, para. 36; Shotter 1993).

SITE III

Conclusions

9

Self-Transformation

Self-identity for us forms a *trajectory* across the different institutional set-tings of modernity over the *durée* of what used to be called the "life-cycle."

Anthony Giddens

One does not simply see more of the world . . . one also accepts the invitation to become a better person.

Chris Rojek and John Urry

In the travel narratives they tell, backpackers re-create themselves as *changed* persons. The great journey, they enthusiastically admit, supplies more than mere recreation and even more than a profound experience per se: rather, it is downright transformative. Upon performing their travel experiences, the backpacking narrators establish a heightened dialogical context that facilitates powerful claims of self-change.

Admittedly, these claims were not apparent from the start; it was well into the research that their salience struck me. This was probably due to the neatly seamless fashion in which they were incorporated in the narration as well as to the obvious ("naturalized") state identity claims have in the discourse of contemporary tourism in general. All in all, twenty-eight (approximately 70 percent) interviewees mentioned self-change spontaneously (as did all the others upon specific questioning). While discussing the backpackers' claims of profound self-change and the intricate way they were tacitly woven into our conversations will be explored at length later, I wish to begin by first attending in general terms to the theme of self-change within personal narratives and second by exploring the relationship between contemporary tourism discourses and identity.

A pervasive genre by means of which individuals articulate identity focuses on the theme of self-change, in which narrators describe a dramatic moment or episode in their biography, one that generated a major and enduring self-change. In such cases, a substantial deflection from the expected life trajectory is depicted, a pivotal moment in which the narrator's identity is altered. Though the raison d'être for the change is rooted in the past, the theme of self-change powerfully engages the present and carries futuristic prospects as well (Langellier 1999; Ochs 1997; Ochs

173

and Capps 1996). In particular, such claims of personal change constitute, by their generic definition, a clear instance of projection into the present and the future, as they performatively carry experiences from past to present. After all, if the change that is depicted is indeed an enduring one and its meaningfulness does not cease, it should only naturally be enacted and displayed in the act of narration.

Although self-change is commonly (and commonsensically) construed as a theme within narratives of personal identity, it is challenging to conceptualize it differently: rather than constituting a pivotal moment across some preassumed progressive trajectory, it is proposed here that the self-change theme may, in fact, be *the only or the primary* instance of identity. If, as suggested by Giddens in the epigraph above, identity is to be thought of as a trajectory, then it is possible that the themes encompassing transformative experiences are the hallmark of late modern times. For if people are continually (trajectorily) becoming, then the pervasive and constitutive means by which people can relate to, articulate, and experience their selfhood is through the mechanism of self-change.

This, indeed, sits well with the exponential growth of international tourism over the last decades. Tourism acts as both a consequence of and an aid to the Western enterprise of engaging in a "panoply of going concerns" (Gubrium and Holstein 2000, 102) that supply the discursive conditions for self-realization. Note that since tourism is commonly perceived as a haven, a recess, from the burdens and constraints of everyday modernized life, and not as additional institutional engagement, it is (uncannily) located in the moments in peoples' lives that are thought of as not "tangled" in discourse, wherein narratives of identity are susceptible to the effects of (trans)formative institutional discourses.

In line with Giddens's observation above, recently we have come to acknowledge the crucial interrelationship that exists between institutions—and the institutional discourses and practices they embody—and identities. Various modern institutions bear a fundamental influence on whom we are continually telling ourselves and others that we have become. As Gubrium and Holstein (2000, 97) appealingly argue, the self is currently "big business, the stock-in-trade of a world of self-constituting institutions, which increasingly compete with each other for discerning and designating identities." This state of affairs is arguably one of the hallmarks of late modernity, when the self is "saturated" by technologically disseminated institutional discourses (Gergen 1991). These discourses are appropriated or consumed by individuals and become resources for the construction of identity (Bruner 1991; Taylor 1989). Put more simply, these institutions supply us with "something (interesting) to talk about."

Yet it is not only that identity is "saturated," or that institutions compete with each other over individuals' and groups' identities. More actively from the consumers' perspective, there is an enormous inventory or arsenal of resources, narratives, and alternatives by which identities may be consumed, elaborated, and performed. Particularly in relation to voluntarily institutional engagements, such as tourism, the point should be made that what consumers choose to pursue is a consequence of the identities they choose to perform.

The literature on tourists in general and on backpackers in particular points to how the myriad experiences of tourists become narrative resources, employed in the capacity of performing and (re)establishing identity. As Elsrud (2001, 606) observes of backpackers, "through establishing a (mythologized) image of Otherness, a story about self-identity can be told" (see also Adler 1989; Bruner 2005; Desforges 2000, 938; Neumann 1992, 1999; Selwyn 1996).

Since the trip is the event with which identity is intimately correlated, claims of touristic identity are performed in terms of a dramatic episode-related self-change; "touristic stories," Desforges (2000, 927) notes, "are used to present new self-identities."

Indeed, as long as tourist excursions are commonly perceived as precisely that—that is, excursions from habitual everyday life—the experiences they endow are seemingly separated from the "rest" of the biography. This structure accounts for why tourist narratives frequently relate to and are framed by the impression of self-change. To refer again to Desforges, touristic stories are used to present new self-identities because by being framed as "touristic" they suggest an excursion from (or intrusion into) the linear progressive trajectory of "normal" biographies. Interestingly, however, due to the processes of commercialization and mediatization, contemporary tourism pervades lives and is in fact a less and less autonomous and secluded practice. This is another way to state—*this time vis-à-vis the language of identity*—that tourism and modern culture(s) are enmeshed.

Identity and Authenticity

Though the structural dimensions of different touristic activities may vary greatly, they share a number of underlying factors. The dazzling array of forms of tourism is actually rooted in a few founding discourses or metanarratives that are the industry's energizing forces. These discourses inspire and shape the touristic experience, by means of which tourists can construct their identities. Thus, although backpackers comprise a more or less formally distinct touristic subgroup (see chapter 1), their experiences and underlying discourses are not unique to this subgroup but are rather shared by other forms of tourism (Richards and Wilson 2004b, 2004c).

Research on tourism indicates that one of the basic motivations of tourists to travel pertains to the theme of "authenticity." According to MacCannell (1976), the modern tourist's primary motivation for travel is the pursuit of authentic experiences. In an alienated, industrialized, and homogenized modern world, individuals romantically seek a pure, original, and unpolluted whole. The search for authenticity is construed not as a matter of (mere) leisure but as a meaningful, existential desire that may endow the individual with a richer and fuller experience of being; it is a much sought-after resource made available by the tourism industry, allowing its consumers an "ecstasy of experience" (Ritzer and Liska 1997, 106).

Tourism has become an "industry of authenticity" (Wang 2000, 71), wherein "existential authenticity becomes a commodity." It plays a restitutive role, by which it purportedly bestows upon the tourist—visiting the Taj Mahal, the Louvre, Niagara Falls, or participating in a safari in Kenya—a sense of realness. Moreover, tourists, while seeking authentic destinations, also engage in the pursuit of "hot authenticity," seeking their own authentic selves (Selwyn 1996, 21–25).

It is with regard to the profound experience bestowed upon tourists by the discourse of authenticity that they are capable of talking about themselves becoming transformed with authority and persuasiveness. The quality of uniqueness, inspired by institutionally constructed authenticity, which is initially associated with the destination, serves as a reality anchor by means of which the claim for the construction of self—and the cultural capital associated with this claim—can be credibly articulated and performed. Within an environment of utter consumerism, the tourist accepts the invitation to change (as noted by Rojek and Urry in the epigraph above) as she or he consumes the discursive commodity that authenticates one's sense of selfhood. The industry circulates and perpetuates identity discourses together with the well-defined practices and itineraries by means of which they are to be pursued. Though usually not overtly (as is the case with, say, psychotherapy), the romanticist perception of authenticity is concerned as much with selfhood as it is with sites and destinations.

"Simply a changed person": Tourist Self-Change Narratives

Following are two excerpts from the interviews with Boaz, who backpacked in Southeast Asia and the Pacific, and with Sharon, who backpacked in Southeast Asia, both for eight months. Both narrators typically explicitly state that they underwent significant self-change upon their return from the trip. Crucially, they locate these statements in the *final parts* of our interview-conversations: after eighty minutes of narration in the first case and sixty-five in the second. As will be shown, the meaningfulness and impact of these sequences rests on the preceding adventurous travel narrative, into which they are tacitly woven and upon which they reflect in hindsight.

Boaz mentions the prevalence of backpacking among his acquaintances, stressing, "everyone, everyone, traveled in South America or in the East." After a pause, he begins:

Boaz: And I returned changed
            quite changed
                    if it's changed as far as life experiences go
                                    that is mmm
    I left—
    I left the country IGNORANT
    I left the country ignorant in that I don't know many cultures
                    I haven't MET with many cultures

perhaps I read about

them or had seen them on television

but I haven't run across them really

physically

and after I return
and after all I see
and after all I hear

that is—

I'll give you an example

I KNEW New Zealand

that is

I knew it's a beautiful country and all—

but I didn't know PARTICULAR SPOTS

when I arrived to travel

there then suddenly

I know a lot more with regard to general knowledge of the country   (quicker)

on the region on the—

people

that is if you ask me today about New Zealand

I'll know MUCH MORE than I knew before

ask me suddenly about the mountains and all the rest

and I'll know more than I knew before   (quickly)

you see— like—

that is you leave the country when you DON'T KNOW MUCH

[and] when you return you

suddenly know EVERYTHING

you also know yourself better because you put yourself in

many situations

like I told you about the volcano suddenly   (quickly)

or in the very difficult physical

conditions at the trek

you simply know yourself differently than you knew

yourself before

you simply stretch inside you the

the limits of your abilities the

limits of your self-knowing

it's exactly like that

you know yourself very good

simply you're much more responsible for yourself for the

people around you

[you are] simply a changed person

Boaz is rather straightforward in indicating how deep and dramatic is the change he has experienced. Attesting that he returned from the trip "simply a changed person" amounts to an explicit claim of self-change. The trip, Boaz asserts, has *truly* ("really, physically") allowed for an encounter with "many cultures"—that is, with the authentic Other—which is what generated self-change. The change is constructed by way of an association, one that the narrator suggests is only natural and consequential to the trip: the true encounter led to a significant enhancement in the alleged knowledge of the destination, which led, subsequently, to a sense of profound knowledge of himself. It is this knowledge that led to a sense of self-change. Boaz stresses that his new knowledge was not gained from afar, nor is it of a general or blurry character anymore. Rather, it is authentic knowledge attained by means of a seemingly *unmediated encounter.* It is founded on close and solid (firsthand) knowledge of "particular spots," as he puts it, which suggest it is a detailed, "factual" type of knowledge.

The dramatic character of the description is established by the forceful invocation of the empty-to-full metaphor, which follows the cyclic course of the trip. Boaz left the homeland "ignorant" and returned "full," in a state in which he now possesses answers, where he now "know[s] everything." The repeated use of the word "suddenly" (four instances) further communicates the sense that change was dramatic. In employing this metaphor, Boaz's narrative is indeed transformative: his life story is retrospectively reconstructed in a dichotomous, dramatic fashion, where the latter, posttrip part—leading up to the present and projecting onward—is viewed positively, even admiringly. In terms of travel-related cultural capital, or narrative capital, Boaz establishes that he has mastered the knowledge engulfed by backpacking (he is asking the interviewer to test him: "ask me") and consequently has gained entitlement rights to an identity story and hence to a claim of self-change.

In the following extract Sharon argues that she has changed, yet she does so in a different, milder tone than Boaz. Her frequent hesitations, pauses, and self-retractions render the segment more reflexive, and the claim lacks the definite, explicit, and "masculine" parlance of Boaz's assertions. Nonetheless, Sharon aims at communicating the same profound message and cleverly accomplishes this goal through the use of a more tacit rhetorical strategy.

Sometime before the extract begins, Sharon mentions that she feels she was not successful in conveying her powerful emotions and experiences to me. She recalls that a day before our meeting she spoke with an acquaintance who had recently returned from the trip who, like her, had been deeply moved by the experience. She pauses and then says:

Sharon: This trip really DOES something to you

                             I can't put my finger on WHAT but it changes your

perception of things in many ways

                   I'm not—

                         it's hard for me to say that I was once this

way and now I'm different

                  that today I see specific matters differently

                     [but] I feel INSIDE MYSELF that some   (quickly)

change has occurred in me but I can't— (quickly)

I can't say WHAT

what has changed

Chaim: mmm but you FEEL it [and—]

Sharon: [and people] see it

certainly

people who know me and others too like—

everyone told

me I've changed

and it's— you know

the trip—

where else can you have such a thing ...

later I DID travel to places that have opened up only recently

I reached less touristic places

it attracts me

you see the pictures you see it's a completely DIFFERENT world

not one that we know of or

even think of ...

it had already begun being touristic but not enough

I KNOW that if I'll travel there NOW it won't be the same anymore

it's clear to me

because people hear about it and so they travel

and in big numbers

Sharon argues that she underwent a meaningful change, that upon her return she was "different." She makes it clear that the impact of the trip on her is to be framed in terms of identity and selfhood, and in this regard it is unmistakably of a positive, wide, and enduring scope. As in Boaz's argument, the change she sensed is narrated in a way so as to indicate it is directly linked to the unique experience of the trip, about which she rhetorically asks, "where else can you have such a thing?"

Yet Sharon indicates that the particular, or even general, domain of the profound changes remains unspecified. Unlike Boaz's straightforward narrative, it is precisely the vagueness or the unspecificity of the description that persuasively communicates Sharon's argument. The two words she chooses to emphasize in the beginning, "really DOES something" and "I can't put my finger on WHAT," are related. They are simultaneous indications of the powerful impact of the trip on her, on the one hand, and of its inherent ineffable (unnarratable) quality, on the other hand. They emphasize what positively *is*—that is, the profoundness of the experience, the authenticity of the personal change—and what *is not*—that is, what is extra-discursive, noncommunicable. The difficulty of putting into words her experience of personal change, a difficulty she previously interpreted as a failure of her communication skills, does not undermine the message she communicates but rather enhances it.

In other words, what could have been paradoxical is complementary in her narrative: the immensity of the experience, Sharon suggests, lies precisely in the fact that it is located *beyond* speech, beyond the possibility of spoken words to articulate and communicate it referentially. By employing this structure of complementary *confirmation and negation,* Sharon establishes a communication that concerns the "ineffability of the immense." What she describes is profound and elusive both simultaneously and consequentially. It is essential to the construction of the experience of self-change and to its successful communication that its impact be located beyond the sayable. The claim she makes about identity is thus also a claim about language and about the various ways it may be manipulated in the performance of self/self-change (Stromberg 1993, 1–16).[1]

When Sharon asserts that she cannot elaborate further on her immense feelings, I feel impelled to confirm her experience, to share *my experience* with her—to indicate that I understand that self-change has indeed occurred and that it rests "inside" her as a "deep" feeling. My assertion that it is inner and experiential in essence ("you FEEL it") compels Sharon to claim that, even though she acknowledges its innermost quality, the change is by no means abstract or invisible. By her correction of me, her insistence that the changes are not only (subjectively) felt but also (objectively) seen, the similarities between Sharon's and Boaz's narratives gradually come to light. What is "visible" for Sharon is "actual" for Boaz: in both cases, claims are made to "actual" manifestations, to their factual quality, which is crucial for communicating a sense of authentic self-change. In both cases the actual changes are construed as the result of a trip (which truly occurred) and the real or "true" encounter with authentic views, cultures, and so on therein.

Finally, soon after Sharon stresses that she arrived at an authentic destination, she evokes a temporal attribute of authenticity ("travel there now"). She suggests that the nearly epiphanic moment she experienced is singular and fleeting. Experiencing authenticity is presented as a matter of arriving at the right place at the *exact* right time. It is not only the unique place she has visited but also the special moment—the last minute—at which she has done so that together amount to what has touched and "influenced" her profoundly. Sharon incorporates a variety of the discourse of time in tourism, whereby the new spoils the old (Cohen 1986; Dann 1996, 218–28). In the convergence of authenticity and identity, it is both the whereabouts and the whenabouts that matter, and it is through the institutional discourse of nostalgia that tourism powerfully draws time, as a commodity that becomes a resource, into the autobiographical time of the lives of tourists (Bruner 1991, 242, 248; and with specific regard to backpackers, Elsrud 1998, 312, 318–19).

Moreover, temporality and evanescence give the impression that Sharon was one of the last to *witness* the uniqueness of which she narrates. She is, thus, a witness of things bygone, and her story is not merely a touristic travel narrative but a testimonial one, bearing witness to that which once was and is no longer. Bearing this witness has affected her profoundly and consequently, she, too, has changed and she, too, will not be the same thereafter. Relying on the hermeneutics of witnessing, Sharon thus draws a parallel between the destination she visited and her inner realms—both of which have altered irreversibly: both of which require a witness to capture the experience and "propagate" it (Barbara Johnson, qtd. in Felman and Laub 1991, 23).

Authenticity Performed: Transcendent Texts and Self-Change

The concern is with performance as . . . creative, realized, achieved, even transcendent of the ordinary course of events.

Dell Hymes

Narrative arguments of this magnitude, wherein the self is construed as undergoing valuable and significant changes, are among the strongest claims that can be asserted by personal narratives. In order for the narrator to speak convincingly of such meaningful occurrences, which, being internal, cannot be observed or measured, their performances need to be sufficiently anchored in culturally powerful and socially persuasive texts. For this reason, narrators draw an association between their experiences and some other authoritative topos of extraordinariness, which authenticates them and renders them credible and valid.

Texts of such type have two prerequisites. First, they must embrace some sort of "transcendent" quality. They relate to and convey some profound realm of meaning, consensually acknowledged as such by members of a socially relevant subgroup. Second, they do not refer to the Self, at least not explicitly, but to some other (or better, Other) realm of meaning. Thus, narratives of dramatic occurrences, which take place "within" the boundaries of the conscious self, correlate with dramatic archnarratives (such as the romanticist travel narrative) pertaining to events that occur "outside" it and that are perceived as being responsible for its vicissitudes. In other words, though transcendent texts are seemingly of other/Other subject matters, they nevertheless inherently revolve around the Self.

The following two excerpts illustrate the employment of transcendent text (Maingueneau 1999) in the context of tourism. They occurred earlier in the conversations than the previous excerpts, when the narrators were describing the sights they saw and the adventures they underwent (the core travel narrative). The first is drawn from Sharon's narrative (preceding the above excerpt by forty minutes) and the second from a narrative by Danit, who describes trekking in the Peruvian Azangate mountain range. In both cases the conversation flows while we look now and then through pictures from the trip. Sharon and Danit describe breathtaking views in what seem to be naïve descriptions, typical of tourists' excited and wordy accounts. However, these descriptive segments can be read as legitimizing sources of the identity claims that follow shortly after. In contrast to the sequences described above, the apparent subject of these segments is not the Self (the "inner" realm) but the impressive sights viewed by tourists (the "external" realm).

Sharon: It's all clouds here. so here I took pictures all the time because
they kept on changing but again. you can't see it in the pictures. it's

not—you know I tried to do [a montage] with the pictures mmm
but it never came out right . . . it's simply the—the change. but you
can't see it. it's not—you know all the time the clouds are moving
and shifting forms and suddenly there's a hole HERE [where light
shines through] and previously there was a hole HÉRE. and—the
shades again they are changing all the time. you see, these pictures
are already more light . . . here you already have the blue. here it's
still all red.

Chaim: Yeah, wow—

Sharon: I don't know it's something (quietly) different. simply different.

While Sharon foregrounds that which is shifting and fleeting—the moving clouds,
Danit concentrates on that which is stationary—the Peruvian mountain chain.
Nonetheless, the scene's dynamic quality is competently communicated.

Danit: There are whole mountains that are—

            or in that red color

            or in the color of dark green

    and then you think that you see—

            that it's only say

                 the MOUNTAIN that's in this color or the

   SAND that covers it

        but NO

          you see whole rocks that are in that RED color or whole rocks that

   are in the green color

       and you simply—

          at some point you reach it and you walk on it and you

   look

     "I'm walking on a RED mountain

     I'm walking on a green mountain"

         simply amazing [there—   (quietly)

Chaim: wow] wow   (quietly)

Danit: amazing

Both Sharon's and Danit's extracts are fine illustrations of the semiotics of the tourist gaze, as they powerfully evoke vision and referential language related to it. These
not only convey but also construct the remarkable, the authentic, which assume in
tourism the shape of peoples or places, urban or natural. In all cases, the moving
gaze endows the tourist with the powerful lived experience of authenticity (Wang
2000). Once they are actually "walking on" authentic places and "knowing" authentic cultures and peoples, to use Danit's and Boaz's excited words, backpackers consume the commodity of constructed authenticity, with the intention of constructing
an identity vis-à-vis a dramatic narrative of self-change.

The breathtaking scenery, the intense experiences it bestows upon the back-packers, and the travel narratives capturing and enacting these experiences amount to what Maingueneau (1999) describes as "self-constitutive discourse." These are powerful transcendent texts that are deeply rooted in modern-Western societies and are "under the control of something transcendent, such as Tradition, Reason, Truth" (190). Of central importance to these texts is what lies *beyond* narrative—that is, the ineffable. What grants them their transcendent authority is precisely their being "under control" of that which is beyond narratability, "bordering on un-speakable meanings," as Maingueneau puts it (183). To use a Turnerian terminology, such discourses are of liminal quality, and their generativity and authority are drawn from being located "betwixt-and-between" (Turner 1967): they are intermediaries between the sayable and the unsayable, between language and the "nonreadable surround" (Silverstein and Urban 1996, 1).

The vivid descriptions provided by Sharon and Danit, which are seemingly re-lated not to the Self but to the scenery, amount to transcendent narratives of back-packers. Their identity claims, which are staked as high as self-change, are viably asserted by being bound to a transcendent text. The narrators summon profound meanings that are perceived as existing independently both of the viewer—that is, the gazing tourist subject—and of language.

Symbolically, the role these narratives play corresponds to that of revelations (Stromberg 1993) or gospels (Harding 1987) in religious evangelic narratives of per-sonal experience and change. Such institutional discourses enable the articulation of selfhood at a (trans)formative moment, endowing the individual's narrative with much-needed validity vis-à-vis claims of transcendence and authenticity.

Transcendent discourses, however, are imbued with authority with regard to particular historical and cultural contexts. In tourism, the romantic (adventur-ous) experience lies at the core of the desire for authentic experiences. This is what grants backpackers' overwhelmed narratives their transcendent quality and is their legitimizing "Source" (Maingueneau 1999). It enables the construction of an iden-tity having "deep interior" (Gergen 1991, 18–47), where the authentic self allegedly lodges and in which its feelings abide. The "deep exterior" reverberates here with the deep interior, both of which are simultaneously constructed as encompassing great depths.

Performing Self-Change:
From the Semiotics of Attraction to the Semiotics of Extraction

In addressing backpackers' performances of self-change, I wish to offer three obser-vations. First, in the settings of their narrations backpackers are granted a "voice" (Shotter 1993, 7–10) or a "speaking role," as Keane (1997, 58) observes in relation to religious experience: "Transformation consists of taking a new role as speaker . . . [of] being transformed from the listener to the speaker . . . the speaker's religious identity is approached . . . as an inhabitable speaking role with all the discursive and moral possibilities that may entail." Those who have heard time and again stories by others before they left for the great journey have now themselves become storytellers. Vis-à-vis the great trip, backpackers shift—transform—from the listener role to the narrator role.

Having a voice, or a speaking role, is crucial for a performance wherein the experience of self-change is induced. In an illuminating discussion of the language of born-again evangelists, Peter Stromberg (1993, 29) observes that the change "occurs as a result of changing embodied aims into articulable intentions." Entering the domain of the articulate, Stromberg suggests, "draw[s] a new part of the subject's experience into the realm of the self," producing a sense of self-change. As pointed out by Maingueneau (1999, 183, 195), too, it is precisely the capacity of allowing permeability of meaning from the ineffable to the effable (from the embodied to the articulable) that characterizes the effect of transcendent texts, and it is that which allows for a self-change narrative to be performed viably.

Hence, the experience of self-change is located within narrative, or narratability. Consequently, the narration of a self-change experience *constitutes its experience.* Language is not employed in this regard only referentially, conveniently located within the effable, but also constitutively: it is through language, in its transformative capacity, that self-change is intersubjectively experienced. Clearly, narratability and the move to the effable require sociocultural conditions of the type that makes performance possible—namely, a community of speakers wherein one can assume and materialize a voice, a speaking role: and, as the earlier chapters showed, wherein the speaker can conjure and perform various social voices *directly* by quotation.

The second observation to be considered is that performance entails the bridging of the experiential (and epistemological) gulf that lies between the there-and-then of the narrated events and the here-and-now of the storytelling occasion. The more fluid and seamless the weaving of the two contexts, the more persuasive and effectual is the performance. There is a unique paradox here that the narrators need to contend with when performing self-change before an audience that *has not* traveled. Because the listeners did not know the narrators prior to the trip and are thus unable to compare the "before" and "after," all they have to go on is the story of the self-change. The backpackers are thus under pressure and are required to persuasively *show* self-change in vivo. They accomplish this performatively by extensively employing metacommunicative allusions addressing the very acts of communication in which they are involved (Bauman and Briggs 1990; Lucy 1993c). These, in turn, affect the pragmatics of the conversation, or "the pragmatics of putting narrative into practice" (Langellier 1999, 127).

In order to implicate their interlocutor(s) in their narratives and bridge the two realms, the backpackers establish performative—interpersonal and intersubjective—communication, by means of which they are able to perform their new speech role, that which instantiates their significant self-change. It is an instance in which narrative points beyond the referential and descriptive and achieves a social action, that of the sense of transformation, within the process of (co-)narration (Ochs 1997; Wortham 2001).

It was only within interactional positioning that I was able to experience and "know," as termed by the backpackers, the sense of self-change they underwent. By merely listening to their stories, within the semiotics of tourism I, too, acquired a conversational position: that of the (implicated) listener. I was uncannily drawn from the storyrealm into the taleworld, feeling that by attending to their stories I also participated in them to a degree (see Harding 1987 and the discussion in chapter 2).

The third and final point I wish to make is that in a performance, transcendent texts are seamlessly woven into the realm of lived (inter)personal experience, thus imbuing the narrative with credibility and authority. The transcendent quality—institutionally constructed authenticity, in the present case—is "imported" from the alleged there-and-then to the here-and-now and is constructed and re-enacted interpersonally as lodging within the (transformed, transcendent) Self. Consequently, the occasion of narration is imbued with features of that which it describes: it describes authenticity and establishes it simultaneously.

In the first extract above, Boaz is consistently referring to himself, until, at a certain point, he addresses me directly for the first time, suggesting two illustrations of his newly gained knowledge. He employs a repetitive structure ("ask me") as he rhetorically invites me to test him. Under the equation that he draws, correlating new knowledge with self-knowledge and subsequently with self-change, establishing detailed familiarity with the destination is crucial.

The problem Boaz faces is that *I did not know him before his trip.* He thus searches for ways to credibly communicate the knowledge he has gained. He stresses that his knowledge was previously only of a general and mediated character ("seen them on television"), while after the trip it is accurate and founded on concrete details. From this point onward, it is me to whom Boaz explicitly refers. He follows the lead he himself has made as he ventriloquizes me into the conversation and suggests answers to the queries that he puts in my mouth.

Interestingly, these queries are only seemingly hypothetical. What Boaz suggests I *could have* asked is in fact what *I indeed asked.* It is the inquiry that lies at the core of our meeting, its underlying motivation. When he suggests that I ask him about New Zealand or "about the mountains," he in fact indexes the context of the interview and the fact that I *did* ask him such questions earlier (the answers to which generated his posttour narrative). This is why he alludes to the core narrative when he reminds me, in a metacommunicative note, that he previously told me about such events ("like I told you").

The way he implicitly indexes the context of our interview meeting constructs the roles and positions we play in it. Elaborating on the experiences and undertakings of the trip positions Boaz as "knowledgeable" and myself as "ignorant." Hence, the emerging rhetorical structure, the transformative before-and-after claim, denotes in the performance not only Boaz's experiences but mine too. After all, the knowledge I presently hold of New Zealand resembles, in kind and scope, the knowledge he had *prior* to the trip. Through conversational positioning, the metaphor is cast dialogically. In this capacity Boaz positions himself as occupying the role of the experienced (full, after) and myself in the role of the novice (empty, before) in an interpersonal, "pedagogical" interaction (Briggs 1988, 82–83).

Note that the word *suddenly* ("ask me suddenly") functions in a metacommunicative capacity. This is the only instance in which it refers to the present context (in its three other occurrences it denotes the narrated events). An analogy is thus drawn between two occasions that carry dramatic and, more important, factual weight: that which occurred during the trip and that which occurred during the performance of the posttour narrative. What *was* dramatic and sudden *is* dramatic and sudden. From the perspective of the self-change claim, which is located at the end of the narration, akin to an evaluative sequence or a coda, both of these contexts are not here-and-now, and are thus alluded to. While I did not participate in the trip, I certainly did play a role in the narration, collaborating with the narrator in the conversation.

In a more profound way, the unspoken understanding we both share is that Boaz has *indeed* traveled—that he has actually participated in the practice. We both take this statement as a true fact and agree, epistemologically, that it "occurred." We agree that traveling amounts to an actual or factual practice, which from the outset led to my desire to meet him, in the same way that, from the perspective of the self-change segment, the narration took place. By the time the narrator arrives at telling her or his transformation, the conversation has an ontic weight of its own, so that the assertion may rest on the *eventfulness of the conversation* itself and on how we both assumed the speaking and listening roles throughout.

At this point in the collaborative storytelling, narrator and audience share the ground they have covered together. The location of the self-change argument toward the end of the interview is thus not coincidental. It stands in epistemological and metapragmatic tension with the events depicted in the core narrative, which itself depicts the "actual" occurrences of the trip.

Moreover, by meeting with him and listening to his travel narrative, I gained substantial knowledge of the destination. And if this knowledge is correlated with self-change, as Boaz contends it is, then the occasion of the interview amounts, in itself, to the commencement of *my own* experience of self-change. Paraphrasing Boaz, I also "put myself in situations" in the present actual/factual encounter with him (as he did with regard to the destination) in which the seeds of self-change are planted. In this sense authenticity and the semiotics of attraction more generally have a "contagious" quality: they travel with the traveler. Hence, the audience is repeatedly constituted in the performance as a traveler. From a performance perspective this perpetuation entails the shift from the "semiotics of attraction" (for example, MacCannell) to the "semiotics of extraction" (for example, Brunner and Kirshenblatt-Gimblett).

Similarly to Boaz, after my reflexive comment ("but you FEEL it"), Sharon employs metapragmatic cueing as she chooses to stress four words: "DID," "DIFFERENT," "KNOW," and "NOW." The first two emphases confirm the fact that she did in fact travel, and, more important, the fact that she arrived at authentic and inspiring destinations previously not visited. Akin to Boaz, she, too, establishes what is agreed upon as factual in our conversation. The position of the third emphasis is only natural—after all, the real and authentic sites inspired a unique experience, one that is captured in the intimacy of her knowing, of her coming to know. The final emphasis evokes the *context of the narration* of the posttour performance. The narrator contends that from the perspective of the present, both the places she visited and her Self have changed irreversibly. As noted earlier, her story has a testimonial quality, and it is she, at the present moment of the conversation, who "knows" and treasures that which has vanished.

The precious singularity of which she narrates also reverberates within the occasion of narration. By listening to her remarkable story, I, too, became a witness (a "second-order" witness, a witness of a witness). As I suggested, the semiotics of extraction are contagious and therefore, in a way, I also get to see that which is transcendent, which now lies within the narrator and not at the destination. As asserted by another backpacker when describing how he descended to the town of Namche at the end of the Everest base camp trek, "I told everyone of my adventures and so I was a kind of an attraction. It was nice. [People] asked me and took my advice."

Though she does so more implicitly than Boaz, Sharon forcefully evokes the sense of self-change with me. Through tacit employment of metapragmatic framing devices, she suggests that my self-change is *already* under way. Her pointing out (and correcting me) that people in fact *see* it (among several other allusions she makes to vision) evokes referentiality and the tourists' gaze. But now she draws the tourist gaze onto herself. *She* is now the one who should be looked at and viewed with appreciation, and it is "within" her Self that an authentic attraction—with its unspecifiable and ineffable characteristics—is located. She establishes a "second-order" type of authenticity: at present, what is worth viewing is (within) Sharon. As she indeed indicates, people actually "see it," both those who "know me and others too . . . everyone" (perhaps alluding to myself/audience).

Again, Sharon faces the need to establish the credibility of the fact she has changed, even though I did not know her previously. Similarly, backpackers commonly assert that upon their return, their inner change was clearly apparent, and that "people would see [it] in my eyes" (in those very eyes that have seen, gazed at, and consumed authenticity). The vicissitudes of authenticity are the vicissitudes of its powerful constructing gaze. In the conversation I am the listener/spectator, I am a tourist of sorts, granting the narrators their role as changed while, at the same time, being implicated in and by that change.

In this regard we should consider the narrator's unique use of the irregular (reflexive) conjugation of the word "change" (*hishtanut*, "some change has occurred"). This specific form appears, in fact, only in Sharon's interview and only twice: once in the self-change assertion and once in the core narrative (in the second extract from Sharon: "it's simply the—the change"), where it refers to the changing contours of the clouds. Akin to Boaz's use of the word *suddenly*, Sharon uses this pivotal word both in the transcendent text *and* in its reflexive, evaluative coda, referring, in the latter, to her self-change (herself change). Thus, what occurs within her is as profound and perhaps as "natural" as the events she witnessed.

Once again, two "destinations" are simultaneously referred to: one at a spatio-temporal distance and the other nearby both in space and in time, being constantly re-created in the fleeing narrative interaction. Semiotically, we can see how the contention that contemporary tourism entails and promotes a blurring of the signifier with the signified is here performed by the tourists' evocation of double reference or twofold "conceptual structures" (Wortham 2001, 36). Consequently, narrating tourists have themselves become potent signifiers of what is worth the tourist's gaze and narrative. After "actually" being there, they become signifiers—not only on-site markers of the attractions but off-site markers as well (Dann 1996, 9–12). They are now metonymically associated with the destination vis-à-vis their own (owned) narratives. In a way, they have now become an "attraction" themselves, while their listener/spectator has transformed, too, and has become a tourist.

Thus, the performance of their transformation is an occasion in its own right and it emerges as homologous with the event of the actual travel. The transformative, metapragmatic force of language begins precisely with the listening role, without which the speaker's role cannot be inhabited later.

As for Sharon's second extract, the depiction of the dynamic play of subtle hues and shifting clouds persuasively conveys the twofold point she has been making: the more spectacular the views, the more elusive and ineffable they are—the harder it is to communicate them. Here, again, the complementary rhetorical structure of confirmation and negation emerges, wherein each evaluative judgment reinforces the other. The confirmation concerns the *experience of witnessing* a spectacular view, and the negation lies in the recurrent expression of dissatisfaction with a referential mode of communication. It amounts to an instance on a metacommunicative evaluation typical of romanticist-idealist language. As observed by Vološhinov (1973, 85), the possibility of expression is negated on the grounds that it can "deform the purity of the inner element"; which is why in relation to singularity and foreignness, language in tourism is problematic, an "enemy," even (as Kirshenblatt-Gimblett writes [1998, 239], following Sontag 1966). In the performance these two aspects converge: the narrator conveys that she or he is overwhelmed and frustrated alternately (or, more accurately, simultaneously).[2]

The three narratives point to what lies beyond the sayable, that which is extradiscursive. They imply that there are no narrative shortcuts, no words to replace acts. To continue the process of my own transformation, I now need to embark upon a trip myself, a practice that has two profound "destinations": sites and self.

Finally, an illustration of how the interlocutor is skillfully implicated in the taleworld is also found in Danit's depiction, which is drawn from the core narrative and does not seemingly concern her self-change (or mine). At first glance Danit seems enthusiastic about sharing her powerful experiences without being preoccupied with their communicability (she stresses how "simply amazing" the views are). Yet a closer reading reveals here, too, the narrator's metacommunicative statements concerning the communicability of her profound experience. Masked as a descriptive sequence, a meaningful mininarrative is embedded within the excerpt, where Danit narrates her gradual, and eventually successful, approach to a colorful mountain.

The narrative points out that the first impression of the view arouses both admiration and suspicion. The remarkable sight arouses doubts about its realness; about whether it is "only" the sand, the mountain's "cover," that is colored. Again, the twofold structure is discernible: the more awesome the spectacle, the more elusive it is for expression. Yet in the narration it is so both in the eyes of the tourist-protagonist *and*, later, in the ears of the interlocutor: the fact that Danit is not sure of the reality and authenticity of the mountain may reflect the audience's hesitation as to whether her self-change is authentic and real or only a "cover," a superficial colorful façade.

The answer Danit provides to her preceding (skeptical) hesitation—a subtle way of ventriloquizing me—is a resounding no: the mountain *is* authentic—its color is natural (its *inside* is red or green). In a particularly excited utterance, Danit describes how sharp and real its colors are and, in the scene's crescendo, how she actually *reached* the colorful mountain and actually walked on it. It is then that she resorts to the use of quotations, which instantiate in the narration the actuality of her being there.

When she describes reaching the mountain ("at some point you reach it"), Danit actualizes her protagonist's voice and tells herself out loud—and, in effect, tells *me*—she is/has actually been there. The quotation, fusing "expression with communication" (Lucy 1993a, 20) through a shift in the spatiotemporal perspective, is a crucial metacommunicative framing device that marks here the convergence of the narrated events with the event of narration and conveys, in a seemingly unmediated ("direct") manner, that she has been there (see chapter 1). It performatively parallels and enacts the narrated fact that she has reached, *in actuality*, what she previously only saw from afar. By arriving at the truly "red" mountain, Danit has reached the inside of the direct quotation, so to speak, a crescendo that I echo sympathetically. Now she—her transformed self—is as enthralling an attraction as is the marvelous mountain. She is speaking from within the experience with a voice that, if I should wish to own it, I would have to travel there for myself. After the trip she establishes having gained not only storytelling rights (Hymes and Cazden 1978; Shuman 1986), but also *quoting rights*.

The double reference here—that is, my witnessing her being within the quotations in the there-and-then (taleworld)—means that at present *I* am the witness of the authentic, already on the track of my own touristic transformation. In the interview situation Danit short-circuits the referential order. She accomplishes this in speech and quotation rather than in gaze and vision. The verb with which she introduces the quotation is "look," which is a play on the usual type of speech verbs. Danit exchanges—transforms, translates—the perceived *immediacy* of vision with that of *direct* quotation. The colors of her changed self are just as authentic and real as the colors of the mountain, and just as she experienced (viewed) the mountain, I experienced (heard) her.[3]

To conclude, backpackers' persuasive narrations of self-change are accomplished through the performative implication of their audience. They do so by manipulating pragmatic aspects of live narrative interaction, which rests on the perception that by seeking to interview them, the researcher is already implicated in their taleworlds.

Posttour storytelling again emerges as a constitutive rite of its own, and not as a by-product of the trip. As a social action, the stories amount to an initiatory rite in the listeners'/yet-to-be backpackers' own search for self/self-change and to the beginning of the construction of their touristic taleworld itinerary. The interlocutor is conversationally positioned and experientially constructed as the novice, occupying the listener role, and the narrating backpacker is cast as the experienced performer, occupying the speaker role. As Bauman (1978, 4) has remarked, narration changes social relationships and categories of identity inside and outside the performative event.

The narrating backpackers cleverly work around the "evidential problem" and around the problem of conveying the fact that they have changed to an audience who did not know them beforehand. In the interactions, their self-change assertions are located toward the end of the core narratives, at a point where conversational roles and identities have already been established. Moreover, the credibility of their argument is gained through the drawing of a parallel between the trip and the core travel narrative, on the one hand, and the latter and the self-change segment, on the other hand. These segments are not organic (narrative) parts of the travel narrative, they are "hanging" evaluative clauses (Labov 1972) and hence are knitted to the narrative via metacommunicative comments. This work of "knitting" parallels the work of overcoming or short-circuiting the epistemological gulf between the core narrative ("discourse"), and the trip ("practice"). It accomplishes important metapragmatic work in the performance.

Further, the backpackers' accounts revolve around the ineffable, insofar as they extradiscursively point toward two nonlinguistic "destinations" simultaneously: sites and selfhood. Both, they suggest, possess a factual quality of the kind language is commonly not accredited with. Their stories suggest (somewhat paradoxically) that there are no narrative shortcuts. No words to replace acts: in order to be viable and valid, self-change claims should be closely associated with practices that are perceived as "extradiscursive": occasions of traveling. Such metapragmatic work is effectively accomplished under shared perceptions of language in the West, particularly the subjectivization of speech (Silverstein 1976; Vološhinov 1973).

This is where the frequent employment of quotations and voices, abundantly presented in the chapters in site II, comes into the picture. In the reported dialogues, others' directly reported words assume the significance of a souvenir. Somewhat paradoxically, these reported words and utterances assume a nondiscursive or extradiscursive status and are as factual and as credible as souvenirs. Although they consist of words, when direct quotations are transported from the spaces of tourists' experiences (in)to the performances "in one piece," as it were, they validate and authenticate the claims made by the narrators.

Finally, the success—credibility and authenticity—of the performance of self-change is intimately tied to the performance's persuasive character and intention (described and discussed in chapter 2). The description of positioning and dialogue in the storytelling occasion presented in this chapter indicates that self-change is persuasive insofar as persuasion is transformatory. The two are dialogically interlocked performances: if you have been persuaded, your self-change has already begun, and if you have started to change, you are in the process of becoming part of the community, and its discourse—part of yours. Put simply, good performances make for good persuasions, and vice versa.

"Garçon, get me someone who speaks Tibetan!"

One of the funniest moments of my life happened during my second trip to India, this time together with my future wife, Orly (who had also backpacked in India a few years before). We spent three wonderful weeks in the northern state of Himachel Pradesh, most of the time in and around the towns of Dharamsala and Mecleodganj, of which we still occasionally reminisce warmly, with the wonderful views and fresh air of the Indian Himalayas.

One evening we went out to dine in an Indian-run Tibetan restaurant. My memories of that evening are blurred and dim. Earlier that evening we met a group of three Israelis, a woman and two men of our age, who immediately seemed to share our lighthearted mood. They, too, were looking for a place to dine. Of the place itself all I can remember was that it seemed quite dark inside. In my memory the scene around us was darkish, with a soft spotlight directed on our table of five tourists. The dinner was long, we had many courses, and the experience was very pleasing.

One of our three companions was extraordinarily funny. I remember thinking: "This guy is a talented comedian." He was born in Israel, where he spent his childhood years, but had lived most of his life in the United States. Consequently, he knew both Hebrew and English fluently, although he had a clear foreign accent in the former and not in the latter. Toward the end of the evening we were getting ready to pay the check, an act that would prove to be an annoyance, because we had ordered and shared more dishes than we could remember and because the waiters did not impress us as being very efficient or orderly. At one point our newly acquired American-Israeli friend exclaimed, in a rolling authoritative voice that imitated and animated a demanding American tourist: "Garçon! Get me someone who speaks Tibetan!" This was terribly funny because it was clear the American tourist he was imitating had no knowledge of the Tibetan language (nor did our friend or, for that matter, any of us) and that he was playing a consumer's game: ordering people, services, and com-

modities around. I guess it was particularly funny for us because we were all familiar with the figure he was caricaturing: a condescending white American male tourist, very loud, who gives the impression that the world is out there to serve him (which, in the context of capitalist tourism, is not inaccurate). It might have been funny also because we ourselves were tourists, and to some degree the point he was making was ironic: there is a loud, demanding, and condescending American inside all of us.

Furthermore, a nuanced appreciation of the expression might also suggest that the caricature, and perhaps the impersonator as well, is searching for something Tibetan: in an Indian-run Tibetan restaurant in a Tibetan town (where the Dalai Lama has a permanent refuge) in the northern Indian state of Himachel Pradesh. In other words, the tourist's demand could be interpreted to mean: "Give me something authentic, some signifier of true Tibetanese." A Babylonian tower was thus instantaneously erected by our friend's expression, in which several languages, as well as echoes of other languages, were evoked within the context of international/multilingual tourism: the lingua franca of global consumption—American English, Hebrew, the French address (indicating that the speaker is competent in the international language of service in restaurants), and the mention of Tibetan.

At any rate, once the check arrived, it was full of errors, which, as we had anticipated, inflated the bill considerably (or at least we thought it was full of errors, although we weren't really in a state to figure it out correctly). So our friend addressed the waiter once again, exclaiming: "There seems to have been a misunderstanding here." Though it was not as funny as the earlier imitation, it was still funny because once more a cliché was evoked: a consumer's complaint. Yet this time the demeanor was more sophisticated and polite.

The next line, however, was the best and was to become truly memorable. The waiter, who seemed puzzled and to some degree uninterested in our complaint, or maybe he did not fully understand what our friend had said, didn't reply. We couldn't judge and weren't sure whether there was a genuine intercultural language barrier or whether the waiter understood full well what was going on and was merely pretending to have difficulties comprehending the language of the tourists who were arguing that the bill had been incorrectly and unfavorably calculated. In any case, upon seeing the waiter's indifferent reaction, our friend exclaimed, still with enthusiasm: "There seems to be an ongoing misunderstanding!"

Now this was incredibly funny. The observation still evoked the customer's clichés, but this was an improvisation. It suggested that the previous cliché hadn't achieved its aim, and there were no more ready-made clichés to be tossed at those providing tourist services. This was the dead end of tourists'/consumers' clichés. It also suggested that there was no use in furthering the discussion because one of the parties literally did not understand what was being said/argued/complained about. It was one of these occasions in life in which the words one is uttering have absolutely no value. Regardless of their content, they are rendered ontologically meaningless because they are emitted within a noncommunicative context.

I'm reminded of a character in one of Herman Melville's stories. In "Bartleby,

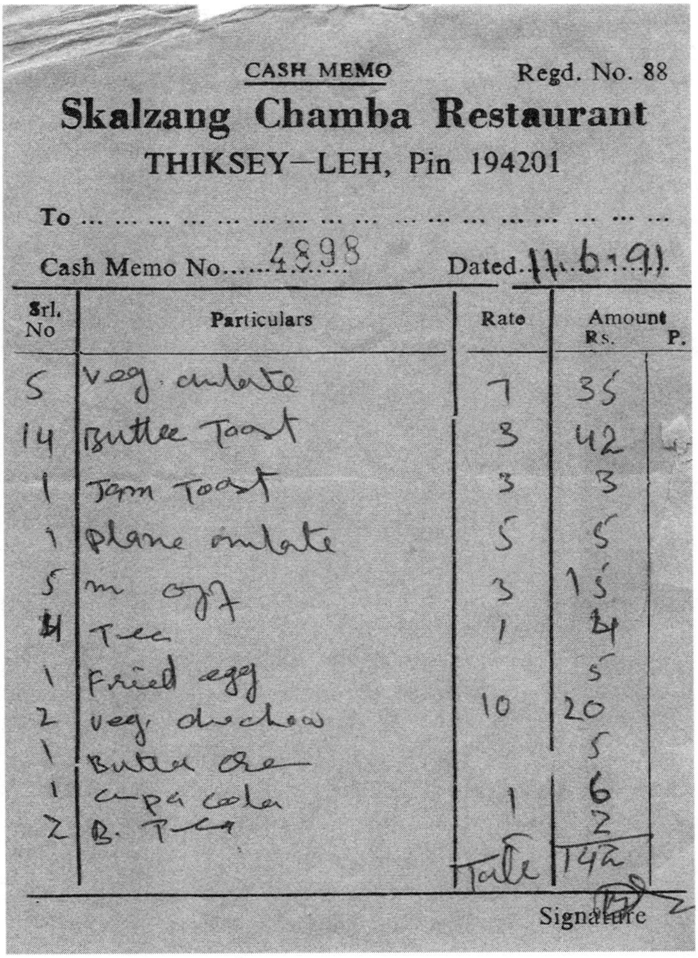

CASH MEMO Regd. No. 88

Skalzang Chamba Restaurant

THIKSEY—LEH, Pin 194201

To ... ...

Cash Memo No......4898 Dated 11.6.91.

Srl. No	Particulars	Rate	Amount Rs. P.
5	veg. omlate	7	35
14	Butter Toast	3	42
1	Jam Toast	3	3
1	plane omlate	5	5
5	m egg	3	15
4	Tea	1	4
1	Fried egg		5
2	veg. chowchow	10	20
1	Butter Tea		5
1	Coca cola	1	6
2	B. Tea		2
		Total	142

Signature

Fig. 4. "An ongoing misunderstanding!" A check from a Tibetan restaurant in India

the Scrivener" (1853/1997), Melville describes a very introverted and quiet person who dies at the end of the story. In the epilogue we learn of the character's past occupation: Bartleby worked in the post office in the Dead Letter Office. Melville conjures this poignant metaphor to indicate states of noncommunicative expressions. He writes of these dead letters: "Sometimes from out the folded paper the pale clerk takes a ring:—the finger it was meant for, perhaps, moulders in the grave; a bank-note sent in swiftest charity:—he whom it would relieve, nor eats nor hungers any more." Regardless of intent or actual expression, these messages did not reach those for whom they were intended and were not effective in making an impact upon or changing the world.

Our friend's expression—"There seems to be an ongoing misunderstanding!"—

had a similar effect (which can be tragic or humorous, depending on the circum-stances). Its competent performance, evoking authoritative and eloquent rolling Eng-lish, did not help. In fact, it merely exposed the tourist to an even greater embarrass-ment, one entailed in a complete misunderstanding of the consumer–service provider interaction and power structure (Robinson and Lynch, 2005)—a misunderstanding that was even greater than that of the waiter. Our friend might just as well have ut-tered this expression to himself.

At the end of the evening Orly and I kept one of the checks as a memento of this memorable occasion.

Epilogue

> I have praised and singled out unapologetically what I particularly cherish.
> These are merely opinions, rooted at times to certain footnotes, but rootless
> in the end—searching out along the horizons, compulsive, yearnful, remem-
> bering, looking forward.
>   Michael Tobias

This book embodies a discursive travel. Like the backpackers' itinerary, the book commences with an inquiry into the dialogics of persuasive narration that govern pretrip storytelling occasions between accomplished and novice backpackers (see chapter 2). The aim achieved by narrative performances extends beyond the pleasure of a well-told story. Covertly—veiled by the heightened atmosphere of the interaction and by the enthusiasm typical of tourist talk—the narrations promote action to be taken by the audience. Although they at first appear to be descriptive, the stories are in fact prescriptive: they amount to literally *moving performances*, propelling the listener to embark on her or his own backpacking rite of passage. In this sense, the stories frame the great journey: they suggest and demonstrate how backpacking leads to narrative capital and to the assumption of a new identity and a new sense of communal belonging. They afford a "visa," as suggested by one of the backpackers, not only to other countries but to sociocultural collectives in Israel as well.

The book concludes by framing the trip retrospectively as a (trans)formative experience. The lively travel narratives compellingly attest to and create in the performance a sense of profound self-change (see chapter 9). This experience is accomplished intersubjectively (Young 1987): the narrators first draw the audience into the adventurous and exciting taleworld and then, by establishing the interaction as a symbolic-ritualistic site in and of itself, the beginning of the audience's travel narrative is inaugurated. The social identity of the audience covertly and uncannily shifts during the interaction from an "unmarked" audience to a yet-to-be backpacker, a potential "candidate" of the rite of passage. Thus, the transformatory experience emerges not only with regard to the trip but also with regard to the interview meeting (we have called it a "second-order" or "contagious" type of transformation). The dialogic genres of persuasion and self-transformation are both effective in a complementary way in the interaction (Noy 2004a).

Indicating that the trip supplies the backpackers with a formative experience and that they consequently change in the course of traveling highlights the effect of this particular tourist practice on the lives of the participants. As noted by Tim Edensor:

> Tourists' narratives are often used biographically to mark episodes in personal life stories. The moment of travel may thus be incorporated into a self-reflexive, serialized account of an individual's development. This is most obvious in particularly symbolic forms of tourism . . . where certain symbolic sites are constructed as worthy of a "once-in-a-lifetime-visit" . . . tourists' sites are important locations where people attempt to make sense of themselves and the world in which they live, where they situate themselves in relation to the symbolic qualities associated with the site. (1998, 70)

Clearly, backpacking is a "symbolic form of tourism," viewed by the backpackers as a precious "once-in-a-lifetime" experience (see the introduction; the exception is "trampoline" backpackers who undergo this "once-in-a-lifetime" experience repeatedly [Noy and Cohen 2005a, 19]). Yet beyond the observation Edensor makes concerning personal biography, the trip also serves to position the backpackers in a collective social biography: Israeli backpackers of the 1980s differ from the backpackers of the 1990s; those who traveled to Asia view themselves differently from those who traveled to South America, and so on—and all of these travelers view themselves differently from those who have not traveled.

Between the rhetoric of persuasion and self-change lies the "actual" rite—the great journey, with all that it encompasses. The bulk of this book is dedicated to (voiced) representations of this phase. The book dwells—as backpackers do—within the scenes of which they narrate, within the many quotations, voices, and dialogues that enliven and authenticate the compelling taleworld of which they speak and in which they protagonize.

In this sense, the book is not centrally concerned with the tourists' biographical stories: with their individual life biographies, with their travel biographies, or even with the narratives of the great journey itself. Rather, the main impression conveyed by their multiple voices—an impression that the process of transcription could not moderate—was the intense intertextual network of humming voices and noises: a communal sonority (see chapter 8) that was performed competently, mostly with the help of the mechanism of quotation.

Quoting a Social Scene:
From Voices of a Community to a Community of Voices

The centerpiece of this book concerns the production of quotations and the evocation of social voices by backpackers. From the personal voice of the narrator-as-character through the choral voice of the small and cohesive group to the authoritative and impersonal voice of the Israeli crowd, backpackers make skilled use of words drawn from their touristic taleworlds to imbue their performances with a constitutive quality and to establish and maintain new social identities.

Analytically speaking, quotations play a dual role in narrative performances and can be discussed both in performative and referential terms. Performatively, the most important task fulfilled by quotations is the dialogical implication of the audience in the taleworld. By allowing the audience to "overhear" words exchanged in a different context between different characters, the listener is positioned *in relation* to the ensuing tale and is drawn into the taleworld. The audience thus becomes a character in the story and is cast or narrativized into the taleworld.

The many quotations and other forms of reported speech and the dialogic interrelations between them lend the stories and the storytelling occasions an almost corpo*real* quality. The repetitions (quotations) amount to plurality and to a polyphonic state. This lively—nearly tangible—polyphony suggests that a crowd of animators inhabits the performance. Thus a social context is established, wherein the dichotomies—narrator/audience, interviewee/interviewer—are augmented to become a social crowd populating the interaction. This, in turn, establishes the prerequisite of a social ritual—the "presence" of absent authoritative actors—and amounts to a populated site of cultural livelihood and change.

Whether the narrators narrativize the audience-as-character into the taleworld or whether they cast the taleworld and its garrulous characters into the interview, overhearing the words of others allows the audience accessibility to the taleworld. Here I employ a Goffmanesque notion, whereby narrators "sell association" (1981, 187) to the stories they recount, to the very taleworlds from which they have emerged. Since the backpackers travel between contexts, they are viewed as credible witnesses who are testifying in one (real) context about something that transpired in another (real) context. Hence, they are credibly selling their association to the touristic taleworld and to its wonders and marvels (see chapter 9).

Obviously, two contexts are required: the one described in the narrative and the one in which its description is performed. Hence, the condition of physical accessibility refers to "both ends": the event of the narrative and the event of its recounting. Thus, through actual physical, embodied access to the performer-tourist, the audience gains "ritual accesses to the subject matter over which the speaker has command" (Goffman 1981, 187). In terms borrowed from tourism discourse, a quotation is akin to an intact souvenir that the audience may access corporeally; it authentically conveys the social "subject matter" commanded by the narrators. Note that these semiotics of performance are true of academic discourse as well: alas, this book, too, offers you—the reader—ritual accesses, a souvenir of sorts (cf. Noy 2003b; Silverstein 1976, 54).

In addition to performative functions, quotations and voices serve referential goals. Reported speech portrays a dialogic collage, a map of social voices, characters, positions, and interactions. The map suggests that the great journey, with all the touristic destinations and attractions visited en route, is the backdrop against which a meaningful social drama occurs. Furthermore, this map demarcates and constructs the very community populated by backpackers, a traveling narrative community that emerges in and from their stories.

On the one hand, a strong communal sense emerges by discursive indications of inclusion and exclusion, which are located at the interface between the community and its exterior and which constantly demarcate the borders of the community. On the other hand, backpackers refer to intracommunal dynamics, complementing the construction of a sense of community. Inclusive and exclusive discourses refer to "natives" or "tourists" of various countries of origin with whom the backpackers cross paths in touristic spaces (see chapter 5). Would-be backpackers ("candidates"), too, are external to the community, but in a profoundly different sense: they define the communal threshold not according to who they *are not* and *cannot be*—the ultimate definition of the Other—but according to who they *can* and *will become* once they commit themselves and become engaged in the rite of passage.

At the same time, a sense of community is also established from "within" through evoking multiple intracommunal voices and dialogues, or "dialogics" (Mannheim and van Vleet 1998). The effect of establishing a community from within stems, first and foremost, from performing the authoritative collective voice. This voice represents the social and existential center of the Israeli backpacking community, embodying and propagating its normative ideology. Evoking the authoritarian instructions of the collective voice allows the performers to construct the community vis-à-vis its center, while at the same time positioning their own individual views in relation to it. Here, languages of conformity and subversion, canonicity and improvisation are evinced. In the former case, the narrators align themselves completely and wholeheartedly with the normative ideology and with the demanding requirements upon the backpackers' bodies. In the latter case, they express various degrees of disagreement, discontent, frustration, and subversion. If, as Bruner (2005, 24) argues, a trip is "a story in the making," and if to travel is "to inscribe the pretour narrative within the body of the tourist," then some backpackers, particularly female backpackers, make use of the occasion of posttrip narrations to contest and reconstruct the great journey's narrative (see chapters 6–7). Moreover, designated as the voice of "Israelis," the collective authority represents something of how the backpackers view the essence of Israeliness and the ideological and normative tenets engendered by it. This essence is established in and through what Virginia Domínguez (1989, 27) calls the "publicness of the dialogue of objectification in Israel." This dialogical-sociodiscursive space is the site where social groups establish notions of collectivity (and "peoplehood") through objectifications of their communal belonging (21–41).

Another set of intracommunal objectifying dialogics occupies the social space between the choral voice and the personal voice, between the group and the individual (see chapter 4). While in some cases the negotiation between the group and the individual metonymically enacts the relationship between the individual and the amorphous "collective," in other cases the individual employs the choral voice in the capacity of her or his social "shelter," as a shield against the normative-collective prescriptions and demands.

Although quotations at times construct the group as an extended self and at other times as a metonymized collective, broader patterns of sociability in Israel suggest the need for a warning note. As observed by Haim Hazan (2001a, 84) of the status of the cohesive group among Israeli youths, "[t]he very essence of the group is a symbol of collectivism. Moreover, for all its individualism and rebelliousness, the group conforms at the end of the day, to the plans of the collectivity." Indeed, skepticism about the emancipatory functions of the choral entity may well be warranted. In this respect, seemingly subversive rhetoric in fact fortifies the sovereignty of the collective by incorporating the dialogics of subversion into the narrative canon. The "snowball" sampling methodology employed in this research, which led me from one contented veteran backpacker to another (with no cases of dismissal), inevitably led this research to explore collectivism. The overlap of the rhetoric of persuasion and the backpackers' lively social chains and networks suggested that despite the blatancy of the voices of defiance, they were necessarily expressed from *within* the collective and are an integral part of its polyphonic discourse. This is why snowball sampling is sometimes called an "ascending methodology" (Faugier and Sargeant 1997). The snowball I eventually had in my hands was indeed the result of ascending from individuals to collectives: it amounted to no less than the mass of the collective itself.

All in all, the above dialogic web demonstrates that quotations are social ties. They function like numerous screws holding the ark of the traveling community together: those "communal webs" (Katriel 1991) that construct and maintain a shared sense of belonging. In and through quotations the narrators performatively illustrate not only "what a community means" but also "what it does" (Hazan 1990, 1); social meaning and social action are here one and the same thing, simultaneously establishing the sense of belonging and the vehicle of belongingness.

Furthermore, the polyphony highlighted in the narratives reveals the social voices by which backpackers are "possessed" (Handelman 2002). From a dialogical perspective, the narratives are dramatized—enacted and embodied—scripts that evoke the social actors and agents who hover in and around the youths' social realms. The great journey, then, serves to author and to enact a lively script of this type, by which a rich cast of new voices populates the travelers' minds—a script by which the narrators can access and possess a set of vibrant voices and dialogues.

The various functions that quotations and voices play in the stories and in their telling—discussed above under the theoretical categories of "performative" and "referential"—are de facto indistinguishable; they augment one another in the creation of a viable social taleworld: without a particular reference, a particular performative state cannot be accomplished.

The Language of Tourists

The very notion of "tourists' language" suggests that there is indeed a discernible register that can characterize the words and the stories recounted by tourists; this, in turn, promotes the idea that there is a definable set of practices indexed by the term *tourism* or *backpacking*. With the emergence of the "end of tourism" paradigm (Urry 1990), however, the autonomic status the semiotics of tourism have enjoyed over the last decade as a cultural site and space is seriously contested. An orthodox adherence to this paradigm would lead to a view of tourists' language as the language of everyday consumption and recreation in general.

Common sense, however, suggests that the term *tourism culture* covers a viable social space and that when tourists recount their (tourist) experiences, discursive aspects of the culture of tourism are evoked. More precisely, there is no all-inclusive "tourism culture" but rather "tourism cultures," with a rich ("within") variance that does not exhaust the delineation between tourism and other institutional high-consumer engagements and discourses. In this sense there is a semi-institutional quality to the stories recounted by tourists.

In this regard, this book is therefore a response to a call for institutionally sensitive research into discourses of identity (Gubrium and Holstein 2001). It sheds light on the still-marginal research of tourism in sociology and anthropology and on the roles played by tourism as a discursive system of signification. It suggests that in affluent societies, in which tourism is so common, tourism institutions serve to "launder" forms of capital: economic or material capital is converted to cultural and narrative capital, by which identity is established.

Furthermore, tourism supplies "instant" narrative resources in the form of ready-made taleworlds. The modern touristic trip is constructed as crossing a mythical geographical and experiential gulf, about which a transcendent narrative can later be told (Elsrud 2001). The persuasive impact of such narratives, as well as the role they play in the construction of identity in touristic discourses, echoes the similar role played by revelation or gospel texts in religious discourses. This should not be surprising, for one of the manifestations of the sublime in late modernity is the authentic, which is, not coincidentally, one of the foundational discourses of the industry, one that is particularly salient in the backpackers' narratives. Although this book did not focus on the interrelations between the roles reserved to language and to experience in the symbolic orders of tourism and religion, these interrelations have surfaced repeatedly. From the charged rhetorics of persuasion and self-transformation (see chapters 2 and 9) to the search for and the manifestation of transcendence (engulfed in the experience of authenticity) and highly authoritative and prescriptive canonic texts (see chapters 6–7), the language of the tourists studied in this research and the semiotics of their performances powerfully echo religious preoccupations.

Indeed, one of the main reasons for the enduring influence on tourism scholarship of Dean MacCannell's 1976 work *The Tourist* has to do with the sharp conceptualization it suggests of the very nature of modernity and of the transformation of religious drives and impulses therein. According to MacCannell, the emergence of mass modern tourism is framed in the context of modern alienation, which emerged with the gradual withdrawal of the divine from modern (Western) everyday life. MacCannell observes that tourism is "functionally equivalent to the sacred text that still serves as the moral base of traditional society . . . [it] contain[s] the representations of good and evil that apply universally to modern man in general" (39–40).

The parallels between touristic discourses and religious discourses, which emerged persistently throughout this book, are also attributed to two other, related sources, which I shall briefly discuss: the intense communal experience of which the backpackers narrate and the youths' cultural background. With regard to the former, it has been noted by sociologists—from Georg Simmel (1959) to Emile Durkheim (1995)—that the symbolic structure typical of "religious" movements (a structure that translates into personal experience [Stromberg 1991]) is sustained by social relations in groups and communities. Indeed, an authoritative voice of the type explored in chapters 6–7, with its moral rights and wrongs and dos and don'ts, can viably emerge only within social contexts that promote frequent social interaction. This condition, as we have seen, is a defining characteristic of backpacking tourism. The relation between groups and symbols is of course tautological: groups create symbolic structures which, in turn, organize them according to the levels of commitment of their members. This is all the more true with regard to traveling people, who have little by way of shared space and place and more by way of shared narratives and organizing metanarratives. These emerge and surface tangibly into the travelers' actual social life, which in the case of the present study assumed the shape of narrative interviews. On these occasions language plays a "strong" (constitutive) role, as it establishes, even momentarily, the participants' communal tenets.

With regard to the latter, the crisis of youth culture in contemporary Israeli society should be considered (see the introduction; Noy and Cohen 2005b). It suffices to note here that one of the attractive cultural alternatives offered to youths and young adults is the experience of being "born again" (see chapter 2). With this alternative in mind, the great journey, with the symbolic quasi-religious structure it engulfs and its quasi-religious rhetoric, is conceived as competing with a variety of "orthodox" and spiritual (New Age) movements over symbolic and narrative capitals, which endow a sense of coherent and meaningful identity.

Related to this issue is the fact that the linguistic register evident in the many excerpts in this book is undoubtedly highly dramatic, recounting many adventurous endeavors and experiences. This language both entails and attempts to reconcile dichotomies, to bridge extremes, in an almost literary manner. The narratives recounted by the backpackers negotiate various opposites: the "here" and the "there," the individual and the collective, the self and the Other, the premodern ("traditional") and the modern, the rural and the urban, the mundane and the extraordinary, and so on. This movement between extremes is precisely what endows the narrations with their undeniably dramatic—and, I would add, ritualistic—quality. It indicates that these stories are "myths," that they have the power to both explicate and reconcile opposites—mediating, negotiating, and fusing them (Levi-Strauss 1963). Because quotations signify the conflation of irreducible contexts, they are a metonymic expression of this mythic tension.

Since quotations are representations (of speech), they carry a playful—liminal and experimental—quality. They express the backpacking youths' ludic experiments with sociocultural material. In this sense, too, they are like myths, or perhaps even like "simulations," providing, as noted by Hazan (2001a, 4), an "easily manipulated cultural form, divorced from personal commitment." While myths are usually solemn and grave, simulations are playful, enabling one to toy reflexively—with a very low dosage of explicit ideology—with representations and imitations of reality (5). As Meirav says in the epigraph to this book's "Itinerary": "So we decided on playing this game. The truth is we invented it on the spot, but I'm sure it was also invented before us."

Although the journey is concluded, the phenomenology of quotations is not exhausted. It can never be, for quotations are the emblem of continuity, enmeshing creativity with repetition that cannot be bound by context.

Quotations as reiterations,
creations,
events,
stories,
trails of stories,
voices,
myths,
memories,
reincarnations

APPENDIX 1: SNOWBALL STEMMATA

Of the forty-four interviewees I met with in the course of this research, I reached eight directly: four through joint acquaintances and four through several visits to a photography store in downtown Jerusalem. Three of these eight backpackers referred me to their friends and acquaintances, thus generating three snowball stemmata, a process that led me to the other thirty-six interviewees.

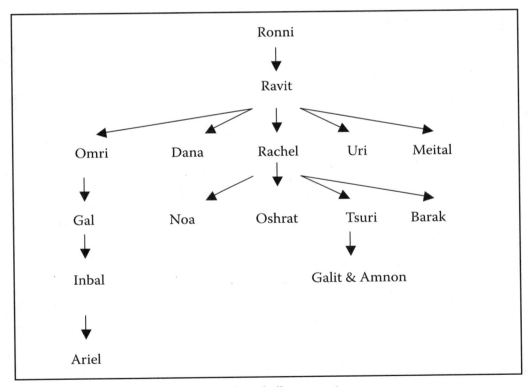

Fig. 5. Snowball stemma 1

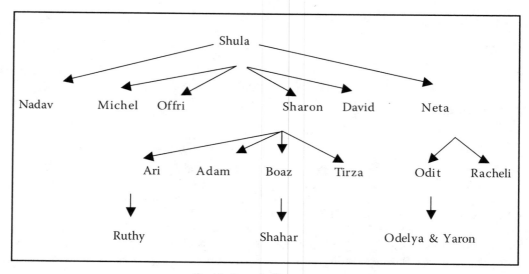

Fig. 6. Snowball stemma 2

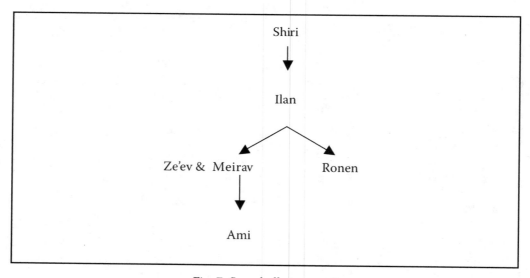

Fig. 7. Snowball stemma 3

APPENDIX 2: QUESTIONS ASKED

The interview conversations typically consisted of three phases. First, I introduced a general question with the intention of eliciting the core travel narrative. The question addressed the interviewee's travel experiences:

- Can you tell me about your experiences from the trip?

I sometimes added that narrating the travel's experiences chronologically, in line with the trip's itinerary, might make the recollection process easier.

The second phase of the interview consisted of clarifications that addressed the topics and the episodes mentioned during the core narrative. I asked the narrators to expand on issues they had touched on earlier. This I did when I felt that the account did not convey the entire picture, when there were silences that interested me, or simply because my curiosity was aroused with regard to particular events and moments.

In the third phase of the interview, I introduced seven preplanned questions. This phase was more structured than the previous phases and was based on pilot research that included twenty short interviews with backpackers. However, this phase, too, was "negoti-ated" (Fontana and Frey, 2000), and I presented the preplanned questions differently to different narrators. Sometimes, if the narrator had already elaborated on an issue about which I was planning to ask, I did not present the question. Also, I tailored the sequence of the questions and often their wording, too, to the particular interviewee.

The questions addressed peak experiences, gendered experiences, the question of whether military service had had an influence on the travel experience and how it was conducted, bodily experiences, gastronomic experiences, social interactions, preparation for the trip, and the experience of returning to Israel:

- Can you tell about particularly meaningful experiences that you had during the trip—both positive and negative experiences?

- Do you think military service affected your trip and its experience?

- Do you remember physical or bodily experiences that were particularly meaningful?

- Can you elaborate on meetings, interactions, and relationships that you had with backpackers and with local people?

- Did you have experiences or incidents that were related to/influenced by your gender?

Do you think the trip is different for women/men?

- Can you tell about a meaningful gastronomic experience you had?
- Can you tell about the preparations for the trip and about how it was to return to Israel—about the experience of returning?

When this phase was concluded, I asked each interviewee whether she or he had any questions or comments. At the very end of the meeting, I collected standard sociodemographic information.

NOTES

Chapter 1

1. It is difficult to estimate the actual number of backpackers (see Loker-Murphy and Pearce 1995; Noy 2006a; Richards and Wilson 2004b). For one thing, the backpacker population is extremely heterogeneous. In addition, border checkpoints do not register the type of leisure practice travelers pursue. Rough estimates made by tourist operators and others working with backpackers in Israel suggest that approximately fifty thousand backpackers travel every year to Asia (Levy-Barzilai, 2003, 2004). Since Mevorach's (1997) extensive survey indicates that the ratio between backpackers in Asia and in South America is 2:1, the approximate number of total Israeli backpackers would be seventy-five thousand (or a little higher if the number of backpackers traveling in Africa is added). This figure, although unsupported (and, in my opinion, somewhat inflated), will have to suffice, because formal reports of the Ministry of Tourism and the Israeli Central Bureau of Statistics tend to be general; specific parameters such as age, length of trip, and country of destination are indicated only intermittently. This figure should be viewed against the general heightened cultural context of travel consumption. In 2001, for instance, the number of departures was approximately three and a half million, which amounts to 54 percent of the total population in Israel (see Noy 2006a).

At any rate, an observation once made by Victor Turner about quantitative demographic data comes to mind: "These figures told me if not a story at least where to go to find stories" (1980, 141).

2. For instance, ages vary as both younger tourists (even prior to their service in the army) and older cohorts (reaching their sixties and seventies) backpack. Curiously enough, it has recently become a custom that backpackers' parents join their offspring to backpack for parts of the lengthy trip. Religious youths are participating in backpacking in unprecedented numbers. Additionally, a pattern of "trampoline" or "serial" backpacking has emerged, whereby travelers return to Israeli to visit and/or to work, only to travel yet again intermittently for years (Noy and Cohen 2005a; Uriely, Yonay, and Simchai 2002).

3. On the unique and symbolic role outdoor adventurous activities played, see Almog 2000; Liebman and Don-Yihya 1983; Schwartz, Zerubavel, and Barnett 1986; Shapira 1999; Zerubavel 1995.

4. It is noteworthy that Masada has become a site of both intranational and international tourism, of the type that is now termed "heritage tourism" (Bruner and Gorfain 1984).

5. Note that the Sabras, who were descendents of European immigrants, were well acquainted with nineteenth-century travel and adventure literature. Hence, through Kipling, Vern, and others, Israeli youths had imagined and then pursued the romanticist-colonial myth.

The legendary Palmah bonfires were also the setting in which an older relative of the present-day backpacking tale was recounted: the *Chizbat* (Oring 1981). The Chizbat is a tall tale of adventures and wonders, often describing humorously mischievous doings. Through evoking excitement and laughter, the performance of the Chizbat, like that of the backpackers' tales of adventure, created and re-created nostalgia and a sense of group togetherness and cohesiveness.

6. The subject of tourist agency has recently become the center of debate, one that lies at the core of how tourists—the "MacCannell tourist," the "Urry tourist," as they are called half humorously—and their experiences are conceptualized (MacCannell 2001). While the debate is partly inspired by empirical data, it is surely a product of the researchers' paradigmatic and disciplinary views as well. In this sense, too, I tend to concur with Bruner, who recently noted that "[t]here are no persons without agency, without active selves. . . . To conceive of tourists without agency, or of natives as objects, would be to write about them as if they are automatons" (2005, 12).

7. Some of the works on the language of tourists and on linguistic performance include Boxill and Hernandez 2002; Bruner 1991, 2005; Cohen and Cooper 1986; Haldrup and Larsen 2003; Kaplan 1980; Moeran 1983; Neumann 1999.

8. The colloquial Hebrew expression designating snowball sampling is *haver mevi haver* (literally, "a friend brings a friend"). This phrase sounds much better in Hebrew, perhaps because it evokes the characteristic qualities of Sabra patterns of socialization (as observed by Katriel [1986]). As I have demonstrated elsewhere (Noy 2005), some of the unique appeal of backpacking for Israeli youths concerns the possibilities embedded in the particular structure of the trip, which promotes intensified interpersonal communication and heightens the role of hearsay and of tight social networks—all of which are characteristic of patterns of socialization in the backpackers' home culture.

9. A few points concerning the three stemmata described in appendix 1 are noteworthy. First, this type of graphic depiction should be viewed as a residue or a trace of lively interactions. Somewhat akin to transcription, a stemma is a two-dimensional "still" picture of an inherently dynamic social process.

Second, although the overall number of women and men interviewed in the present study was balanced, a brief examination of the stemmata indicates that women are positioned in social (referral) junctions. This finding is not surprising. It corresponds with the socialization patterns of women, which they are required to demonstrate as a part of the social roles they assume in various institutions (as feminists have noted; see Ruddick 1989, 87). As a native Israeli, it is my impression that from military service to adult social and familial life, women are generally expected to assume the role of those who maintain the social ties of the social system in which they participate (for an elaboration of this point see Noy 2006b).

Third, it should be pointed out that the stemmata are in fact incomplete. They include only those referrals that were materialized in the form of interviews. A more comprehensive depiction and discussion of snowball sampling and stemmata would require indicating *all* the referrals made by *all* the interviewees (even by those with whom I only spoke over the phone).

Chapter 2

1. Cuzco is a city in the south of Peru from which many treks depart, and Azangate is a name of one of these trekking routes.

2. *Chola* is a Spanish word designating indigenous Indian women in the Andes. The term, popular among tourists, has a colonial history and derogatory and racial connotations (see Gotkowitz 2003).

3. The high social status accorded to longtime veteran backpackers was recently evinced in a heated exchange, including allegations and accusations, between two men, each of whom claims the "title" (their word) of having been the "first backpacker" (see www. akkonet.co.il/forums/viewtopic.php?t=2637, and the response, published in the letters to the editor section, *Ha'aretz,* May 5, 2006).

4. A transliteration note: Throughout the book I used the symbol *h* to correspond to both *het* and the *khaf* of the Hebrew alphabet. Regardless of the backpackers' socioethnic backgrounds, the pronunciation of these letters was indistinguishable (this is also the case with the letters *aleph, ayin,* and to some degree even *he*). This state reflects a general blurring of the unique pronunciation of guttural consonants in spoken Hebrew, particularly so among speakers who are second- and third-generation Israeli-born and who were educated in urban centers (middle class). I am grateful to Yael Maschler and Esther Schely-Newman for their comments on this issue.

5. For more on persuasive discourses, see in linguistics works that derive from speech act theory (Austin 1962; Searle 1969) regarding "perlocutive" acts (Gaines 1979) and the communicational value of speech acts (Geis 1995); in psychology (Green and Brock 2000, about "transportation theory"); in religious studies (Hinze 1996; Mack and Robbins 1989); and, more closely related to our discussion, in conversation and communication analysis (Gaines 1979; Johnstone 1986, 1989; Keane 1997; Lakoff 1982; Schmidt and Kess 1986).

6. Persuasion has as its aim not only certain activities within a certain trip but also the participation in additional grand excursions (cf. "trampoline" or "serial" backpackers; see note 2 in chapter 1).

7. Arguably, the term was initially employed in the discourse of drug rehabilitation and expressed self-empowerment aimed at preventing individuals from being "weak" and "falling back" into addiction.

8. On the larger effects of repetition in and on culture and social life, see the interesting works of Deleuze (1994); Derrida (1988); and Fischer (1994).

Chapter 3

1. In Hebrew the word designating quotations marks (*gersha'im*) etymologically stems from the verb *g, r, sh,* meaning "to expel." Thus, quotation marks literally mark the utterance as that which is "expelled" from its surrounding (con)text.

2. Concerning prosodic aspects of reported speech, see Couper-Kuhlen 1999; Couper-Kuhlen and Klewitz 1999; Couper-Kuhlen and Selting 1996; Holt 1996, 1999.

3. Since MacCannell's works (1973, 1976), wherein authenticity in tourism was conceived of as the modern embodiment of the age-old universal human concern with the sacred, the concept has received an impressive number of formulations. Authenticity was, and very much still is, at the center of various scholarly discussions (some of which are quite heated), undoubtedly amounting to one of the paradigms of the discipline. For recent discussions of authenticity and its implications for tourists' experiences—from authenticity-

seeking romanticist tourists to "posttourists" who take delight in inauthentic attractions—
see Bruner 2005; Kirshenblatt-Gimblett 1998; Noy 2004b; Olsen 2002; Wang 2000.

Chapter 4

1. Note that the pioneers' social "families" substituted in a way the biological families they left in their countries of origin. Although backpacking is a tourist practice, not an immigrational one, cultural intergenerational reverberations are tellingly evinced (cf. Hazan 2001a, 2001b).

2. While intense social interaction is a defining feature of backpacking tourism, it is by no means limited to this type of tourism. As shown by Harrison, social interactions, encounters, and groupings (sometimes designated by the term *families*), are an important part of the tourist social experience. Social connectedness, Harrison (2003, 48) elaborates, "was experienced in myriad forms, all remembered and valued by the travel enthusiasts: to the human family at its broadest level, to a particular cultural linage or heritage, to those who lived in the past but had walked the same ground . . . to fellow tourists, to relatives and friends visited, to those left behind at home, to all travellers through time, to travelling companions . . . to oneself."

3. Borrowed from Arabic, the word *yalla* is a common exclamatory term in colloquial Hebrew, meaning "Come on!" or "Let's!"

4. Note that elitist rhetoric, albeit presently aimed at locating the backpacker advantageously within his or her community, is generally characteristic of and inherent in several types of tourism ideologies (romanticism in particular). As recently observed by Bruner, "To participate in such a tour in the Third World is to butt into and reinforce a story of unequal power relations, neocolonialism, and elitism" (2005, 21; see also Urry 1990, 86, for elitism among romanticist tourists).

5. Alternatively, three social characters can in fact be designated in the scene Meirav depicts: The protagonist, the anonymous female hiker ("she"), and the group. According to this reading, the second female character had also left the group, even if only "momentarily" (unlike Meirav). An interesting conflict is embodied here between Meirav, who decided to continue leaving the group, and the faceless female character, who decided on being part of the group. Silence arises here in relation to the "she" character, who is a mirror image of the protagonist, hovering between the social possibilities of individuality, on the one hand, and collectivity, on the other hand. I am indebted to Gonen Hacohen for suggesting this reading.

6. Note that Inbal points at an institutional conflation of identities: the men are not discharged, veteran soldiers, they are on temporary leave from active service. This conflation became possible as a result of a recent amendment to military law that permits officers on active duty to take longer leaves from the army and travel abroad (usually joining their discharged friends' backpacking trips). On a different level, Inbal's indication implies an interpermeation of the two institutions: tourism (backpacking) and army (combat units).

Chapter 5

1. The terms *tourist* and *native* are in quotation marks to indicate that they are employed as such by the backpackers (emically, that is).

2. These "quantitative anecdotes" recall the "demographic issue" troubling nationalist politicians in Israel. From the number of Jews who perished in the Holocaust to current

"demographic" anxieties concerning the Palestinian population in Israel, numbers are established signifiers of identity. This is related to the fact that on three occasions backpackers employed "sand" as a metaphor to refer to Israelis' ubiquity, thus echoing the biblical promise granting Jews "demographic advantage."

3. A transliteration note. In the original utterance Rachel repeats the sound "vi" (and not "x" as appears in the text), commonly indicating in Hebrew that an activity or chore has been checked off.

4. The term *havay* (indicating the folklore that emerges from a positive close social atmosphere) subtly alludes to the Sabra-Hebrew register and indicates the warm feeling generated by a group (Katriel 2004). Its frequent use indicates that the backpackers are aware of the shared experience that social bonding nurtures.

Chapter 6

1. Note that the crescendo effect is achieved also by the incorporation of the word "and" *into* the last quotative, while in the preceding three instances the word is located outside the reported speech (which it frames). By including "and" in the quotation (an incorporation of what was ex- or metaquotative), Ravit is terminating the voice of the narrator—a performance that produces a dramatic and concluding effect.

2. The term *canonic* is employed hereafter to designate a popular corpus of texts whose tenets are ideological and hegemonic. Exploring the canonic quality with regard to the collective voice is enriching, especially so when considering that literary (and discursive) canons are often authoritative. They come to embody "the location, the index, and the record of the struggle for cultural representation" (Michael Bérubé, cited in Gluzman 2003, 1).

3. In the sense that Barak speaks of remedying a state of meager knowledge, his extract can be read as elevating the consumption of foods to a symbolic level. Later in the narrative Barak refers to collective quotations as "nurturing" or "feeding" (*mezinim*) and to other narrators as "they nurture you" (*mezinim otha*). According to this metaphor (which is indeed oral-regressive in line with the tourist context), stories, recommendations, tips, suggestions, and warnings are consumed like nutrient substances. The extract, then, bears not only on the material substances "out there," which can be consumed and incorporated—that is, that are pure or impure—but also on the nurturing substances that are supplied by the collective (voice) in the form of satisfying informational assertions. In line with the canonic quotations' phonic form, they also have an *oral quality* and can be thus consumed. According to Barak they are pure nutrients, necessary for the sustenance of the backpackers in a "foreign land." It is as though the backpackers can sustain themselves primarily by consuming and incorporating these "fleshy" quotations. Besides being kosher, these quotations-as-products (akin to any other evangelist product), are more than recyclable, they are regenerative.

4. The notion of multiple collectives brings to mind one of the funniest sketches performed by the legendary satire group Ha-Hamishiya Ha-Kamerit, which aired during the 1990s in Israel. In the sketch, the actors are discussing whether they themselves (i.e., the Ha-Hamishiya Ha-Kamerit), with their bitter criticism of society, have become a focus of collective consensus and admiration (as it admittedly had). One of the characters explains to the other that in Israel, "there are big consensuses and small consensuses, but one *must* have a consensus or be affiliated with one." "And if someone doesn't want to be in/have a consensus?" asks the other. "Then he must leave Israel," is the reply. "Here, you must have a consensus."

5. The discussion of word of mouth as "off-site" markers (see the introduction) is true of negative off-site markers as well, which are far more scarce than positive markers and direct tourists *away* from the sites they signify.

Meirav and many other backpackers revert occasionally to the many pictures they shot during the trip and naturally entwine these visual representations into their performances. While a significant amount of research has been conducted on the semiotics of photography and picture taking in tourism (mostly under Urry's [1990] prevalent conceptualization of the "tourist gaze"; see Edensor 1998; Haldrup and Larsen 2003), to the best of my knowledge no work has yet examined backpacker photography culture and ideology in particular.

Note that pictures amount to one part of the overall visual material that backpackers produce and disseminate during the extended trip. From digital cameras and photographic cellular telephones to digital video cameras, a rich array of visual material circulates between the backpackers, usually instantaneously through the Internet and by e-mail communication. It seems that the role these types of visual data play within backpacker communities is highly interesting and bears some parallels to the textual sippurei dereh (the former perhaps the successors of the latter). While a few of the backpackers interviewed for this study mentioned that they had refrained from taking (many) pictures, so as to "truly experience the moment," expressing thus a romanticist ideology, others boasted of the number of pictures they had taken (one mentioned he shot nine hundred pictures during the trip) and used the number of pictures taken at any particular site or activity to be a quantified indicator showing how impressive their experience was.

6. A broad discussion of the terms by which gender categories are indexed in Hebrew is beyond the present scope. Suffice it to point out that the terms *bat* (or *banot*, pl.) and *ben* (or *banim*, pl.) are used by the backpackers almost solely to designate females and males, respectively. These terms do not have satisfactory equivalents in English. They are reserved to index a certain age cohort, which is older than a boy/girl (*yeled*/*yalda*) but younger than a man/woman (*ish*/*isha*). Because, literally, the words *ben* and *bat* mean "son" and "daughter"; they connote familial identities. Most likely, they reflect the categories used earlier in the youths' lives, during schooling, a period to which they return within the regressive setting of tourism after their service in the military (Dann 1996, 101–9).

Chapter 7

1. Though most of the sites where travelers' books are found are located abroad, a few such sites exist in Israel. Particularly, the legendary Hametayel store, located in the center of Tel Aviv, is one such site. The store, which was established in the early 1980s, is a social center customarily visited by many backpackers before the trip and sometimes after they return (Jacobson 1987). A significant part of the time spent in the store is dedicated to reading letters that backpackers sent to the store during the trip. In recent years, the store has become a chain with branches in many cities, all of which have special spaces designated to reading these volumes (including, of course, virtual spaces on the Internet that are dedicated to backpacking; see Noy 2006a).

2. The simun shvilim system pertains to maps that include, in addition to the standard topographical legend, colored marks signifying hiking trails. These marks correspond with same-color marks appearing in visible spots along the trails (a colored line, some fifteen centimeters long, located between two white lines, marked every few hundred meters or so).

3. The popularity of the simun shvilim marking system has raised a polemic. On one

side are those who promote frequent use of markers and signs for the benefit of outdoor recreationists. Not surprisingly, one of the influential spokesmen of this position, Ori Dvir (who also headed the Committee for Trail Marking), evokes the "traditional" role trail marking has played in Zionist history. His argument is nostalgic, suggesting that present-day marking practices are related to and echo past traditions of outdoor hiking (Dvir 1993, 38-39; also Birger 1993, 36-37).

On the other side are those who claim that demarcation is presently far too extensive (and indeed is decided upon by irrelevant ideological considerations), and that it should be pursued in a more restricted fashion. Menahem Marcus, a spokesman of the latter view, opposes what he terms the "megalomaniac ritual of trail marking" (Marcus 1993, 43). At stake in this discussion is a variation of the nature/culture question, and specifically the issue of the colonizing of nature by signs and marks.

4. Yet backpackers mention that occasional Hebrew graffiti is visible along the trails as well as along the collective enclaves. Such inscriptions usually include reference to the inscribers' military occupation and unit affiliation. They make for an up-to-date, extranational variety of the notorious "Baruch Gamili" graffiti of the 1948 Independence War.

Chapter 8

1. The specific allusion to German travelers here is not coincidental and evokes (cross-)cultural images. In depicting "sterility," a notorious stereotype of Germans is evoked, one that pertains to interpersonal distance, coldness, and impersonality. This is done not for the purpose of distinguishing Germans from other tourists but for precisely the opposite reason: it powerfully exemplifies how "tourists" differ from "Israelis," and how the former are not as interpersonally close and warm as the latter. It is interesting to observe how, through distinguishing between "Germans," "Swiss," "Europeans," and other tourists, and comparing Israelis with them, various types and stereotypes of foreignness are employed in the aim of constructing identity.

2. Note that Ari does not need to report the neighborhood's name, because we immediately learn that the silent locator lives in the same neighborhood. As was the case with Bella (in chapter 6), who did not specify names of hotels but chose to indicate generic labels ("X"), so, too, Ari's aim is not to acquaint us with specifics but to make a point: "people meet their neighbors abroad".

3. The issue of social noisiness and impoliteness also carries *ethnic* hues in Israeli culture. In several cases, narrators implicitly draw an association between loudness and vulgarity, on the one hand, and *mizrahi* (Oriental) identity, on the other hand. For instance, when they mention that Israelis are noisy (*ra'ashnim*), they pronounce the vowel "a" throatily. They thus evoke a cultural stereotype according to which Oriental Jews, some of whom pronounce some vowels throatily, are the epitome of vulgarity in their supposedly "un-Western" throaty pronunciation.

4. The Hebrew expression Odit uses (*bekol tru'a rama*), together with *kishkushim* (in the previous excerpt), *birburinm, palavrot,* and the like, calls to mind Katriel's (1986, 25) observation concerning the "proliferation of metalinguist terms" in Sabra Hebrew.

5. According to a survey quoted by Shavit, the respondents indicated that the "road" was the place where Israelis behaved most vulgarly (38 percent). Interestingly, the "trip abroad" was in second place (19 percent)!

6. Late in the production stage of this volume (summer 2006), a war in Lebanon was

launched. During this period—due to rocket attacks by the Hezbollah on northern Israel—
the net of wartime sirens was activated repeatedly. Note that the soundscapes created by
these sirens were selective and covered mainly Jewish settlements and cities in northern
Israel.

Chapter 9

1. The use of opaque language and the avoidance of explicit statements of transformation serve also to avoid, or rebuff, potential allegations of a downright religiouslike (born-
again) transformation narrative. Since the backpackers are viewed in their home society
as "secular," and since the trip is perceived as a recreational practice rather than a religious
pilgrimage, narrators generally do not wish to convey a total transformative experience too
explicitly. In this sense Sharon's narration differs from Boaz's, and she manages to grasp
both ends of the stick: while successfully conveying a meaningful experience of self-change,
she simultaneously refutes potential claims that her story is of a fundamental, born-again
nature. (See chapter 2.)

2. Note that shortly before the extract Sharon mentioned an acquaintance she met
who backpacked with her and shared her experience. Thus, when she communicates her
frustration with her inability to convey the trip's meaningfulness to an interlocutor (myself)
whom she presumes has *not* backpacked, she is possibly alluding to an alternative genre: one
in which the personal experience is shared by both sides.

3. The alteration in the senses accomplished by Danit reminds me of a peculiar sen-
tence that I (like many generations of commentators) have puzzled over ever since I read
it in my undergraduate Old Testament studies. In Exodus 20:14, immediately after the Ten
Commandments are given to the People of Israel, it is written: "When the people saw the
thunder" (*vehol ha'am ro'im et ha-kolot;* literally, "And all the people are seeing the voices").
Perhaps the alteration Danit accomplished as she *performatively* transforms the different
modes of perception is as close as I can come to understanding what "seeing the voices"
means. Within a heightened performative state, the same semiotic effect can be reached
through different modalities and senses.

WORKS CITED

Adler, Judith. 1989. Travel as performed art. *American Journal of Sociology* 94 (6): 1366–91.

Aitchison, Cara. 2001. Theorizing Other discourses of tourism, gender, and culture: Can the subaltern speak (in tourism)? *Tourist Studies* 1 (2): 133–47.

Almog, Oz. 1997. *Ha-Tsabar: Dyokan.* Tel Aviv: Am Oved.

———. 2000. *The Sabra: The creation of the new Jew.* Trans. H. Watzman. Berkeley: University of California Press.

Alneng, Victor. 2002. The Modern does not cater for Natives: Travel ethnography and the conventions of Form. *Tourist Studies* 2 (2): 119–42.

Anteby-Yemini, Lisa, Keren Bazini, Irit Gerstein, and Gali Kling. 2005. "Traveling cultures": Israeli backpackers, deterritorialization, and reconstruction of home. In *Israeli backpackers and their society: A view from afar,* ed. Chaim Noy and Erik Cohen. Albany: State University of New York Press.

Appadurai, Arjun. 1996. *Public worlds.* Vol. 1 of *Modernity at large: Cultural dimensions of globalization.* Minneapolis: University of Minnesota Press.

Auerbach, Erich. 1953. *Mimesis: The representation of reality in Western literature.* Trans. W. R. Trask. Princeton: Princeton University Press.

Austin, John L. 1962. *How to do things with words.* Oxford: Clarendon.

Azmon, Yael, ed. 2001. *Will you listen to my voice? Representations of women in Israeli culture.* Jerusalem: Van Leer Jerusalem Institute and Hakibbutz Hameuchad House.

Babcock, Barbara A. 1993. At home, no women are storytellers: Ceramic creativity and the politics of discourse in Cochiti Pueblo. In *Creativity/Anthropology,* ed. Smadar Lavie, Kirin Narayan, and Renato Rosaldo. Ithaca, N.Y.: Cornell University Press.

Badone, Ellen, and Sharon R. Roseman. 2004. Approaches to the anthropology of pilgrimage and tourism. In *Intersecting journeys: The anthropology of pilgrimage and tourism,* ed. Ellen Badone and Sharon R. Roseman. Urbana: University of Illinois Press.

Bakhtin, Mikhail M. 1968. *Rabelais and his world.* Trans. H. Iswolsky. Cambridge, Mass.: MIT Press.

———. 1981. Discourse in the novel. In *The dialogic imagination: Four essays.* Trans. C. Emerson and M. Holquist. Austin: University of Texas Press.

———. 1984. *Problems of Dostoevsky's poetics.* Trans. C. Emerson. Minneapolis: University of Minnesota Press.

———. 1986. The problem of speech genres. In *Speech genres and other late essays.* Trans. V. W. McGee. Ed. M. Holquist. Austin: University of Texas Press.

———. 1990. *Art and answerability: Early philosophical essays.* Trans. V. Liapunov. Ed. M. Holquist and V. Liapunov. Austin: University of Texas Press.

Bamberg, Michael, ed. 1997. Oral versions of personal experience: Three decades of narrative analysis. Special issue, *Journal of Narrative and Life History* 7 (1-4).

Banfield, Ann. 1973. Narrative style and the grammar of direct and indirect speech. *Foundations of Language* 10: 1–39.

Bar-Tal, Daniel, and Dikla Antebi. 1992. Siege mentality in Israel. *International Journal of Intercultural Relations* 16: 251–75.

Barthes, Roland. 1986. *The rustle of language.* Trans. R. Howard. New York: Hill and Wang.

Basso, Ellen B. 1985. *A musical view of the universe: Kalapalo myth and ritual performances.* Philadelphia: University of Pennsylvania Press.

Basso, Keith H. 1984. "Stalking with stories": Names, places, and moral narratives among the western Apache. In *Text, play, and story: The construction and reconstruction of self and society,* ed. Edward M. Bruner. Washington, D.C.: American Ethnological Society.

Baum, Tom, and Svend Lundtorp, eds. 2001. *Seasonality in tourism.* Amsterdam: Pergamon.

Bauman, Richard. 1978. *Verbal art as performance.* Rowley, Mass.: Newbury House.

———. 1986. *Story, performance, and event: Contextual studies of oral narrative.* Cambridge: Cambridge University Press.

———. 2004. *A world of others' words: Cross-cultural perspectives on intertextuality.* Malden, Mass.: Blackwell.

Bauman, Richard, and Charles L. Briggs, 1990. Poetics and performances as critical perspectives on language and social life. *Annual Review of Anthropology* 19: 59–88.

Baynham, Mike, and Stef Slembrouck. 1999. Speech representation and institutional discourse. *Text* 19 (4): 439–57.

Bazzanella, Carla, ed. 1996. *Repetition in dialogue.* Tubingen: Niemeyer.

Becker, Alton L. 1988. Language in particular: A lecture. In *Linguistics in context: Connecting observation and understanding,* ed. Deborah Tannen. Norwood, N.J.: Ablex.

Ben-Ari, Eyal. 1998. *Mastering soldiers: Conflict, emotions, and the enemy in an Israeli military unit.* New York: Berghahn.

Ben-Ari, Eyal, and Edna Levi-Schreiber. 2000. Body-building, character-building, and nation-building: Gender and military service in Israel. *Studies in Contemporary Judaism* 16: 171–90.

Benjamin, Walter. 1968. *Illuminations.* New York: Harcourt.

Berger, Peter L., and Thomas Luckmann. 1967. *The social construction of reality: A treatise in the sociology of knowledge.* London: Penguin.

Bhattacharyya, Deborah P. 1997. Mediating India: An analysis of a guidebook. *Annals of Tourism Research* 24 (2): 371–89.

Bijsterveld, Karin. 2001. The diabolical symphony of the mechanical age: Technology and symbolism of sound in European and North American noise abatement campaigns, 1900–40. *Social Studies of Science* 31 (1): 37–70.

Binder, Jana. 2004. The whole point of backpacking: Anthropological perspectives on the characteristics of backpacking. In *The global nomad: Backpacker travel in theory and practice,* ed. Greg Richards and Julie Wilson. Clevedon, Eng.: Channel View.

Birger, Hillel. 1993. Nothing new under the sun and we're not the first [in Hebrew]. *Teva va-*

Aretz 254 (93/3): 35-37. (Orig. pub. 1949.)

Blake, Susan L. 1990. A women's trek: What difference does gender make? *Women's Studies International Forum* 13 (4): 347–55.

Bloch, Linda R. 1998. Communicating as an American immigrant in Israel: The Freier phenomenon and the pursuit of an alternative value system. *Research on Language and Social Interaction* 31 (2): 177–208.

———. 2000a. Mobile discourse: Political bumper stickers as a communication event in Israel. *Journal of Communication* 50 (2): 48–76.

———. 2000b. Setting the public sphere in motion: The rhetoric of political bumper stickers in Israel. *Political Communication* 17: 433–56.

———. 2003. Who's afraid of being a Freier? The analysis of communication through a key cultural frame. *Communication Theory* 13 (2): 125–59.

Blondheim, Menahem. 2005. Why is this book different from all other books? The orality, the literacy, and the printing of the Passover *Haggadah.* Unpublished manuscript.

Blum-Kulka, Shoshana. 1992. The metapragmatics of politeness in Israeli society. In *Politeness in language: Studies in its history, theory, and practice,* ed. R. J. Watts, S. Ide, and K. Ehlich. New York: Mouton de Gruyter.

———. 1997. *Dinner talk: Cultural patterns of sociability and socialization in family discourse.* Mahwah, N.J.: Lawrence Erlbaum.

Boxill, Ian, and Edith Hernandez. 2002. How tourism transforms language: The case of Playa del Carmen, Mexico. *Social and Economic Studies* 51 (1): 47–60.

Briggs, Charles L. 1988. *Competence in performance: The creativity of tradition in Mexicano verbal art.* Philadelphia: University of Pennsylvania Press.

Bruner, Edward M. 1991. The transformation of self in tourism. *Annals of Tourism Research* 18 (2): 238–50.

———. 2005. *Cultures on tour: Ethnographies of travel.* Chicago: University of Chicago Press.

Bruner, Edward M., and Phyllis Gorfain. 1984. Dialogic narration and the paradoxes of Masada. In *Text, play, and story: The construction and reconstruction of self and society,* ed. Edward M. Bruner. Washington, D.C.: American Ethnological Society.

Butler, Judith. 1990. *Gender trouble: Feminism and the subversion of identity.* New York: Routledge.

———. 1993. *Bodies that matter: On the discursive limits of "sex".* New York: Routledge.

———. 1997a. *Excitable speech: A politics of the performative.* New York: Routledge.

———. 1997b. Sovereign performatives in the contemporary scene of utterance. *Critical Inquiry* 23 (2): 350–77.

Buttny, Richard. 1997. Reported speech in talking race on campus. *Human Communication Research* 23 (4): 477–506.

———. 1998. Putting prior talk into context: Reported speech and the reporting context. *Research on Language and Social Interaction* 31 (1): 45–58.

———. 1999. Discursive constructions of racial boundaries and self-segregation on campus. *Journal of Language and Social Psychology* 18 (3): 247–68.

Buttny, Richard, and Princess L. Williams. 2000. Demanding respect: the uses of reported speech in discursive constructions of interracial contact. *Discourse and Society* 11 (1): 109–33.

Cain, Carole. 1991. Personal stories: Identity acquisition and self-understanding in Alcoholics Anonymous. *Ethos* 19 (2): 210–53.

Carter, S. 1998. Tourists' and travellers' social construction of Africa and Asia as risky locations. *Tourism Management* 19 (4): 349–58.

Clifford, James. 1992. Traveling cultures. In *Cultural studies*, ed. L. Grossberg, C. Nelson,
and P. Treichler. London: Routledge.

———. 1997. *Routes: Travel and translation in the late twentieth century.* Cambridge, Mass.:
Harvard University Press.

Cohen, Erik. 1972. Toward a sociology of international tourism. *Social Research* 39: 164–
89.

———. 1973. Nomads from affluence: Notes on the phenomenon of drifter tourism. *International Journal of Comparative Sociology* 14: 89–103.

———. 1979. A phenomenology of tourist experiences. *Sociology* 13 (2): 179–201.

———. 1986. Tourism and time. *World Leisure and Recreation* 28: 13–16.

———. 1992a. Pilgrimage and tourism: Convergence and divergence. In *Sacred journeys: The
anthropology of pilgrimage*, ed. A. Morinis. Westport, Conn.: Greenwood.

———. 1992b. Pilgrimage centers: Concentric and excentric. *Annals of Tourism Research* 19:
33–50.

———. 1993. The study of touristic images of native people: Mitigating the stereotype of a
stereotype. In *Tourism research: critiques and challenges*, ed. D. G. Pearce and R. Butler. London: Routledge.

———. 2000. *The commercialized crafts of Thailand: Hill tribes and lowland villages.* London: Curzon.

Cohen, Erik, and Robert L. Cooper. 1986. Language and tourism. *Annals of Tourism Research* 13 (4): 533–63.

Coleman, Simon, and Mike Crang, eds. 2002. *Tourism: Between place and performance.*
New York: Berghahn.

Corradi, Consuelo. 1991. Text, context, and individual meaning: Rethinking life stories in a
hermeneutic framework. *Discourse and Society* 2 (1): 105–18.

Corradi, Fiumara G. 1995. *The other side of language: A philosophy of listening.* London:
Routledge.

Couper-Kuhlen, Elizabeth. 1999. Coherent voicing: On prosody in conversational reported
speech. In *Coherence in spoken and written discourse: How to create it and how to describe it*, ed. L. Wolfram, Uta Ventola, and E. Ventola. Amsterdam: John Benjamins.

Couper-Kuhlen, Elizabeth, and Gabriele Klewitz. 1999. Quote-unquote? The role of prosody
in the contextualization of reported speech sequences. *Pragmatics* 9 (4): 459–85.

Couper-Kuhlen Elizabeth, and Margret Selting, eds. 1996. *Prosody in conversation: Interactional studies.* Cambridge: Cambridge University Press.

Crawford, James. 1992. *Language loyalties: A source book on the official English controversy.*
Chicago: University of Chicago Press.

Dann, Graham. 1996. *The language of tourism: A sociolinguistic perspective.* Wallingford,
Eng.: CAB International.

Davidson, Donald. 1984. Quotation. In *Inquiries into truth and interpretation.* Oxford: Oxford University Press. (Orig. pub. 1979.)

Deleuze, Gilles. 1994. *Difference and repetition.* New York: Columbia University Press.

Delph-Janiurek, Tom. 1999. Sounding gender(ed): Vocal performances in English university
teaching spaces. *Gender, Place, and Culture* 6 (2): 137–53.

Derrida, Jacques. 1976. *Of grammatology.* Trans. G. C. Spivak. Baltimore: Johns Hopkins

University Press.

———. 1981. *Positions.* Trans. A. Bass. Chicago: University of Chicago Press.

———. 1982. *Margins of philosophy.* Trans. A. Bass. Chicago: University of Chicago Press.

———. 1988. *Limited Inc.* Evanston, Ill.: Northwestern University Press.

Desforges, Luke. 2000. Traveling the world: Identity and travel biography. *Annals of Tourism Research* 27 (4): 926–45.

Domínguez, Virginia R. 1989. *People as subject, people as object.* Wisconsin: University of Wisconsin Press.

Dundes, Alan, and E. O. Arewa. 1975. Proverbs and the ethnography of speaking folklore. In *Analytic essays in folklore,* ed. Alan Dundes. The Hague: Mouton. (Orig. pub. 1964.)

Duranti, Alessandro. 1997. *Linguistic anthropology.* New York: Cambridge University Press.

———. 2003. Language as culture in U.S. anthropology: Three paradigms. *Current Anthropology* 44 (3): 323–47.

Durkheim, Emile. 1995. *The elementary forms of religious life.* Trans. Karen E. Fields. New York: Free Press.

Dvir, Ori. 1993. A debate on both banks of the trail [in Hebrew]. *Teva va-Aretz* 254 (93/3): 38–39.

Edensor, Tim. 1998. *Tourists at the Taj: Performance and meaning at a symbolic site.* London: Routledge.

Elsrud, Torun. 1998. Time creation in travelling: The taking and making of time among women backpackers. *Time and Society* 7 (2): 309–34.

———. 2001. Risk creation in traveling: Backpacker adventure narration. *Annals of Tourism Research* 28 (3): 597–617.

Fanon, Frantz. 1986. *Black skin, white masks.* London: Pluto.

Faugier, Jean, and Mary Sargeant. 1997. Sampling hard to reach populations. *Journal of Advanced Nursing* 26 (4): 790–97.

Feld, Steven. 1982. *Sound and sentiment: Birds, weeping, poetics, and song in Kaluli expression.* Philadelphia: University of Pennsylvania Press.

Felman, Shoshana, and Dori Laub. 1991. *Testimony: Crises of witnessing in literature, psychoanalysis, and history.* New York: Routledge.

Fischer, Andreas, ed. 1994. *Repetition.* Tubingen: Gunter Narr.

Fiske, John. 1989. *Understanding popular culture.* Boston: Unwin Hyman.

Fontana, Andrea, and James H. Frey. 2000. From structured questions to negotiated text. In *Handbook of qualitative research,* 2nd ed., ed. N. K. Denzin and Y. S. Lincoln. London: Sage.

Fortuna, Carlos. 2001. Soundscapes: The sounding city and urban social life. *Space and Culture* 11–12 (December): 70–86.

Frank, Arthur W. 1991. For a sociology of the body: An analytical review. In *The body: social process and cultural theory,* ed. Michael Featherstone, M. Hepworth, and Brian S. Turner. London: Sage.

Gaines, Robert N. 1979. Doing by saying: Toward a theory of perlocution. *Quarterly Journal of Speech* 65: 207–17.

Geis, Michael L. 1995. *Speech acts and conversational interaction.* Cambridge: Cambridge University Press.

Gergen, Kenneth J. 1991. *The saturated self: Dilemmas of identity in contemporary life.* New York: Basic Books.

Giddens, Anthony. 1984. *The constitution of society: Outline of the theory of structuration.* Berkeley: University of California Press.

——. 1991. *Modernity and self-identity: Self and society in the late modern age.* Stanford, Calif.: Stanford University Press.

Gilligan, Carol. 1982. *In a different voice: Psychological theory and women's development.* Cambridge, Mass.: Harvard University Press. Gluzman, Michael. 2003. *The politics of canonicity: Lines of resistance in modernist Hebrew poetry.* Stanford, Calif.: Stanford University Press.

Goffman, Erving. 1974. *Frame analysis: An essay on the organization of experience.* Boston: Northeastern University Press.

——. 1981. *Forms of talk.* Philadelphia: University of Pennsylvania Press.

Gotkowitz, Laura. 2003. Trading insults: Honor, violence, and the gendered culture of commerce in Cochabamba, Bolivia, 1870s–1950s. *Hispanic American Historical Review* 83 (1): 83–118.

Graburn, Nelson H. H. 1983. The anthropology of tourism. *Annals of Tourism Research* 10 (1): 9–33.

——. 1989. Tourism: The sacred journey. In *Hosts and guests: The anthropology of tourism,* ed. V. L. Smith. Philadelphia: University of Pennsylvania Press.

Green, Melanie C., and Timothy C. Brock. 2000. The role of transportation in the persuasiveness of public narratives. *Journal of Personality and Social Psychology* 79 (5): 701–21.

Gubrium, Jaber F., and James A. Holstein. 2000. The self in a world of going concerns. *Symbolic Interaction* 23 (1): 95–115.

——. 2001. *Institutional selves: Troubled identities in a postmodern world.* New York: Oxford University Press.

Gumperz, John J. 1992. Contextualization and understanding. In *Rethinking context: Language as an interactive phenomenon,* ed. A. Duranti and C. Goodwin. Cambridge: Cambridge University Press.

——. 1995. Mutual inferencing in conversation. In *Mutualities in dialogue,* ed. I. Markova, C. F. Graumann, and K. Foppa. Cambridge: Cambridge University Press.

Gurevitch, Zali, and Gideon Aran. 1991. *Al Hamakom* (Israeli anthropology). *Alpayim* 4: 9–44.

Haldrup, Michael, and Jonas Larsen. 2003. The family gaze. *Tourist Studies* 3 (1): 23–45.

Handelman, Don. 2002. The interior sociality of self-transformation. In *Self and self-transformation in the history of religions,* ed. D. D. Shulman and G. A. G. Stroumsa. Oxford: Oxford University Press.

Handelman, Don, and Lea Shamgar-Handelman. 1997. The presence of absence: The memorialism of national death in Israel. In *Grasping land: Space and place in contemporary Israeli discourse and experience,* ed. E. Ben-Ari and Y. Bilu. Albany: State University of New York Press.

Harding, Susan F. 1987. Convicted by the Holy Spirit: The rhetoric of fundamental Baptist conversion. *American Ethnologist* 14 (1): 167–85.

Harrison, Julia D. 2003. *Being a tourist: Finding meaning in pleasure travel.* Vancouver: UBC Press.

Haviv, Ayana S. 2005. Next Year in Kathmandu: Israeli backpackers and the formation of a new Israeli identity. In *Israeli backpackers and their society: A view from afar,* ed. Chaim Noy and Erik Cohen. Albany: State University of New York Press.

Hazan, Haim. 1990. *A paradoxical community: The emergence of a social world in an urban renewal setting.* Contemporary Ethnographic Studies. Greenwich, Conn.: JAI Press.

———. 2001a. *Simulated dreams: Israeli youth and virtual Zionism.* New York: Berghahn.

———. 2001b. That's how we were: Individual, group, and collective in the Tel Aviv of "Late Summer Blues." In *language and communication in Israel,* ed. H. Herzog and E. Ben-Refael. New Brunswick: Transaction. (Orig. pub. 1993.)

Heckathorn, Douglas D. 1997. Respondent-driven sampling: A new approach to the study of hidden populations. *Social Problems* 44 (2): 174–99.

Heckathorn, Douglas D., and Joan Jeffri. 2001. Finding the beat: Using respondent-driven sampling to study jazz musicians. *Poetics* 28 (4): 307–29.

Hinze, Bradford E. 1996. Reclaiming rhetoric in the Christian tradition. *Theological Studies* 57 (3): 481–500.

Holmes, Janet. 1986. Functions of "you know" in women's and men's speech. *Language in Society* 15 (1): 1–21.

Holsanova, Jana. 1998. The use of quotations in discourse about ethnicities. In *Dialog-analyse VI,* ed. S. Cmejrkova, J. Hoffmannova, O. Muellerova, and J. Svetla. Tubingen: Niemeyer.

Holt, Elizabeth. 1996. Reporting on talk: The use of direct reported speech in conversation. *Research on Language and Social Interaction* 29 (3): 219–45.

———. 1999. Just gassing: An analysis of direct reported speech in a conversation between employees of a gas supply company. *Text* 19 (4): 505–37.

Hymes, Dell H. 1974. *Foundations in sociolinguistics: An ethnographic approach.* Philadelphia: University of Pennsylvania Press.

———. 1975. Breakthrough into performance. In *Folklore: performance and communication,* ed. D. Ben-Amos and K. S. Goldstein. The Hague: Mouton.

Hymes, Dell, and Courteney Cazden. 1978. Narrative thinking and storytelling rights: A folklorist's clue to a critique of education. *Keystone* 22 (1–2): 21–36.

Jacobson, Yehuda. 1987. Secular pilgrimage in the Israeli context: The journey of young Israelis to distant countries. Master's thesis, Tel Aviv University.

Jakobson, Roman. 1960. Closing statement: Linguistics and poetics. In *Style in language,* ed. T. A. Sebeok. Cambridge: Technology Press of Massachusetts Institute of Technology.

———. 1966. Gramatical parallelism and its Russian facet. *Language* 42: 398–429.

Jakobson, Roman, and Morris Halle. 1971. *Fundamentals of language.* 2nd ed. The Hague: Mouton.

Jakobson, Roman, and Krystyna Pomorska. 1983. *Dialogues.* Cambridge, Mass.: MIT Press.

Janssen, A. J. M. Theo, and Wim van der Wurff. 1996. Introductory remarks on reported speech and thought. In *Reported speech: Forms and functions of the verb,* ed. A. J. M. Theo Janssen and W. Wurf. Amsterdam: John Benjamins.

Johnston, Lynda. 2001. (Other) bodies and tourism studies. *Annals of Tourism Research* 28 (1): 180–201.

Johnstone, Barbara. 1986. Arguments with Khumeini: Rhetorical situation and persuasive style in cross-cultural perspective. *Text* 6: 171–87.

———. 1989. Linguistic strategies and cultural styles for persuasive discourse. In *Language, communication, and culture,* ed. S. Ting-Toomey and F. Korzenny. London: Sage.

Kapchan, Deborah A. 2002. Possessed by culture/possessing culture: Giving flesh to voice. www.sas.upenn.edu/folklore/center/voiceover/possessed.html.

Kaplan, Max. 1980. A new language for a new leisure. *Communications* 6 (1): 33–42.

Katriel, Tamar. 1986. *Talking straight: Dugri speech in Israeli Sabra culture.* Cambridge: Cambridge University Press.

——. 1990. Celebrating language: The "Hebrew Language Year" as cultural performance. *Text and Performance Quarterly* 10 (4): 321–23.

——. 1991. *Communal webs: Communication and culture in contemporary Israel.* Albany: State University of New York Press.

——. 1993. Lefargen: A study in Israeli semantics of social relations. *Research on Language and Social Interaction* 26 (1): 31–53.

——. 1995. Touring the land: Trips and hiking as secular pilgrimages in Israeli culture. *Jewish Ethnology and Folklore Review* 17 (1–2): 6–13.

——. 2004. *Dialogic moments: From soul talks to talk radio in Israeli culture.* Detroit: Wayne State University Press.

Katriel, Tamar, and Pearla Nesher. 1986. Gibush: The rhetoric of cohesion in Israeli school culture. *Comparative Education Review* 30 (2): 216–31.

Keane, Webb. 1997. Religious language. *Annual Review of Anthropology* 26: 47–71.

Kharraki, Abdennour. 2001. Moroccan sex-based linguistic difference in bargaining. *Discourse and Society* 12 (5): 615–32.

Kimmel, Michael S. 1996. *Manhood in America: A cultural history.* New York: Free Press.

Kimmerling, Baruch. 2001. *The invention and decline of Israeliness: State, society, and the military.* Berkeley: University of California Press.

Kimmerling, Baruch, and Irit Backer. 1985. *The interrupted system: Israeli civilians in war and routine times.* New Brunswick, N.J.: Transaction.

Kirshenblatt-Gimblett, Barbara. 1974. The concept and varieties of narrative performance in East European Jewish culture. In *Explorations in the ethnography of speaking,* ed. Richard Bauman and Joel Sherzer. Cambridge: Cambridge University Press.

——. 1998. *Destination cultures: Tourism, museums, and heritage.* Berkeley: University of California Press.

Kvale, Steinar. 1996. The 1,000-page question. *Qualitative Inquiry* 2: 275–84.

Labov, William. 1972. *Language in the inner city: Studies in the black English vernacular.* Philadelphia: University of Pennsylvania Press.

Lacan, Jacques. 1977. *Écrits: A selection.* Trans. A. Sheridan. New York: Norton.

Lakoff, Robin T. 1982. Persuasive discourse and ordinary conversation, with examples from advertising. In *Analyzing discourse: Text and talk,* ed. D. Tannen. Washington, D.C.: Georgetown University Press.

Landau, Rachel. 1993. Hatsitut ketexnika retorit beneumeyhem shel rabanim bnei zemaneinu. *Am Vasefer* 8: 50–63.

Lang, Paul. 1995. *The English language debate: One nation, one language?* Springfield, N.J.: Enslow.

Langellier, Kristin M. 1999. Personal narrative, performance, performativity: Two or three things I know for sure. *Text and Performance Quarterly* 19 (2): 125–44.

Lash, Scott, and John Urry. 1994. *Economies of signs and space.* London: Sage.

Lavie, Smadar, Kirin Narayan, and Renato Rosaldo. 1993. Introduction to *Creativity/Anthropology,* ed. Smadar Lavie, Kirin Narayan, and Renato Rosaldo. Ithaca, N.Y.: Cornell University Press.

Lee, Yew-Jin, and Wolff-Michael Roth. 2004. Making a scientist: Discursive "doing" of identity and self-presentation during research interviews. *Forum of Qualitative Social Re-*

search 5 (1): art. 12. http://www.qualitative-research.net/fqs-texte/1-04/1-04leerothe. htm.

Lerner, Gene H. 1992. Assisted storytelling: Deploying shared knowledge as a practical matter. *Qualitative Sociology* 15 (3): 247–71.

———. 1993. Collectivities in action: Establishing the relevance of conjoined participation in conversation. *Text* 13 (2): 213–45.

Levelt, Willem J. M. 1989. *Speaking: From intention to articulation.* Cambridge, Mass.: MIT Press.

Levi-Strauss, Claude. 1963. *Structural anthropology.* Trans. C. Jacobson and B. G. Schoepf. New York: Basic Books.

Levy-Barzilai, Vered. 2003. ha'im mishehu natan leha mashehu leha'avir? *Ha'aretz,* December 19, 2003.

———. 2004. They call someone who takes drugs *"sarut"* (scratched). www.thehandstand. org/archive/january2004/articles/youngdrugdeals.htm.

Lieblich, Amia. 1989. *Transition to adulthood during military service: The Israeli case.* Albany: State University of New York Press.

Liebman, Charles S., and Eliezer Don-Yihya. 1983. *Civil religion in Israel: Traditional Judaism and political culture in the Jewish state.* Berkeley: University of California Press.

Loker-Murphy, Laurie, and Philip L. Pearce. 1995. Young budget travelers: Backpackers in Australia. *Annals of Tourism Research* 22 (4): 819–43.

Lomsky-Feder, Edna. 1996. The personal meaning of the experience of war: Life stories of Israeli men. *Megamot* 38: 48–73.

Longacre, Robert E. 1994. The dynamics of reported speech in narrative. *Word* 45 (2): 125–43.

Lucy, John A. 1993a. Metapragmatic presentationals: Reporting speech with quotatives in Yucatec Maya. In *Reflexive language: Reported speech and metapragmatics,* ed. John A. Lucy. Cambridge: University Press.

———. 1993b. Reflexive language and the human disciplines. In *Reflexive language: Reported speech and metapragmatics,* ed. John A. Lucy. Cambridge: Cambridge University Press.

———, ed. 1993c. *Reflexive language: Reported speech and metapragmatics.* Cambridge: Cambridge University Press.

MacCannell, Dean. 1973. Staged authenticity: Arrangements of social space in tourist settings. *American Journal of Sociology* 79 (3): 589-603.

———. 1976. *The tourist: A new theory of the leisure class.* New York: Schocken.

———. 1984. Reconstructed ethnicity: Tourism and cultural identity in third world communities. *Annals of Tourism Research* 11 (3): 375–91.

———. 2001. Tourist agency. *Tourist Studies* 1 (1): 23–37.

Mack, Burton, and Vernon Robbins K. 1989. *Patterns of persuasion in the gospels.* Sonoma, Calif.: Polebridge.

Maingueneau, Dominique. 1999. Analyzing self-constituting discourses. *Discourse Studies* 1 (2): 175–99.

Mandelbaum, Jenny. 1987. Couples sharing stories. *Communication Quarterly* 35 (2): 144–71.

———. 1989. Interpersonal activities in conversational storytelling. *Western Journal of Speech Communication* 53 (2): 114–26.

Mannheim, Bruce, and Krista van Vleet. 1998. The dialogics of southern Quechua narrative. *American Anthropologist* 100 (2): 326–46.

Maoz, Darya. 2004. The conquerors and the settlers: Two groups of young Israeli backpackers in India. In *The global nomad: Backpacker travel in theory and practice,* ed. Greg Richards and Julie Wilson. Clevedon, Eng.: Channel View.

Marcus, Menahem. 1993. It's possible without ritual of signs [in Hebrew]. *Teva va-Aretz* 254 (93/3): 42–45.

Markus, Thomas A., and Deborah Cameron. 2001. *The words between the spaces: Buildings and language.* London: Routledge.

Maschler, Yael. 2001. "*Veke'ilu haraglayim sh'xa nitkaot bifnim kaze*" ("and like your feet get stuck inside like"): Hebrew *kaze* ("like"), *ke'ilu* ("like") and the decline of Israeli dugri ("direct") speech. *Discourse Studies* 3 (3): 295–326.

———. 2002a. On the grammaticization of *ke'ilu* "like," lit. "as if," in Hebrew talk-in-interaction. *Language in Society* 31 (2): 243–76.

———. 2002b. The role of discourse markers in the construction of multivocality in Israeli Hebrew talk-in-interaction. *Research on Language and Social Interaction* 35 (1): 1–38.

———. 2003. The discourse marker *nu:* Israeli Hebrew impatience in interaction. *Text* 23 (1): 89–128.

Mazali, Rela. 2001. *Maps of women's goings and stayings.* Stanford, Calif.: Stanford University Press.

Melville, Herman. 1997. *Bartleby, the scrivener: A story of Wall Street.* New York: Simon and Schuster. (Orig. pub. 1853.)

Metcalf, Peter. (2002). *They lie, we lie: Getting on with anthropology.* London: Routledge.

Mevorach, Oded. 1997. The long trip after the military service: Characteristics of the travelers, the effects of the trip, and its meaning [in Hebrew]. Ph.D. diss., Hebrew University of Jerusalem.

Minh-Ha, Trinh, T. 1994. Other than myself/my other self. In *Travellers' tales: Narratives of home and displacement,* ed. G. Robertson, M. Mash, L. Tickner, J. Bird, B. Curtis, and T. Putnam. London: Routledge.

Moeran, Brian. 1983. The language of Japanese tourism. *Annals of Tourism Research* 10 (1): 93–108.

Murphy, Laurie. 2001. Exploring social interactions of backpackers. *Annals of Tourism Research* 28 (1): 50–67.

Myerhoff, Barbara G. 1978. *Number our days.* New York: Dutton.

Myers, Greg. 1999. Unspoken speech: Hypothetical reported discourse and the rhetoric of everyday talk. *Text* 19 (4): 571–90.

Nash, Dennison. 1989. Tourism as a form of imperialism. In *Hosts and guests: The anthropology of tourism,* ed. Valene L. Smith. Philadelphia: University of Pennsylvania Press.

Neumann, Mark. 1992. The trail through experience. In *Investigating subjectivity: Research on lived experience,* ed. Carolyn Ellis and M. G. Flaherty. London: Sage.

———. 1999. *On the rim: Looking for the Grand Canyon.* Minneapolis: University of Minnesota Press.

Nietzsche, Friedrich Wilhelm. 1967. *On the genealogy of morals.* Trans. W. Kaufmann and R. J. Hollingdale. New York: Vintage.

Noy, Chaim. 2002. The Great journey: Narrative analysis of Israeli trekking stories [in Hebrew]. Ph.D. diss., Hebrew University of Jerusalem.

———. 2003a. Narratives of hegemonic masculinity: Representations of body and space in Israeli backpackers' narratives [in Hebrew]. *Israeli Sociology* 5 (1): 75–102.

———. 2003b. The write of passage: Reflections on writing a dissertation in narrative/ qualitative methodology. *Forum of Qualitative Social Research* 4 (2). http://www. qualitative-research.net/fqs-texte/2-03/2-03noy-e.htm.

———. 2004a. From persuasion to self-transformation: Dialogical genres of narration in a tourist speech community. *Texas Linguistic Forum* 48: 149–65. http://studentorgs. utexas.edu/salsa/ salsaproceedings/salsa12/index.htm.

———. 2004b. "The trip really changed me": Backpackers' narratives of self-change. *Annals of Tourism Research* 31 (1): 78–102.

———. 2005. Israeli backpackers: Narrative, interpersonal communication, and social construction. In *Israeli backpackers and their society: A view from afar,* ed. Chaim Noy and Erik Cohen. Albany: State University of New York Press.

———. 2006a. Israeli backpacking since the 1960s: Institutionalization and its effects. *Tourism Recreation Research* 31 (3): 1–17.

———. 2006b. Qualitative sampling tactics: The hermeneutics of snowball sampling. Unpublished manuscript.

———. Forthcoming. Traversing hegemony: Gender, body, and identity in the narratives of Israeli female backpackers. *Tourism Review International* 11 (2).

Noy, Chaim, and Erik Cohen, eds. 2005a. Introduction: Backpacking as a rite of passage in Israel. In *Israeli backpackers and their society: A view from afar,* ed. Chaim Noy and Erik Cohen. Albany: State University of New York Press.

———. 2005b. *Israeli backpackers and their society: A view from afar.* Albany: State University of New York Press.

Ochs, Elinor. 1997. Narrative. In *Discourse as structure and process,* ed. T. A. Van Dijk. London: Sage.

Ochs, Elinor, and Lisa Capps. 1996. Narrating the self. *Annual Review of Anthropology* 25: 19–43.

O'Leary, Zina. 2004. *The essential guide to doing research.* London: Sage.

Olsen, Kjell. 2002. Authenticity as a concept in tourism research: The social organization of the experience of authenticity. *Tourist Studies* 12 (2): 159–82.

Oring, Elliott. 1981. *Israeli humor: The content and structure of the Chizbat of the Palmah.* Albany: State University of New York Press.

Parker, Sara. 1999. Speaking your piece: A cross-cultural comparison of use of direct speech in Erie County, Pennsylvania to dugri speaking of Israeli Sabra. *Dissertation Abstracts International, A: The Humanities and Social Sciences* 60 (3): 594–A.

Pratt, Mary L. 1992. *Imperial eyes: Travel writing and transculturation.* London: Routledge.

Propp, Vladimir I. A. 1968. *Morphology of the folktale.* 2nd ed. Austin: University of Texas Press.

Radner, J. Newlon, and Susan S. Lancer. 1993. Strategies of coding in women's cultures. In *Feminist messages: Coding in women's folk culture,* ed. J. N. Radner. Urbana: University of Illinois Press.

Rapoport, Tamar, and Tamar El-Or. 1997. Cultures of womanhood in Israel: Social agencies and gender production. *Women's Studies International Forum* 20 (5–6): 573–80.

Raz, Aviad E., and Rina Shapira. 1994. A symbolic interactionist user's guide to the answering machine: 22 reflections on vocal encounters in an emerging social world. *Symbolic*

Interaction 17 (4): 411–29.

Richards, Greg, and Julie Wilson, eds. 2004a. *The global nomad: Backpacker travel in theory and practice.* Clevedon, Eng.: Channel View.

———. 2004b. The global nomad: Motivations and behavior of independent travellers worldwide. In *The global nomad: Backpacker travel in theory and practice,* ed. Greg Richards and Julie Wilson. Clevedon, Eng.: Channel View.

———. 2004c. Widening perspectives in backpacker research. In *The global nomad: Backpacker travel in theory and practice,* ed. Greg Richards and Julie Wilson. Clevedon, Eng.: Channel View.

Ricoeur, Paul. 1984. *Time and narrative.* Chicago: University of Chicago Press.

Riley, Pamela J. 1988. Road culture of international long-term budget travelers. *Annals of Tourism Research* 15 (3): 313–28.

Ritzer, George, and Allan Liska. 1997. "McDisneyization" and "post-tourism": Complementary perspectives on contemporary tourism. In *Touring cultures: Transformations of travel and theory,* ed. Chris Rojek and John Urry. London: Routledge.

Robertson, George, Melinda Mash, Lisa Tickner, Jon Bird, Barry Curtis, and Tim Putnam, eds. 1994. *Travellers' tales: Narratives of home and displacement.* London: Routledge.

Robinson, Martha, and Paul A. Lynch. 2005. Hospitality through poetry: Control, fake solidarity, and breakdown. Unpublished manuscript.

Rodaway, Paul. 1994. *Sensuous geographies: Body, sense, and place.* London: Routledge.

Roeh, Izhak, and R. Nir. 1990. Speech presentation in the Israeli radio news: Ideological constraints and rhetorical strategies. *Text* 10 (3): 225–44.

Rojek, Chris, and John Urry, eds. 1997. *Touring cultures: Transformations of travel and theory.* London: Routledge.

Roniger, Luis, and Michael Feige. 1992. From pioneer to Freier: The changing models of generalized exchange in Israel. *European Journal of Sociology* 33 (2): 280–307.

Rosenthal, Gabriala. 1993. Reconstruction of life stories: Principles of selection in generating stories for narrative biographical interviews. *Narrative Study of Lives* 1: 59–91.

Ruddick, Sara. 1989. *Maternal thinking: Toward a politics of peace.* Boston: Beacon.

Said, Edward W. 1978. *Orientalism.* New York: Pantheon.

Salamon, Hagar. 2001. Political bumper stickers in contemporary Israel: Folklore as an emotional battlefield [in Hebrew]. *Jerusalem Studies in Jewish Folklore* 21: 113–44.

Savarese, Rossella. 2000. "Infosuasion" in European newspapers: A case study on the war in Kosovo. *European Journal of Communication* 15 (3): 363–81.

Schely-Newman, Esther. 1999. "I hear from people who read torah . . .": Reported speech, genres, and gender relations in personal narrative. *Narrative Inquiry* 9 (1): 49–68.

Schiebe, Karl. 1986. Self narratives and adventure. In *Narrative psychology: The storied nature of human conduct,* ed. Theodore R. Sarbin. New York: Praeger.

Schiffrin, Deborah. 1984. Jewish argument as sociability. *Language and society* 13 (3): 311–35.

Schmidt, J., and J. F. Kess. 1986. *Television advertising and televangelism: Discourse analysis of persuasive language.* Amsterdam: John Benjamins.

Schwartz, Barry, Yael Zerubavel, and Bernice M. Barnett. 1986. The recovery of Masada: A study in collective memory. *Sociological Quarterly* 27 (2): 147–64.

Searle, John R. 1969. *Speech acts: An essay in the philosophy of language.* London: Cambridge University Press.

Seeger, Anthony. 1987. *Why Suya sing: A musical anthropology of an Amazonian people.*

Cambridge: Cambridge University Press.

Selwyn, Tom. 1996. *The tourist image: Myths and myth making in tourism.* Chichester, Eng.: John Wiley.

Sered, Susan Starr. 2000. *What makes women sick? Maternity, modesty, and militarism in Israeli society.* Hanover, N.H.: Brandeis University Press.

Shapira, Anita. 1999. *Land and power: The Zionist resort to force, 1881–1948.* Stanford, Calif.: Stanford University Press.

Shilling, Chris. 1993. *The body and social theory.* London: Sage.

Shotter, John. 1993. Becoming someone: Identity and belonging. In *Discourse and lifespan identity,* ed. C. Nikolas and J. F. Nussbaum. London: Sage.

Shuman, Amy. 1986. *Storytelling rights: The uses of oral and written texts by urban adolescents.* Cambridge: Cambridge University Press.

———. 1992. "Get outa my face": Entitlement and authoritative discourse. In *Responsibility and evidence in oral discourse,* ed. J. H. Hill and J. T. Irvine. Cambridge: Cambridge University Press.

Silverstein, Michael. 1976. Shifters, linguist categories, and cultural description. In *Meaning in anthropology,* ed. Keith H. Basso and S. A. Henry. Albuquerque: University of New Mexico Press.

———. 1979. Language structure and linguistic ideology. In *The elements: A parasession on linguistic units and levels,* ed. P. R. Clyne, W. F. Hanks, and C. L. Hofbauer. Chicago: Chicago Linguistic Society.

———. 1996. The secret life of texts. In *Natural histories of discourse,* ed. Michael Silverstein and Greg Urban. Chicago: University of Chicago Press.

———. 2001. The limits of awareness. In *Linguistic anthropology: A reader,* ed. A. Duranti. Malden, Mass.: Blackwell. (Orig. pub. 1977.)

Silverstein, Michael, and Greg Urban. 1996. The natural histories of discourse. In *Natural histories of discourse,* ed. Michael Silverstein and Greg Urban. Chicago: University of Chicago Press.

Simmel, Georg. 1959. *Sociology of religion.* Trans. Curt Rosenthal. New York: Philosophical Library.

———. 1997a. The sociology of space. In *Simmel on culture: Selected writings,* ed. D. Frisby and Michael Featherstone. Thousand Oaks, Calif.: Sage. (Orig. pub. 1903.)

———. 1997b. Sociology of the senses. In *Simmel on culture: Selected writings,* ed. D. Frisby and Michael Featherstone. Thousand Oaks, Calif.: Sage. (Orig. pub. 1907.)

Smith, Valene L. 1992. Hosts and guests revisited. *American Behavioral Scientist* 36 (2): 187–99.

Sontag, Susan. 1966. *Against interpretation and other essays.* New York: Farrar.

Sørensen, Anders. 2003. Backpacker ethnography. *Annals of Tourism Research* 30 (4): 847–67.

Stein, Rebecca L. 2002. "First contact" and other Israeli fictions: Tourism, globalization, and the Middle East peace process. *Public Culture* 14 (3): 515–43.

Sternberg, Meir. 1982. Proteus in quotation-land: Mimesis and the forms of reported discourse. *Poetics Today* 3 (2): 107–56.

Stewart, Kathleen. 1996. *A space on the side of the road: Cultural poetics in an "other" America.* Princeton: Princeton University Press.

Stewart, Susan. 1993. *On longing: Narratives of the miniature, the gigantic, the souvenir, the collection.* Durham, N.C.: Duke University Press.

Stromberg, Peter G. 1991. Symbols into experience: A case study in the generation of commitment. *Ethos* 19(1): 102–26.

———. 1993. *Language and self-transformation: A study of the Christian conversion narrative.* Cambridge: Cambridge University Press.

Sturma, Michael. 1999. Packaging Polynesia's image. *Annals of Tourism Research* 26 (3): 712–15.

Tannen, Deborah. 1984. *Conversational style: Analyzing talk among friends.* Norwood, N.J.: Ablex.

———. 1989. *Talking voices: Repetition, dialogue, and imagery in conversational discourse.* Cambridge: Cambridge University Press.

Taylor, Charles. 1989. *Sources of the self: The making of the modern identity.* Cambridge, Mass.: Harvard University Press.

Tedlock, Dennis. 1983. *The spoken word and the work of interpretation.* Philadelphia: University of Pennsylvania Press.

Theophano, Janet. 2002. *Eat my words: Reading women's lives through the cookbooks they wrote.* New York: Palgrave.

Tobias, Michael. 1979. A history of imagination in the wilderness. In *The mountain spirit,* ed. Michael Tobias and Harold Drasdo. Woodstock, N.Y.: Overlook.

Torronen, Jukka. 2000. The passionate text: The pending narrative as a macrostructure of persuasion. *Social Semiotics* 10 (1): 81–98.

Turner, Victor W. 1967. Betwixt and between: The liminal period in rites de passage. In *Forest of symbols,* ed. Victor W. Turner. Ithaca, N.Y.: Cornell University Press.

———. 1969. *The ritual process.* Chicago: Aldine.

———. 1980. Social dramas and stories about them. *Critical Inquiry* 7 (1): 141–68.

———. 1982. Liminal and liminoid. In *From ritual to theatre,* ed. Victor W. Turner. New York: Performing Arts Journal Publications.

Tusting, Karin, Robert Crawshaw, and Beth Callen. 2002. "I know, 'cos I was there": How residence abroad students use personal experience to legitimate cultural generalizations. *Discourse and Society* 13 (5): 651–72.

Tyler, Stephan. 1986. Post-modern ethnography: From document of the occult to occult document. In *Writing culture: The poetics and politics of ethnography,* ed. James Clifford and George E. Marcus. Berkeley: University of California Press.

Urban, Greg. 1984. Speech about speech in speech about action. *Journal of American Folklore* 97 (385): 310–28.

———. 1996. Entextualization, replication, and power. In *Natural histories of discourse,* ed. Michael Silverstein and Greg Urban. Chicago: University of Chicago Press.

Uriely, Natan, Yaniv Yonay, and Dalit Simchai. 2002. Backpacking experience: A type and form analysis. *Annals of Tourism Research* 29 (2): 520–38.

Urry, John. 1990. *The tourist gaze: Leisure and travel in contemporary societies.* London: Sage.

———. 1999. Sensing the city. In *The tourist city,* ed. D. R. Judd and S. S. Fainstein. New Haven, Conn.: Yale University Press.

van den Abbeele, Georges. 1980. Sightseers: The tourist as theorist. *Diacritics: A Review of Contemporary Criticism* 10 (4): 3–14.

van Doorn, Joseph W. M. 1989. A critical assessment of sociocultural impact studies of tourism in the third world. In *Towards appropriate tourism: The case of developing countries,* ed. T. V. Singh, H. L. Theuns, and F. M. Go. Frankfurt: P. Lang.

van Gennep, Arnold. 1960. *The rites of passage.* Trans. M. Vizedon and G. Caffee. Chicago: University of Chicago Press. (Orig. pub. 1909.)

Veijola, Soile, and Eava Jokinen. 1994. The body in tourism. *Theory, Culture, and Society* 11 (3): 125-51.

————. 1998. The death of the tourist: Seven improvisations. *European Journal of Cultural Studies* 1 (3): 327-51.

Vološhinov, Valentin N. 1973. *Marxism and the philosophy of language.* Trans. L. Matejka and I. R. Titunik. New York: Seminar.

Wang, Ning. 2000. *Tourism and modernity: Sociological analysis.* Amsterdam: Pergamon.

Weiss, Meira. 1997. War bodies, hedonist bodies: Dialectics of the collective and the individual in Israeli society. *American Ethnologist* 24 (4): 813–32.

Weizman, E. 1998. Emet or bedaya? dibur yashir ba'itonut hayomit haktuva. *balshanut ivrit* 43: 29–42.

Welk, Peter. 2004. The beaten track: Anti-tourism as an element of backpacker identity construction. In *The global nomad: Backpacker travel in theory and practice,* ed. Greg Richards and Julie Wilson. Clevedon, Eng.: Channel View.

Wickens, Eugenia. 2002. The sacred and the profane: A tourist typology. *Annals of Tourism Research* 29 (3): 834–51.

Wilson, Julie, and Greg Richards. 2004. Backpacker icons: Influential literary "nomads" in the formation of backpacker identities. In *The global nomad: Backpacker travel in theory and practice,* ed. Greg Richards and Julie Wilson. Clevedon, Eng.: Channel View.

Wortham, Stanton E. F. 2001. *Narratives in action: A strategy for research and analysis.* New York: Teachers College.

Young, Katharine G. 1987. *Taleworlds and storyrealms: The phenomenology of narrative.* Dordrecht: Martinus Nijhoff.

————. 1991. Perspectives on embodiment: The uses of narrativity in ethnographic writing. *Journal of Narrative and Life History* 1 (1–2): 213–43.

Wittgenstein, Ludwig. 1998. *Culture and value.* Ed. G. H. von Wright and H. Nyman. Trans. P. Winch. Oxford: Blackwell. (Orig. pub. 1977.)

Zerubavel, Yael. 1995. *Recovered roots: Collective memory and the making of Israeli national tradition.* Chicago: University of Chicago Press.

GENERAL INDEX

adventure, vii, 5, 10, 33, 63; and masculinity, 73, 124; and narrative, 8, 10, 18, 39, 110, 208n. 5; and Sabra culture, 6–8

agudot meshotetim (groups of wanderers), 6

Annapurna Mountain Chain, vii, 82, 84, 144. *See also* Nepal

Argentina, 3, 19; Buenos Aires, 109, 110

army (military), 3, 5, 61, 74, 205, 210n. 6. *See also* militarism

Asia, 3, 4, 19, 40, 196, 207n. 1

authenticity: constructed, 176, 182, 185, 187; and authority, 88, 92; and discourse, 51, 131, 136, 168; of experience, 56, 124, 152, 157, 176, 181; and liminality, 167; and performance, 34, 51, 55, 108, 186, 190–91; and sanctity, 209n. 3; of sites, xii, 3, 92, 94, 167, 180–92 (passim)

authority, viii, 32, 107, 183; and authenticity, 88, 92; and performance, xii, 15, 107; group (choral), 67, 74–77, 103; collective (communal), viii, 103–7, 112–27, 130, 136, 198; of collective documents, 129–30, 143

bargaining, 156–60. See also *Freier*

body, 74, 124, 136, 141, 198; and gender, 74, 123, 127; collective (communal), 103, 120; socially constructed, 120, 123, 126

Bolivia, 75, 96, 97, 135, 137, 142

Brazil, 3, 19, 109

canon, 92, 112, 115, 211n. 3; and authority, 45, 103, 129–36 (passim); and the collective, 103–8, 112, 129–34, 138, 211. 2; narrative (*see* narrative); normative, 123–24

capital: cultural, 35, 134, 176, 178, 200; narrative. *See* narrative capital

Chile, 3, 19, 73, 101; Torres del Paine, 64, 116–17

Clifford, James, 9, 121

collective. *See* community

Colombia, 3, 124

colonial, 5, 6, 94, 123, 157; neocolonial, 81, 95; in tourism, 81, 85, 86, 210n.4

community: and authority (*see* authority; canon); borders of, 35, 43, 79–80, 151, 165, 198; and communication, 20, 39–44 (passim), 106, 111, 142, 156; diasporic, 90; entering, 19, 34, 43, 138, 155, 191; evangelist, 34, 38, 40, 42, 43; *havay* of, 97; and hierarchy, 16, 17, 31, 44, 106, 159; inside/outside of, 31, 33, 88, 93, 94, 198; knowledge of, 46, 132, 142; norms of, 104, 107, 114–19, 130; and persuasion, 42–44, 191; socially constructed, xii, 20, 198; sounds of (*see under* sound); of tourists, vii, ix, 113, 199; of voices 49, 15, 197. *See also* polyphony

Deixis, 50, 51, 97, 132, 154, 155

demographic anecdote, 88, 90

dialogue, 56, 117–18, 168, 195–97; field of, 92, 105, 198; dialogics, 59, 77, 195, 198; and monologue, 13, 166; persuasive, ix, 38–41, 45, 195

discourse, 11, 46, 58, 106, 116, 209n. 7; and gender, 74, 120; inclusive/exclusive, 198; institutional, 174, 180, 183, 198, 200; in Israeli culture, 81, 82, 120, 134, 160; and persuasion, 40–44, 54, 155, 209n. 5; and quotation, 49, 50, 76, 117; religious, 183, 200–201; self-constituting, 46, 183; as souvenir, 55; in tourism, 20, 74, 104, 140, 168, 180; written/oral, 129

discourse markers, 52, 125

AUTHOR INDEX